NICK COHEN is a columnist for the *Observer*, *New Statesman* and *Evening Standard*. In his Channel Four documentaries and general media appearances, he has proved himself to be the witty and excoriating voice of the left. He commands a loyal readership, as his groaning weekly postbag attests. He is the author of two books: *Cruel Britannia: Reports on the Sinister and the Preposterous*, a collection of his journalism and *Pretty Straight Guys*, a dissection of the Blair leadership.

Visit his website: www.nickcohen.net

Visit www.AuthorTracker.co.uk for exclusive information on your favourite HarperCollins authors.

From the reviews of *What's Left?*:

'Nick Cohen is in a great tradition of English radical writing and right on target. His is a powerful and contemporary voice'
MELVYN BRAGG

'Exceptional and necessary…Do not feel you have to be a leftist or liberal to read it, because it engages with an argument that is crucial for all of us, and for our time'
CHRISTOPHER HITCHENS, *Sunday Times*

'A roaring polemic of outrage against the moral and political crisis of the liberal tradition. It is already one of the most discussed current affairs books of the year'
MARTIN KETTLE, *Guardian*

'Angry and splendid'   DAVID AARONOVITCH, *The Times*

By the same author

Cruel Britannia: Reports on the Sinister and the Preposterous
Pretty Straight Guys

NICK COHEN

What's Left?

HOW THE LEFT LOST ITS WAY

HARPER PERENNIAL

London, New York, Toronto and Sydney

Harper Perennial
An imprint of HarperCollins*Publishers*
77–85 Fulham Palace Road
Hammersmith
London W6 8JB

www.harperperennial.co.uk

This edition published by Harper Perennial 2007
1

First published in Great Britain by Fourth Estate in 2007

A catalogue record for this book is
available from the British Library

ISBN 978-0-00-722970-3

Set in Minion

Printed and bound in Great Britain by Clays Ltd, St Ives plc

In memory of Hadi Saleh,
the last of the socialists
(1949 to 2005)

Lest we should see where we are,
Lost in a haunted wood,
Children afraid of the night
Who have never been happy or good.

W. H. Auden

CONTENTS

INTRODUCTION

IN THE EARLY SEVENTIES, my mother searched the super-markets for politically reputable citrus fruit. She couldn't buy Seville oranges without indirectly subsidizing General Francisco Franco, Spain's fascist dictator. Algarve oranges were no good either because the slightly less gruesome but equally right-wing dictatorship of António Salazar ruled Portugal. She boycotted the piles of Outspan from South Africa as a protest against apartheid, and although neither America nor Israel was a dicta-torship, she wouldn't have Florida or Jaffa oranges in the house because she had no time for the then American President, Richard Nixon, or the Israeli occupation of the West Bank and Gaza.

My sisters and I did not know it, but when Franco fell ill in 1975, we were in a race to the death. Either he died of Parkinson's disease or we died of scurvy. Luckily for us and the peoples of Spain, the dictator went first, although he took an unconscionably long time about it.

Thirty years later, I picked up my mother from my sister Natalie's house. Her children were watching a Disney film; *The Jungle Book*, I think.

'It's funny, Mum,' I said as we drove home, 'but I don't remember seeing any Disney when I was their age.'

'You've only just noticed? We didn't let you watch rubbish from Hollywood corporations.'

'Ah.'

'We didn't buy you the *Beano* either.'

'For God's sake, Mum, what on earth was wrong with the *Beano*?'

'It was printed by D. C. Thomson, non-union firm.'

'Right,' I said.

I was about to mock her but remembered that I had not allowed my son to watch television, even though he was nearly three at the time. I will let him read the *Beano* when he is older – I spoil him, I know – but if its cartoonists were to down their crayons and demand fraternal support, I would probably make him join the picket line and boycott it as well.

I come from a land where you can sell out by buying a comic. I come from the Left.

I'm not complaining, I had a very happy childhood. Conservatives would call my parents 'politically correct', but there was nothing sour or pinched about their home, and there is a lot to be said for growing up in a political household in which everyday decisions about what to buy and what to reject have a moral quality.

At the time, I thought it was normal and assumed that all civilized people lived the same way. I still remember the sense of dislocation I felt at 13 when my English teacher told me he voted Conservative. As his announcement coincided with the shock of puberty, I was unlikely to forget it. I must have understood at some level that real Conservatives lived in Britain – there was a Conservative government at the time, so logic dictated that there had to be Conservative voters. But it was incredible to learn that my teacher was one of them when he gave every appearance of being a thoughtful and kind man. To be good you had to be on the Left.

Looking back, I can see that I got that comforting belief from my parents, but it was reinforced by the experience of living through the Thatcher administration that appeared to reaffirm the Left's monopoly of goodness. The embrace first of monetarism and then of the European Exchange Rate Mechanism produced two recessions that Conservatives viewed with apparent composure because the lives wrecked by mass unemployment and business failure had the beneficial side effect of destroying trade union power. Even when the Left of the Eighties was clearly in the wrong – as it was over unilateral nuclear disarmament – it was still good. It may have been astonishingly dunderheaded to believe that dictators would abandon their weapons systems if Britain abandoned hers, but it wasn't wicked.

Yet for all the loathing of Conservatives I felt, I didn't have to look at modern history to know that it was a fallacy to believe in the superior virtue of the Left: my family told me that. My parents joined the Communist Party but left it in their twenties. My father encouraged me to read Alexander Solzhenitsyn's exposés of the Soviet Union and argue about them at the dinner table. He knew how bad the Left could get, but this knowledge did not stop him from remaining very left wing. He would never have entertained the notion that communism was as bad as fascism. In this, he was typical. Anti-communism was never accepted as the moral equivalent of anti-fascism, not only by my parents but also by the overwhelming majority of liberal-minded people. The Left was still morally superior. Even when millions were murdered and tens of millions were enslaved and humiliated, the 'root cause' of crimes beyond the human imagination was the perversion of noble socialist ideals.

Every now and again, someone asks why the double standard persists to this day. The philosophical answer is that communism did not feel as bad as fascism because in theory, if not in practice, communism was an ideology which offered universal emancipation, while only a German could benefit from Hitler's Nazism and only an Italian could prosper under Mussolini's fascism. I'm more impressed by the matter-of-fact consideration that fascist forces took over or menaced Western countries in the Thirties and Forties, and although there was a communist menace in the Cold War, the Cold War never turned hot and Western Europe and North America never experienced the totalitarianism of the Left.

There were many moments in the Thirties when fascists and communists cooperated – the German communists concentrated on attacking the Weimar Republic's democrats and gave Hitler a free run, and Stalin's Soviet Union astonished the world by signing a pact with Nazi Germany in 1939. But after Hitler broke the terms of the alliance in the most spectacular fashion by invading the Soviet Union in 1941, you could rely on nearly all of the Left from nice liberals through to the most compromised Marxists to oppose the tyrannies of the far right. Consistent anti-fascism added enormously to the Left's prestige in the second half of the twentieth century. A halo of moral superiority hovered over it because if there was a campaign against racism, religious fanaticism or neo-Nazism, the odds were that its leaders would be men and women of the Left.

For all the atrocities and follies committed in its name, the Left possessed this virtue: it would stand firm against fascism. After the Iraq war, I don't believe that a fair-minded outsider could say it does that any more.

Iraqis have popped up throughout my life – indeed, they were popping up before I was born. My parents had Iraqi communist friends when they were students who came along to their wedding in the late Fifties. God knows where they are now. My mother certainly doesn't. Saddam's Baath Party slaughtered the Iraqi left and in all likelihood the Baathists murdered her friends years ago and dumped their bodies in unmarked graves.

I grew up in the peace and quiet of suburban Manchester, started out in newspapers in Birmingham and left for Fleet Street in 1987 to try my luck as a freelance. I wangled myself a desk next to a quiet and handsome young Iranian called Farzad Bazoft in the old *Observer* newsroom round the corner from St Paul's Cathedral. In 1989, he went to Iraq. Extraordinary reports were coming out about Saddam Hussein imitating Adolf Hitler by exterminating tens of thousands of Iraqi Kurds with poison gas. Farzad was a freelance like me, and perhaps he was looking for a scoop to make his name and land himself a staff job. More probably, he was just behaving like a proper reporter. He had heard about a sensational story of gigantic explosions at secret rocket bases and wanted to nail it down regardless of the risk or reward. The secret police caught him, and after taking him to a torture chamber, they murdered him, as they had murdered so many before.

It is hard to believe now but Conservative MPs and the Foreign Office apologized for Saddam in those days. Tories excused Farzad's execution with the straight lie that he was an Iranian spy – and one reptilian Thatcherite declared that he 'deserved to be hanged'. By contrast, Saddam Hussein appalled the liberal-left. When I went to leftish meetings in the late Eighties, I heard that Iraq encapsulated all the loathsome hypocrisy of the supposedly 'democratic' West. Here was a blighted land ruled by a terrible regime that followed the example of the European dictatorships of the Thirties. And what did the supposed champions of democracy and human rights in Western governments do? Support Saddam, that's what they did. Sold him arms and covered up his crimes. Fiery socialist MPs denounced Baathism, while playwrights and poets stained the pages of the liberal press with their tears for his victims. Many quoted the words of a brave and meticulous Iraqi exile called Kanan Makiya. He became a hero of the Left because he broke through the previously impenetrable secrecy that covered totalitarian Iraq and described in awful detail how an entire population was compelled to inform on their family and friends or face the consequences. All decent people who wanted to convict the West of subscribing to murderous double standards could justifiably use his work as evidence for the prosecution.

The apparently sincere commitment to help Iraqis vanished the moment Saddam invaded Kuwait in August 1990 and became America's enemy. At the time, I didn't think about where the Left was going. I could denounce the hypocrisy of a West which made excuses for Saddam one minute and called him a 'new Hitler' the next, but I didn't dwell on the equal and opposite hypocrisy of a Left which called Saddam a 'new Hitler' one minute and excused him the next. All liberals and leftists remained good people in my mind. Asking hard questions about any of them risked giving aid and comfort to the conservative enemy and disturbing my own certainties. I would have gone on anti-war demonstrations when the fighting began in 1991, but the sight of Arabs walking around London with badges saying 'Free Kuwait' stopped me. When they asked why it was right to allow Saddam to keep Kuwaitis as his subjects, a part of me conceded that they had a point.

I didn't do much with that thought, but carried on through the Nineties holding the standard left-wing beliefs of the day. By the time New Labour was preparing for power, I was a columnist on the *Observer*, and my writing was driven by disgust at the near-uniform good press Blair got in his early years. I felt the adulation unmerited and faintly sinister and became one of the few journalists to bang on about the dark side of the shiny happy people who had moved into Downing Street. My pet topic was the treatment of asylum seekers. I was infuriated by the sight of New Labour pretending Britain welcomed the victims of genuine persecution while all the time quietly rigging the system to stop genuine refugees reaching Britain. Once again, I ran into Saddam Hussein. I had to. It was inevitable because among asylum seekers fleeing genuine persecution were countless Iraqis the Baathists had driven to pack their bags and run for their lives.

I got to know members of the Iraqi opposition in London, particularly Iraqi Kurds whose compatriots were the targets of one of the last genocides of the twentieth century. They were democratic socialists whose liberal-mindedness extended to opposing the death penalty, even for Saddam Hussein. Obviously, they didn't represent the majority of Iraqi opinion. Equally obviously, they shared the same beliefs as the over-whelming majority of the rich world's liberals and leftists and deserved our support as they struggled against fascism. Not the authoritarianism of a tinpot dictator but real fascism: a messianic one-party state; a Great Leader, whose statue was in every town centre and picture on every news bulletin; armies that swept out in unprovoked wars of foreign aggrandizement; and secret policemen who organized the gassing of 'impure' races. The Iraqi leftists were our 'comrades', to use a word that was by then so out of fashion it was archaic.

When the second war against Saddam Hussein came in 2003, they told me there was no other way to remove him. Kanan Makiya was on their side. He was saying the same things about the crimes against humanity of the Baath Party he had said twenty years before, but although his arguments had barely changed, the political world around him was unrecognizable. American neo-conservatives were his champions now, while the Left that had once cheered him denounced him as a traitor.

Everyone I respected in public life was wildly anti-war, and I was struck by how their concern about Iraq didn't extend to the common courtesy of talking to Iraqis. They seemed to have airbrushed from their memories all they had once known about Iraq and every principle of mutual respect they had once upheld.

I supposed their furious indifference was reasonable at the time. They had many good arguments that I would have agreed with in other circumstances. I assumed that once the war was over they would back Iraqis trying to build a democracy while continuing to pursue George W. Bush and Tony Blair to their graves for what they had done. I waited for a majority on the liberal-left to offer qualified support for a new Iraq, and I kept on waiting because it never happened – not just in Britain, but also in the United States, in Europe, in India, in South America, in South Africa...in every part of the world where there was a recognizable liberal-left. They didn't think again when thousands of Iraqis were slaughtered by 'insurgents' from the Baath Party, which wanted to re-establish the dictatorship, and from al-Qaeda, which wanted a godly global empire to repress the rights of democrats, the independent-minded, women and homosexuals. They didn't think again when Iraqis defied the death threats and went to vote on new constitutions and governments. Eventually, I grew tired of waiting for a change that was never going to come and resolved to find out what had happened to a Left whose benevolence I had taken for granted.

All right, you might say, but the reaction to the second Iraq war is not a good enough reason to write a book. The American and British governments sold the invasion to their publics with a false bill of goods and its aftermath was a bloody catastrophe.

It was Utopian to hope that leftists and liberals could oppose George W. Bush while his troops poured into Iraq – and killed their fair share of civilians – while at the same time standing up for the freedoms of others. There was too much emotional energy invested in opposing the war, too much justifiable horror at the chaos and too much justifiable anger that the talk of weapons of mass destruction turned out to be so much nonsense. The politically committed are like football fans. They support their side come what may and refuse to see any good in the opposing team. The liberal-left bitterly opposed war, and their indifference afterwards was a natural consequence of the fury directed at Bush.

It is a fair argument, which I've heard many times, although I wince at the implied passivity. People don't just react to a crisis: they choose how they react. If a man walks down the street trying to pick a fight, you can judge those he confronts by how they respond. Do they hit back, run away or try to calm him down? The confrontation is not of their making, but they still have a choice, and what choice they make reveals their character and beliefs.

If you insist on treating the reaction to the second Iraq war as a one-off that doesn't reveal a deeper sickness, I'll change the subject. This book isn't all about Iraq or mainly about Iraq. It raises questions about morbid symptoms on the liberal-left which were there before George W. Bush and Tony Blair came to power and show every sign of flourishing long after they have gone.

Why is it that apologies for a militant Islam which stands for everything the liberal-left is against come from the liberal-left? Why will students hear a leftish post-modern theorist defend the exploitation of women in traditional cultures but not a crusty conservative don? After the American and British wars in Bosnia and Kosovo against Slobodan Milosevic's ethnic cleansers, why were men and women of the Left denying the existence of Serb concentration camps? As important, why did a European Union that daily announces its commitment to the liberal principles of human rights and international law do nothing as crimes against humanity took place just over its borders? Why is Palestine a cause for the liberal-left, but not China, Sudan, Zimbabwe, the Congo or North Korea? Why, even in the case of Palestine, can't those who say they support the Palestinian cause tell you what type of Palestine they would like to see? After the 9/11 attacks on New York and Washington why were you as likely to read that a sinister conspiracy of Jews controlled American or British foreign policy in a superior literary journal as in a neo-Nazi hate sheet? And why after the 7/7 attacks on London did leftish rather than right-wing newspapers run pieces excusing suicide bombers who were inspired by a psychopathic theology from the ultra-right?

In short, why is the world upside down? In the past conservatives made excuses for fascism because they mistakenly saw it as a continuation of their democratic right-wing ideas. Now, overwhelmingly and everywhere, liberals and leftists are far more likely than conservatives to excuse fascistic governments and movements, with the exception of their native far-right parties. As long as local racists are white, they have no difficulty in opposing them in a manner that would have been recognizable to the traditional left. But give them a foreign far-right movement that is anti-Western and they treat it as at best a distraction and at worst an ally.

A part of the answer is that it isn't at all clear what it means to be on the Left at the moment. I doubt if anyone can tell you what a society significantly more left wing than ours would look like and how its economy and government would work.

(Let alone whether a majority of their fellow citizens would want to live there.) Socialism, which provided the definition of what it meant to be on the Left from the 1880s to the 1980s, is gone. Disgraced by the communists' atrocities and floored by the success of market-based economies, it no longer exists as a coherent programme for government. Even the modest and humane social democratic systems of Europe are under strain and look dreadfully vulnerable.

It is not novel to say that socialism is dead. The argument of this book is that its failure has brought a dark liberation to people who consider themselves to be on the liberal-left. It has freed them to go along with any movement however far to the right it may be, as long as it is against the status quo in general and, specifically, America. I hate to repeat the over-used quote that 'when a man stops believing in God he doesn't then believe in nothing, he believes anything', but there is no escaping it. Because it is very hard to imagine a radical left-wing alternative, or even mildly radical alternative, intellectuals in particular are ready to excuse the movements of the far right as long as they are anti-Western.

It is not only the lost souls of the old far left who are scurrying rightwards, but mainstream liberal-leftists, although for different reasons. The mainstream didn't only argue about economics but had a parallel programme from the Sixties on to promote equal rights for women, homosexuals and ethnic minorities. And on that, the liberal-left won spectacularly. Although prejudice with its attendant miseries continues in the rich world, the liberal-left achieved the political victory of securing equal legal rights in law for groups which had been despised and persecuted for millennia. But victory is a kind of death because it leaves you with no purpose once the old battles are over. Despite their talk of supporting equality, mainstream liberals found it uncomplicated to make excuses for anti-liberal movements because the triumph of their philosophy carried with it a poisonous and despairing legacy. If the dictatorial leaders of a foreign state or radical movement, or the usually unelected leaders of a 'community' or religious group said that their culture demanded the oppression of women and homosexuals, for example, twenty-first-century liberals were tripped over by the thought that it was racist to oppose them. They could be all for the emancipation of women in London, Paris and New York while indifferent to the misogynies of the Middle East, Africa and Asia.

The reverse side of the debased coinage of modern leftish thinking is a poignant spectacle. Democrats, feminists and socialists in the poor world, who are suffering at the hands of the extreme right, turn for support to the home of democracy, feminism and socialism in the West, only to find that the democrats, socialists and feminists of the rich world won't help them or acknowledge their existence.

For all the nihilism brought by the end of socialism and the exhaustion of the liberal agenda, you shouldn't underestimate the advantages the absence of a principled political pro-gramme for liberals and leftists brings. Their philosophy – or lack of a philosophy – suits modern consumerism. You don't have to commit to a vision of society and test it by standing for election. You don't have comrades you are obliged to stick by when times are hard. Like a shopper walking through a mall, you have no loyalties and no duties and can breeze into any store that takes your fancy. All you must be is against your own Western government and against America. As your own government is going to be foolish and unjust at times, and as America naturally attracts resentment and suspicion because it is the world's only superpower, and can also behave foolishly and unjustly at times, these are not high bars for the consumer of politics to jump.

Conservative readers could complain that I cite the indulgence for ideas and movements of the far right as the worst sin of today's liberal-left. Why single out fascism when the far left is as bad as the far right? I accept that if you want to be an accountant about it and get your calculator out, left-wing dictators murdered many millions more than right-wing dictators did in the twentieth century. I also agree that what unites totalitarian movements is more important than what divides them. My case is simply that when liberal-minded people make excuses for a totalitarian right that they would once have considered taboo, a deep fever has taken hold.

What follows is a critical history of how the symptoms of the malaise began in obscure groups of Marxists and postmodern theorists; how the sickness manifested itself in the failure to confront genocide in the Middle East and Europe until it grew into the raging fever of our day. It is also an argument for recovering the best of the liberal-left's democratic and internationalist traditions that have been neglected for too long.

A note on terminology

I use *the Left* as a generalization. It is not an exact term because it is very hard to say what it means, but you know the Left when you see it, and there were times when it felt like the right word. Overall, however, I try to be specific. The *far left* refers to the few remaining Leninists who still believe, or pretend to believe, that they can seize power and introduce a totalitarian state. If they stood alone, they wouldn't be worth bothering with, but they have merged into a much wider and more incoherent alliance which has little to offer beyond a rootless rage. Academics, students, readers of and writers for most leftish newspapers and all but the bravest Muslim and poor world intellectuals share this group's defining unwillingness to condemn crimes that can't be blamed on the West. Occasionally I call them *Chomskyans*, after Noam Chomsky, the American linguist whose flighty behaviour I look at in Chapter 6. At other times, I call them *nihilists* because of their wilful refusal to put an agenda before the public. Because they don't have a positive programme, it is difficult to think of a better label, although I accept that one is needed because they are the dominant left-wing force today.

A difference as large as the gulf between the democratic and totalitarian left is that between the working-class left, which generally fights for better pay and conditions, and the middle-class left which tends to be more interested in social and sexual liberalism. I call the trade unions and their supporters in the labour and social democratic parties the *old left*. For all the condescension directed at them, they are often the people who behave best in a crisis, as we shall see in Chapter 10. I call the middle-class left *the liberals*, not in the derogatory manner of American conservatives, but so I can talk about progressive middle-class opinion as a whole, and include Liberal Democrats in Britain, liberal-minded Christian Democrats and Gaullists in Europe and Democrats in the United States, as well as middle-class supporters of the labour and social democratic parties.

The one movement that I found very hard to classify is *New Labour*, which is probably why it won so many elections.

I use the *liberal-left* as a cover-all term for every shade of left opinion.

I accept that there are dozens of other tribes and traditions on the Left, but if I acknowledged them all I would lose you in a forest of footnotes. You can't write clearly without generalizations, and these are mine.

PART ONE

Morbid Symptoms

Yet it is a great mistake to suppose that the only writers who matter are those whom the educated in their saner moments can take seriously. There exists a subterranean world where pathological fantasies disguised as ideas are churned out by crooks and half-educated fanatics for the benefit of the ignorant and superstitious. There are times when this underworld emerges from the depths and suddenly fascinates, captures, and dominates multitudes of usually sane and responsible people, who thereupon take leave of sanity and responsibility.

Norman Cohn, 1996

CHAPTER ONE

An Iraqi Solzhenitsyn

When an opponent declares, 'I will not come over to your side,' I calmly say, 'Your child belongs to us already...What are you? You will pass on. Your descendants, however, now stand in the new camp. In a short time they will know nothing else but this new community'.

Adolf Hitler, 1933

YOU'RE NOT meant to say it, but great men and women still matter. Even in the modern age when elitism is a sin and the media labour to show the famous are no better than they ought to be, people still need heroes and heroines.

The politically committed need them more than most. They are partisans whose passions can make them appear unhinged. The babble of the therapists and the daytime TV hosts about each of us being special in our own unique way cannot disguise the banal reality that, like everyone else, the politically committed are not especially good or intelligent. Self-doubt creeps in. Why should others believe them when they say their plans for society won't end in the usual mess? Why should they believe themselves? Heroes make them feel comfortable. When they go to a meeting and hear a fine mind who knows more than they can ever know telling them that their cause is just, they are gladdened. When they turn on the television and see a brave woman abandoning her easy life to fight their battles, they know their battles are worth winning.

Until 2 August 1990, Kanan Makiya was a hero of the Left. We looked at him and felt good. It wasn't just that he was eloquent, courteous and intelligent, Kanan Makiya stood out because he did what the Left was meant do. He exposed in horrendous detail the mechanics of a totalitarian state without a thought for the consequences. Complacent foreign ministers practising the debased art of 'realism' and the executives of companies growing fat on arms contracts didn't want to hear what he had to say. Public opinion knew little and cared less about his cause. He wasn't downhearted. He would be heard.

As befitted a Left that said it believed in universal principles, Kanan Makiya was born into a cosmopolitan family in 1949. His father, Mohamed Makiya, was a Shia Arab and one of the first Iraqis to qualify as an architect. Mohamed founded the University of Baghdad's school of architecture and taught his students to create a new style for the Arab world by combining the motifs of his beloved Islamic tradition with the techniques of modernism. While he was studying at Liverpool University in 1941, he met Margaret Crawford, a history student and the daughter of a strict Derbyshire headmaster. To the horror of her conventional parents, they fell in love. When they said she must choose between him and them, she made matters worse by marrying Mohamed and moving to Iraq. Her family renounced her, and Kanan grew up without knowing his English relatives. Margaret was as much a part of the Left of the Forties as Kanan was of the Left of the 1968 generation. (If you were a nice Derbyshire girl from a good family, you had to be very left wing sixty years ago to defy your parents and run off with an Arab.) While they were students, she would take Mohamed away from his town planning classes to hear Bertrand Russell talk on philosophy and the socialist intellectual Harold Laski lecture on the new world which was coming.

The Makiyas were members of what people at that time called the 'progressive middle class' or the 'intelligentsia'. They brought fresh ideas with them when they settled in Baghdad. Mohamed's fusion of old and new styles began to make him a leader of Arab architecture. Margaret organized the first modern art exhibition in Baghdad. They had the self-confidence of a young and bright couple who see a future full of possibilities in front of them.

Kanan admired his parents and wanted a cosmopolitan education of his own. He won a place at the Massachusetts Institute of Technology and arrived in America as the protests against the Vietnam war were swelling. Family tradition and his own radical temperament made joining them an easy choice. From Prague to Los Angeles, the Left was in revolt in 1968, against war, oppression, racism and the creaking religious taboos that repressed human sexuality.

The attempted Arab invasion of Israel in 1967 had proved to be a spectacular miscalculation when the Six Day War ended in a stunning Israeli victory and the occupation of the West Bank and Gaza. For Kanan, as for so many other Arabs of his generation, the Israeli subjugation of a large Palestinian population was a great radicalizing moment. He had no time for nationalism – Palestinian, Arab or Israeli – and embraced a Trotskyist variant of Marxism, which promised to provide answers for all the peoples of the world regardless of colour or creed.

At a teach-in on the plight of the Palestinians, Kanan met his future wife Afsaneh Najmabadi, an Iranian physicist. 'He didn't look like an Arab,' Najmabadi told Lawrence Weschler, Makiya's biographer. 'He had incredibly bushy brown hair in those days, like a halo, and I thought he must be an American Jew, and was struck by the progressive stands he was advancing. I went up to him and introduced myself, and told him where I was from. He gave his name – Kanan Makiya – and said he was an Iraqi. "But Shia," he immediately added to put me, an Iranian, at ease.'

Kanan was following the standard course for a leftist of his class and generation. His enemies were Iran and the other pro-American dictatorships of the Middle East, Israeli colonialism and, more broadly, 'capitalism'. We remember the movements of 1968 he joined as a failed revolution. The student protests in Paris did not bring a change of government; and it was far from clear that any conceivable French government however socialist or anarchic could have satisfied the confused demonstrators. Soviet tanks flattened the attempt by the gallant Czechs to break the grip of communism. America's war in Vietnam continued despite the protests, although to give the demonstrators their due they increased the pressure on Washington to pull out. Historians put the revolts of 1968 in the same box as the revolutions of 1848: failed uprisings that none the less had lasting and unintended consequences on culture and politics. The historians don't quite get it right, however. One country had a successful revolution. Unfortunately, it was a fascist putsch.

In 1968 the Baath Party seized power in Iraq and forced Kanan Makiya to think about a subject very few leftish men and women of the time wanted to discuss: the possibility that fascism had not died in the Forties, but had lived on and flourished in the poor world.

Ominous forces were buffeting his father. The design dearest to his heart was a commission to build a university in the Shia city of Kufa. Shia businessmen had bought the land, while Mohamed and other Shia architects and builders had offered their services *pro bono*. Within months of the coup, the Baath Party nationalized the university. They did not intend to allow Shia students to have an independent education. Instead, the new development minister came up with a kitsch money-making scheme and ordered Mohamed to design a hideous resort on the site of ancient Babylon.

Mohamed told him, 'This is crazy. You are asking me to turn Babylon into a tourist trap with a Ziggurat hotel. This is a crime against history! The man was my worst enemy at the time – he was the one who had ordered Kufa shut down – but he listened, and I managed to convince him. Later, they killed him'.

Iraq became dangerous for the Makiyas. While her husband was abroad on business, Margaret received word that the Baath Party had his name on a list of subversives. His crime was to be a member of a sinister conspiracy of Freemasons.

Er, Freemasons?

Her husband wasn't a Freemason. Even if he had been, the charge would have made no sense. What kind of ideology believes that men who roll up their trouser legs and greet each other with funny handshakes are plotting to overthrow the state? She was mystified.

Margaret had taught English at Baghdad University for twenty-seven years. Half the Iraqi elite were her former pupils, and it didn't take her long to find well-connected friends who knew what the new regime had against Mohamed. Their explanation was the strangest story she had heard. In the Fifties, a British colonel had served as a military adviser to the old Iraqi monarchy. He was a meticulous man who kept records of every trivial event in his life and stored them in his strong box. He fled when the army overthrew the monarchy in 1958, leaving his box behind. It sat in Baghdad for twelve years until the Baathists decided to look inside.

The commonplace has supernatural significance to the conspiratorial mind, and the Baathists found evidence of an abominable intrigue in the humdrum files of a middle-aged Englishman. The records showed that the colonel had been a Freemason. They also showed he had invited hundreds of Iraqis for drinks at his home over the years. Mohamed was a neighbour living in the old British quarter of Baghdad. He spoke excellent English and was a graduate of a British university. It should have surprised no one that the colonel had asked him to one of his many parties. The Baathists put two and two together and concluded that the box revealed a vast conspiracy of Freemasons and British imperialists against the Arab nation. Secret policemen were preparing to arrest Mohamed and 400 others named in the dusty files.

'Don't laugh, they're serious,' Margaret's ex-pupils told her. 'Get out *now*.'

The urgency in her informants' voices was authentic, and Margaret realized that her husband was in mortal danger. Fortunately, he was abroad working on a project in Bahrain. She told him to stay there and used her connections to ship her family and their belongings out of the country

A Baath official requisitioned the Makiyas' home.

Later, they killed him.

The Makiyas found asylum in Britain and Mohamed set up the architectural practice of Makiya Associates in London. Kanan worked for his father's business while running campaigns to protect the Iraqi Kurds from Saddam Hussein's campaigns of racial persecution that were heading towards genocide. Mohamed was a good businessman as well as an excellent architect, and Makiya Associates won contracts from many Middle Eastern countries, with the obvious exception of Iraq.

In 1980, however, his pariah status changed. By then Saddam had total control of the Baath Party and with it Iraq. He wanted glory. He wanted to destroy Iran and make himself the undisputed master of the region. The Conference of Non-Aligned Nations was to meet in Baghdad in 1982, and he wanted the poor world's prime ministers and presidents to look on the works of his new city – and despair. Like many a totalitarian leader before him, he had a craving for triumphal architecture. Unfortunately, most of Iraq's architects were unavailable for work. After ludicrous show trials of alleged 'economic saboteurs', they were either dead or among the millions of refugees who had fled abroad.

Desperate to find alternative talent, Saddam's officials wrote to Makiya Associates to tempt Mohamed into reshaping Baghdad. Saddam was prepared to forget about his part in the global scheme of British Freemasons against the Arab nation, they told him, and shower him with lucrative commissions. Mohamed was wary, but few architects can resist the chance to follow Christopher Wren and Baron Haussmann and stamp their mark on their capital. 'My mother was the one who was interested in politics,' Kanan told me. 'My father went along with her, but all that really mattered to him was architecture. He was an architect to his bones. He wanted to build.'

The Baathists could not have been more attentive when the exile returned. They waved away the customs officers at Baghdad airport and treated Mohamed as a VIP. A member of the Revolutionary Command Council gave an unctuous speech on how proud Iraqis were of Mohamed's achievements.

'He was a very nice man,' Mohamed recalled.

'Later, they killed him.'

Makiya Associates' willingness to build for Saddam provoked Kanan into a savage argument with his father. 'This is for history,' Mohamed snapped. 'It's not for the people there now. It's got nothing to do with them – they'll be gone. This is for the future.'

Kanan couldn't stand it. He hated the thought that by working for Makiya Associates he was helping Saddam create his city of the future. The Iranian Afsaneh Najmabadi, who was his wife by 1979, needed a break, too. Her world had stopped making sense.

The West's support for dictators convinced leftists of Kanan Makiya and Afsaneh Najmabadi's generation that its democracy was a laughable fraud. Nowhere was the contrast between idealistic rhetoric and sordid politics clearer than in Najmabadi's native Iran. At the bidding of Britain, America had overthrown Iran's popular government because it had threatened to nationalize the Anglo-Iranian Oil Company. The West installed Mohammad Reza Pahlavi as Shah of Iran and allowed him to reign as an autocrat whose love of grandiose uniforms and glittering medals would have been ridiculous had it not been combined with the cruel suppression of dissent.

To Kanan, Afsaneh and their friends it was natural to expect that an illegitimate monarch doing the bidding of the West would provoke a revolution. And in 1979 there was a revolution in Iran. It was as profound and shocking as the French and Russian revolutions. Its consequences were as far-reaching – you hear of them daily on the evening news. But it was a revolution of a kind the modern world had never seen. Instead of being led by workers demanding fair shares for all or middle-class radicals demanding human rights and democratic elections, Iran had an Islamist revolution led by priests determined to impose their god's law on men and women (especially women).

Iranian leftists went along with them, somewhat stupidly as events were to turn out. Although they didn't agree with the Ayatollah Khomeini's belief that everything the human race needed to know was revealed in a seventh-century holy book, they reasoned that any revolution was better than none. The mania for Islam would pass, they thought. Religious exuberance was just a craze that flared up every now and again, then disappeared. All serious people knew that religion was hardly worth thinking about. Once the priests had discredited themselves, the scales would fall from the eyes of the masses and they would turn to the true faith of socialism. Everything the Left thought it knew stopped it from understanding that their socialism was dying, while militant religion was taking its place. Kanan stayed in London and watched from afar, but Afsaneh Najmabadi went back to fight with her comrades for a new Iran. The leaders of the Iranian left assured them that they could safely ignore the black-clad fanatics who were fanning out across the country. 'We have criticised Islamic fanaticism – we are against the non-progressive ideas of the conservative elements,' said Noureddin Kianouri, leader of the Marxist Tudeh Party, as he explained how he had weighted the options. 'But for us, the positive side of Ayatollah Khomeini is so important that the so-called negative side means nothing.'

Later they arrested him along with tens of thousands of his comrades, paralysed his arms, broke his fingers and made him confess on television to being a Soviet spy. The ayatollahs crushed the Left, the liberals and the feminists, and imposed a religious tyranny far more terrible and far harder for women to endure than the Shah's persecutions.

Afsaneh Najmabadi had been far more sceptical about the wisdom of leftists going along with holy misogynists, and had the good sense to leave and get back to Kanan in London. The news from Iran got no better on her return. In 1980 Saddam Hussein took advantage of the revolutionary chaos and began an unprovoked war to grab what Iranian oil fields he could. It turned into the longest conventional war of the twentieth century. Across trenches reminiscent of Passchendaele, the Ayatollah Khomeini sent wave after wave of martyrs. Young men marched towards the Iraqi guns, apparently welcoming the chance of death and admission to paradise and all its gorgeous virgins. With tactics again reminiscent of Passchendaele, Saddam met them with poison gas.

The strains in the Makiya family were becoming intolerable. By working in his father's London office on the plans for Saddam's new capital, Kanan was by extension working for a fascistic dictator, who had launched a war of imperial aggression. His wife was seeing her hopes for a socialist Iran destroyed by reactionary clerical forces, while being reminded every morning that her husband was going to work for the tyrant of Iraq whose armies were slaughtering her fellow Iranians.

Something had to give, and to her relief Kanan resigned from Makiya Associates and determined to piece together what had happened to Iraq by talking to refugees.

London is the place to find them. Constables from the Metropolitan Police hear slogans in strange tongues when they shepherd demonstrators through the streets. City bankers who think themselves men of the world would hear stories to make them shudder if they bothered to talk to the migrant women who clean their floors. The scruffy pedant, who insists on dragging out a wearisome meeting at the London School of Economics, becomes a new head of a new state. The preacher in the inner-city mosque with the fancy-dress beard and hook for a hand seems a post-modern parody until the police arrest him for inciting terrorism.

London is a city of exiles: pay attention and you will hear the woes of the world.

'The truth is that before 1980 Kanan hadn't been all that involved in Iraq,' Afsaneh Najmabadi told Weschler. 'Lebanon and Palestine and, later, Iran were far to the fore in what we were struggling over. But then it was as if the Baath came to him. If his father had not been invited back to Iraq, Kanan would probably never have written that book. It was him being involved, even tangentially, in designing the Baath Party headquarters that actually got him thinking, seriously thinking about the Baath . . . There is a great irony here.'

Ms Najmabadi didn't know it, but 'ironic' wouldn't begin to cover the course of the next twenty-five years.

As an aperitif, the money Saddam Hussein was paying his father gave Kanan the time and space to ask very good and very simple questions: What do the Baathists believe? Where do they come from? Why do they kill so many people?

A private income aside, Kanan had one other advantage. He slowly grasped a truth about totalitarianism that Albert Camus, George Orwell, Hannah Arendt and Robert Conquest had grasped before him: the terror *isn't* a side effect of the system; the terror *is* the system. Once a political or religious totalitarian movement has momentum, it has an irrational life and logic of its own which can't be explained away. It kills because its ideology says it has to kill. The massacres will be worthwhile because when it exterminates the enemies of the proletariat or the master race or the one true religion, all the conflicts of the human condition will be resolved in an earthly paradise.

Because he was a Marxist, Makiya might never have recognized the obvious, and no one apart from a handful of friends would have read him. The Marxist tradition has created many mass murderers, but it is hopeless at explaining them. It is not that Marxists have bad consciences about the mounds of corpses – in my experience they rarely do; rather, Marxism assumes that rational economic interests and class conflicts move the world and cannot cope with the lusts for power, murder and martyrdom. A typical left-wing analysis of Iraq from the Eighties argued that 'a bureaucratic bourgeoisie' which depended on 'the depletion of the state's resources, whether by legal, quasi-legal or illegal means' ruled the country. It was a parasitic class which increased its wealth by fostering 'dependence on the multi-nationals' and 'the militarization of the economy'. The forgotten writer was not all wrong, Saddam Hussein, like all other totalitarian dictators, needed loot to reward his followers and equip his armies. Without it, he would never have survived. Yet you can only get so far in explaining Saddam Hussein or any of the other great criminals of the twentieth century by looking at the economies of their countries, their distribution of favours to clients and the national traumas and humiliations that allowed them to seize power. Once you have exhausted all comprehensible reasons for a great crime there remains a gap. The 'root causes' take you to its edge, but then wave goodbye and leave you peering into an unfathomable abyss. The famines Stalin, Mao and the Ethiopian colonels unleashed, Pol Pot's extermination of anyone who could read or write, Hitler's annihilation of the Jews, gypsies, gays and Slavs, Saddam's regime of torture and genocide and the Islamist cult of death aren't rationally explicable. You can cross over to the other side of the abyss only if you shrug off your reasonable liberal belief that every consequence has an understandable cause and accept that enthusiasm for the ideologies of absolute power isn't always rationally explicable.

It took Makiya several years to realize he was looking

through the wrong end of the telescope. He decided to call his exposure of Baathist Iraq *Republic of Fear*, and its first chapter was going to be on Iraq's economy. As a good Marxist he believed that the 'root causes' of Saddam Hussein lay in the arrangement of classes and patterns of economic exploitation. The longer he researched, the lower down the book's running order the chapter on economics fell. In the end, he binned it. His preconceptions were getting in the way.

Makiya also abandoned the pseudo-sophisticated journalist's question, 'Why is this lying bastard lying to me?' He worked on the sensible assumption that despite 'the proclivity of those in public office to propaganda, rhetoric, chicanery and lies, on the whole even they usually end up saying what they mean and meaning what they say'. He not only interviewed exiles, but also dug out the speeches of Saddam Hussein and the pamphlets of his supporters from obscure archives in London and New York and read them not as propaganda but as evidence of what his fellow Iraqis had to believe on pain of death.

He took on the Baath Party by paying it the compliment of taking what it said seriously.

A group of Arab nationalists founded the Baath ('Renaissance') Party in Damascus on 24 July 1943. Like the tightly organized totalitarian parties of inter-war Europe, it had a military structure which allowed it to operate as an underground army. It seized power in Syria in 1963, and remains in sole charge of the one-party state to this day. What happened to Syria was grim, but Makiya faced an organizational problem in describing the greater horror of what the Baath did to Iraq. To print all the available evidence of murder and bestiality would have turned *Republic of Fear* into an unmanageably large book that ran the risk of descending into the pornography of violence. With

31

admirable restraint, he confined the snuff-movie side of Baathism to one relatively dry account of one small bout of extermination by Baathist forces written by a historian working from official sources. It read:

> The Nationalist Guard's Bureau of Special Investigation had alone killed 104 persons, the bodies of 42 of whom were found in 1963–64 buried in al Jazirah and al-Hawash districts. In the cellars of al-Nihayyah Palace, which the bureau used as its headquarters, were found all sorts of loathsome instruments of torture, including electric wires with pincers, pointed iron stakes on which prisoners were made to sit, and a machine which still bore traces of chopped-off fingers. Small heaps of bloodied clothes were scattered about, and there were pools on the floor and stains over the walls.

Those killings were in 1963, the year the Iraqi Baathists joined the Syrian Baathists in seizing power. The Iraqi army threw them out, but they returned in the successful putsch of 1968. By 1980, when Kanan's father flew back to Iraq, Saddam Hussein had become the undisputed master of both party and state. By the time Americans and their allies overthrew him in 2003, the Baathists had murdered around 400,000 Iraqis in internal persecutions, while Saddam's unprovoked wars against Iran and Kuwait led to the killing of a further one million or so. Baathists then joined with Islamists from al-Qaeda to form what delicate euphemists called the 'insurgency', and carried on murdering tens of thousands of Iraqis. The history of modern Iraq is of a systematic depredation and destruction of the human spirit that has lasted four decades. Future historians who decide to chart it are going to need strong stomachs.

The resemblances to European fascism and communism did not stop with the state-sponsored sadism of the all-powerful ruling party. The all-powerful party also had an all-encompassing totalitarian ideology. Michel Aflaq and Salah al-Din, the Baath's chief ideologues, were pan-Arabists who wanted a single state for all the Arabs of the Middle East. Theirs seemed a benign ambition at first glance, but nationalists always have the seeds of tyranny in them. They are just as likely to want to tyrannize their own people as their people's enemies because their own people can let them down badly. The theory holds that the Arabs or the Germans or the Serbs are strong and brave, and ready by biological inheritance or cultural superiority to rule themselves and others. In practice, the people can be lazy and less than thrilled by the prospect of dying for the greater good of the nation. In these circumstances, their manifest destiny can be realized only if they obey orders.

Baathism allowed no room for malcontents who would contradict the party line. In a speech in 1977, Saddam Hussein told history teachers what the Baath expected of them:

> Those researchers and historians who call themselves objective might very well be presenting different viewpoints and possibilities to explain one event...leaving it to the reader to draw his or her own conclusions...The Baathist must never deal with history and all other intellectual and social questions in this way ...They must take on the same specificity as our Baathist way; in other words, the writing of Arab history should be from our point of view with an emphasis on analysis and not realistic story telling.

The truth was what the Baathists said it was. Adults would have memories of different truths from before the Baathists took power, but the Baathists would be able to control their children and mould them into a new type of Arab, conditioned from infancy to obey. In Iraq's case, indoctrination began at primary school where textbooks presented Saddam Hussein as *Baba* – 'father' – Saddam, an alternative object of love and loyalty to their parents. Spies watched to see if pupils participated in Baathist rallies and kept files on the political reliability of their mothers, fathers, grandparents and so on to cousins of the third degree.

The regime's aim was to dissolve family bonds so children would be ready to turn against their parents. The wise Iraqi learned not to talk politics in front of the little ones. After the fall of Baghdad, the argument that Hind Aziz had with her 9-year-old daughter, Dalia, was typical of arguments all over the country. The child wanted to know why she was only now learning that Saddam was a killer.

'Why didn't you tell me the truth?'

'I had to explain to her that if I did, she might have told her friends, and then Mummy would have been executed, Daddy would have been executed, and Grandpa would have been executed, too,' the mother explained.

Her father showed an Australian journalist how deep the indoctrination had gone.

'Who is your father, Dalia?' he asked.

'Baba Saddam,' she replied, robotically.

Saddam's punishment of parents wasn't a corruption of power, a late degeneracy after years of dictatorship. It was a natural consequence of the original Baathist programme. Aflaq explained that the Baathists expected the people to devote themselves to the party like lovers to an impulsive mistress. Laying down the law to Arab intellectuals in 1959, he said: 'The nationalism we are calling for is love before anything else.

He who loves does not ask for reasons.' Blind faith was in the genes, Aflaq believed, a natural part of the Arab Islamic culture.

As theology or history this may have been nonsense, but as a recipe for dictatorship Aflaq's demand for unconditional love was bound to create a tyranny because Iraq was more diverse than any other Arab nation. If Iraq could function as a free society, it could do so only as a federal democracy. If the Baathists tried pan-Arab nationalism instead, they would have to answer the question, where are your Arabs? About one-fifth of Iraq's population were not Arabs but Kurds and Turks. The majority of Iraq's Arabs were Shia Muslims, estranged from the Sunni Arabs since the early days of Islam. Sunni Arabs were a mere 20 per cent of the population, so Sunni Arab nationalism would mean either an apartheid system, with the Sunnis as the 'whites', or a merciless dictatorship, which was what Iraq got for decades.

The contours of that dictatorship ought to have been familiar to European eyes. In his purges of the Baath Party Saddam modelled himself on Stalin. The Baath Party's rhetoric was often a straight copy of communist propaganda, while the Soviet Union was Saddam's largest supplier of arms. Yet Baathist ideology also took the complete conspiracy theory of the European counter-revolution. Like the clerical and aristocratic opponents of the Enlightenment in the eighteenth century and Adolf Hitler, Francisco Franco and the European fascists of the twentieth century, it held that democracy and human rights were a sham that hid the secret workings of sinister conspiracies, and not only those of the Freemasons. Makiya quoted Fadhil al-Barak, one of the regime's apologists, who explained that because Jews had been living in what is now Israel since the seventh century BC, they had been in an anti-Arab conspiracy since then. The Persian Iranians weren't far behind. They had been conspiring against Iraqi Arabs since 539 BC, which was a surprisingly early date to begin plotting given that the Arabs did not invade what is now Iraq until 637 AD, a thousand years or so later. Baathist historical works reeked of racism and included the charming *Three Whom God Should Never Have Created: Persians, Jews and Flies*. Al-Barak naturally took the tsarist forgery *The Protocols of the Elders of Zion* to be a genuine exposé of a Jewish plot to control the world.

Despite all his good work in unmasking subversives, al-Barak was himself unmasked by his rivals in the Baath Party. Under torture, he confessed to being a spy for the Soviet Union and East Germany.

Later, they killed him.

His death in no way diminished the appetite for conspiracy theory. One of the first acts of the Baath Party after 1968 was to turn on Iraq's Jews. They accused them of helping Israel defeat the Arabs in the Six Day War of 1967 – a conflict in which Iraqi soldiers distinguished themselves by their unwillingness to fight. To explain the humiliation and get popular prejudice on the side of the new dictatorship, Ahmad Hasan al-Bakr, the first Baathist president, revealed a Jewish conspiracy to a huge crowd in central Baghdad.

'They aim to create malicious rumour and disturbances employing for this end killings, sabotage and undertaking operations behind the front line of our heroic army.

'What do you want?' he screamed.

'Death to the spies!' the mob screamed back.

The pogrom began. The Baath accused Iraq's Jews of plotting with Israel, Britain, the Freemasons and the Iranians. The Kurds were Zionism's bankers, who funnelled Israeli money to Iraqi Jews.

In 1968, seventeen Jewish 'spies' went on trial. The defendants got a taste of the Baath's idea of due process when their own lawyer opened the case for the defence by apologizing to the prosecution. He wanted it on the record that he 'would not like to see them go unpunished'. The press bench howled with laughter when the defendants pleaded 'not guilty'. The protestations of innocence died when the authorities 'persuaded' them to confess.

Later, they killed them and strung up their corpses in Baghdad's Liberation Square for the edification of hundreds of thousands of spectators who streamed in from across the country to see the sights of the big city.

Makiya despaired as he went through the records. In the Fifties, the optimistic artists and intellectuals of his parents' generation had imagined a future Kurdish–Arab partnership in a common Iraqi homeland. The Baath had shown it was possible to blow away years of rubbing along in a few months. 'Common sense was dying in Iraq,' he wrote, 'along with civil society.' Although the early racist campaigns were undoubtedly popular, Iraq's new masters were also teaching the population a lesson common to all varieties of totalitarianism: nothing is true and everything is permissible. Frenzy quickly turned to fear. People kept dying mysteriously and the Baath Party used their deaths to justify a police state. The newspapers reported that saboteurs were bombing Baghdad. Sometimes the state-controlled media were so on top of the story they reported the explosions before the bombs went off. The Baathists deployed the politics of race to persuade Iraqis to support them and the politics of fear to warn Iraqis of the dangers of defying them.

First they came for the Jews, then they came for the communists. The Soviet leadership wanted Iraq on its side in the Cold War. It ordered Iraqi communists to form an alliance with the Baath Party in the early Seventies, a manoeuvre Saddam made the Iraqi communists regret when he welcomed their support, embraced them as allies, waited for a while and then arrested the entire politburo of the Iraqi Communist Party along with an uncounted number of militants. They, too, were tortured. A few brave men and women stayed strong, but most broke and appeared on television to confess their crimes.

Show trials, televised confessions and plots by Freemasons and Jews stretching back across the millennia . . . these were the raging totalitarian frenzies of fascism and communism rolled into one and adapted to fit local conditions.

Makiya readily conceded that Saddam Hussein was an imitator of European totalitarianism, not an innovator. 'Nevertheless, his legacy has already been assured by the consistency and determination with which he brought such trends to bear inside Iraq. Above all, his particular achievement was the placement of an inordinate emphasis on a revised conception of political crime, one that made it ever more loose and all-inclusive' so that 'police work logically became the substitute for politics'.

Or as Saddam pithily explained, 'The revolution chooses its enemies.'

God and the devil dwell together in the detail of great crimes. The more you know about monstrosities the more likely you are to make a commitment to fight them. For it is one thing to hear the screaming paranoia in the speeches of a dictator and realize that life in his country must be grim, quite another to know the names of the camps and of the torturers and the details of what they do to the camps' captives.

Totalitarian systems do not have freedom of information

acts. At the time of writing, I guess that the worst place in the world is North Korea. There are reports of millions dying in slave camps, gas chambers, mass executions and famines. But it is impossible to be sure. The few who get out, escape to communist China. They have to keep their heads down and mouths shut for fear the Chinese will send them back. Journalists, diplomats and workers for human rights organizations cannot move freely and interview whom they please. North Korea hovers at the back of the public mind. People joke about the cult of the personality of Kim Jong-Il, 'the dear leader', and the 100 per cent turnout in uncontested elections; they worry about his drive to become a nuclear power; but they have few facts to detain them further.

'For every nugget of truth some wretch lies dead on the scrapheap,' said H. L. Mencken. In his extravagant way, he had it right. Getting uncomfortable facts on to the record is the toughest struggle for journalists in democracies. To prove that this minister took a bribe or that policeman beat a suspect requires time and money. Reporters can spend months trying to nail down what they know to be true only for secrecy, the law or the nervousness of their employers to defeat them.

Consider how much tougher it is to get to the truth in a dictatorship where the penalty for saying a word out of turn is death. Asymmetries in access to information have the paradoxical effect of making it easier to expose the abuses of power in open societies than dictatorships. Daniel Patrick Moynihan, a former US ambassador to the United Nations, came up with 'Moynihan's Law' to encapsulate the distorted vision that follows. It holds that the number of complaints about a nation's violation of human rights is in inverse proportion to its actual violation of them. To put it another way, you can find out what is happening in America's prison cells in Guantánamo Bay if you work very hard, but not in Kim Il-Sung's prison cells in Pyongyang.

In the Eighties, I picked up a copy of *Saddam's Iraq: Revolution or Reaction*, a collection of essays by Ann Clwyd, a Labour MP, and her fellow left-wing activists. On re-reading, what struck me was how little they knew. Clwyd was a good friend to the cause of Iraqi democracy, who never ran for cover when the going got rough. She and her colleagues did not intend to give Saddam Hussein an easy ride and correctly noted that he had built the cult of the personality of the classic totalitarian tyrant. But Moynihan's Law meant they had no guide to the terror to tell them who was torturing whom and where. Blank spaces were all over their map. They suspected that 'there be dragons' but couldn't identify the monsters and invite an insouciant world to face them.

Makiya's achievement was to fill the gaps on the map of the police state. He described how the Soviet Union helped the Baath create the *Amn*, or state internal security department, and supplied it with surveillance and interrogation equipment. He reported the crimes of the *Estikhbarat*, or military intelligence, which the Baath based in Iraqi embassies to arrange the intimidation and assassination of potential leaders of the opposition among the millions of Iraqi refugees. Above all, he detailed the power of the *Mukhabarat*, the political secret police, which combined domestic and foreign intelligence gathering and spied on any part of the bureaucracy that might provide cover for a potential challenger to Saddam, including its rival intelligence services.

The whole country was under surveillance. In 2003, Steve Boggan of the London *Evening Standard* went into Baghdad with the American forces. He and his interpreter scouted the ruins of a burnt-out police station. Fortunately for them, Stasi spies from East Germany had helped train the Baathist secret police, and Saddam's goons had adopted the German habit of meticulously recording every detail of their work. The Iraqi interpreter started reading papers going back decades and then stopped in astonishment. 'Hairdressers,' he exclaimed. '*Hairdressers!*'

Boggan got him to translate and heard how hairdressers in Baghdad had to report subversive remarks made by women under the driers. What was a hairdresser to do if her sensibly wary customers steered clear of politics? For how long could she keep telling the secret police that she had nothing to report, without running the risk of the spies marking her down as uncooperative?

Makiya described how it was dangerous to show curiosity in a country gripped by fear. People vanished. Weeks later the police returned their corpses to their families in sealed boxes. They gave them death certificates which stated that X had died in a fire or Y had died in a traffic accident. The procedures were correct in all respects except one. The police told the families that they must on no account open the boxes and look at the real injuries on the corpses. For their own safety, they had to obey and become complicit in spreading the official lie when they gave their friends and neighbours the reason for the deaths of their relatives.

Beyond the spies were the party's militia, the regular police and the armed forces. Beyond the direct instruments of violence were the state's employees and the million members of the Baath Party. All had to be ready to condemn others to torture and murder for fear that the same fate would meet them if they did not collaborate.

When Makiya added up the forces of oppression, he found

there was one agent of the state for every twenty Iraqis, but I don't think he understood the implications of his calculation until the Nineties.

Alexis de Tocqueville said of the French Revolution: 'It is almost never when a state of things is the most detestable that it is smashed, but when, beginning to improve, it permits men to breathe, to reflect, to communicate their thoughts with each other, and to gauge by what they already have the extent of their rights and their grievances.'

All the attempted coups and insurrections in Iraq failed because the Baath had too many spies dedicated to stopping people breathing. There was no space to organize, no one to trust with your thoughts, and Saddam knew it. In 1971 he told the Baath that 'with our party methods, there is no chance for anyone who disagrees with us to jump on a couple of tanks and overthrow the government'.

The hideous choice for Makiya, Iraq and all those who professed to believe in human rights was this: either they would have to wait for his death and the deaths of his sadistic sons Qusay and Uday, or they had to accept that the only way to remove the Baath was foreign invasion.

By the time he approached Mohamed Makiya, Saddam had closed down the alternative prospect of a rival faction within the party taking control and moderating Baathism as Khrushchev had moderated Soviet communism. In 1979, he became 'the leader', the undisputed master of both party and country, and staged a horror show that taught Iraqis that from now on anyone could be the torturer and anyone could be the torturer's victim.

Saddam ordered the kidnapping of the families of one-third of the members of the Revolutionary Command Council and purged their supporters in the bureaucracy. He told his colleagues to cooperate or see his interrogators rape their wives and daughters.

They cooperated.

The 'ringleaders' were marched to a lecture hall to confess to their counter-revolutionary crimes before an audience of 1,000 party members and a camera crew Saddam had instructed to record the scene for posterity.

The film shows Saddam as a trusting and simple man who is overwhelmed with grief by the perfidy of colleagues he took to be friends. He tells the audience: 'After the arrest of the criminals, I visited them in an attempt to understand the motive for their behaviour. "What political differences are there between you and me?" I asked. "Did you lack any power or money? If you had a different opinion why did you not submit it to the Party since you are its leaders?" They had nothing to say to defend themselves. They just admitted their guilt.'

Mystifying, really.

Saddam looks at the unsuspecting audience, produces a list and proclaims, 'The people whose names I am going to read out should repeat the party slogan and leave the hall.' To its astonishment, the audience realizes that Saddam believes there are traitors among them.

A party official goes down the list. After he announces each of the sixty-six names, armed guards force each doomed apparatchik to cry 'One Arab nation with a holy message! Unity, freedom and socialism!' before dragging him from the hall. Saddam enjoys the spectacle. He puffs on a cigar as panic floods the room. When his arrested colleagues try to protest their innocence, he dismisses them with a wave of his hand. No one knows who will be next. No one knows what real or imagined slight to Saddam will be a death sentence.

When the last name has been read and the list has been put

away, the survivors of the purge weep with hysterical gratitude at their escape from murder. 'Long live the father of Uday!' screams one. 'Saddam is too lenient,' screams another.

As a gesture of solidarity, Saddam condescends to sit among them. 'We don't need Stalinist methods to deal with traitors here,' he says. 'We need Baathist methods.'

The Baathist method is something special. Saddam asks the survivors to execute the 'traitors'. Personally execute them, that is, by joining him in a firing squad. His was a new totalitarian tactic in a century that seemed to have exhausted the possibilities of brutality. Stalin made Molotov divorce his wife and then vote to have her imprisoned as a Zionist agent. Even that master of cruelty did not think to have him murder her.

By forcing the Iraqi elite to be the executioners of their colleagues, Saddam was binding them to him. They were criminals now, his made men, who had to sink or swim with the big boss. The purge over, Saddam ordered his armies to begin a war against Iran that was, for once, all about oil. Makiya watched the body count run towards a million and the Iraqi economy collapse. He heard of the generals Saddam had shot for lowering his prestige by losing battles and the generals Saddam had shot for rivalling his prestige by winning battles. Makiya concluded that now, surely, the madness would pass and the dictatorship would collapse.

He finished his book in 1986 with a peroration on the war. It was, he said, 'Saddam's final catastrophe'.

It was the last time he gave him the benefit of the doubt.

CHAPTER TWO

'Sacrificed So Much for This Animal'

I will kill them all with chemical weapons! Who is going to say anything? The international community? Fuck them!

Ali Hassan al-Majid, 'Chemical Ali', 1988

IN 1989 the University of California Press brought out *Republic of Fear* by one Samir al-Khalil. The author acknowledged that he was working under a pseudonym. 'I owe a handful of very dear friends a great deal in writing this book. But things being what they are under the Baath, I can no more mention their names than I can write under my own.'

Kanan Makiya knew that critics of Saddam felt bullets hit the back of their heads wherever they lived. When he appeared on radio to promote his book, he wore a wig and insisted the sound engineers distorted his voice.

In its own way, *Republic of Fear* was a risky venture for the University of California Press. Dozens of publishers had rejected it. The ethical problem for reputable houses was how to deal with an author who refused to reveal his identity and left them wide open to the risk of being taken in by a hoaxer. Lynne Withey, an editor at the University of California Press, was prepared to take a chance. She thought the book was too important to ignore and agreed to consider the manuscript after Afsaneh Najmabadi swore her husband was not a conman. 'Lynne never talked to me,' said Kanan. 'The University of California Press had never published an anonymous book before, let alone a book written under a pseudonym. It took great courage and a special decision at the level of the board of directors.'

There was also a more straightforward commercial obstacle. The publishers who turned down Makiya reasoned that few cared about Iraq, and they were right. The great powers wanted an Iraqi strongman to check the revolutionary threat of Islamist Iran, and their politicians, diplomats, spies and publics were not willing to look too closely at the consequences of *realpolitik*.

A wave of bad faith engulfed the rich world's liberals after the second Iraq war, and they took the indifference of the Western elites of the Eighties as proof that Saddam was the fault of Britain and America – the West's monster and the West's puppet. On the rare occasions they forced themselves to confront his crimes, they had always to add the caveat that they had been committed with Western aid. Even on 19 October 2005 when the worst tyrant she would see in her life went on trial, even as she stood among the graves of the Kurds of Halabja, Caroline Hawley of the BBC was adamant that 'each headstone here represents a family wiped out with weapons that Saddam Hussein bought from the West'.

It was tosh, of course. Saddam was not left in power so he could keep the profits flowing to Anglo-American arms manufacturers. Nor was he any more America's puppet than Hitler was a pawn of MI6. For an Iraqi, the charge of being an agent of American imperialism or British Freemasonry was as dangerous as the charge of being a Zionist spy. After the fall of Baghdad, the Stockholm International Peace Research Institute examined the records of 'actual deliveries of major conventional weapons' to Iraq between 1973 and 2002, and found that 57 per cent of Saddam's weapons came from the Soviet Union, 13 per cent from France and 12 per cent from China. The United States sold about half of 1 per cent, while Britain's sales were worth $79 million, or about one-fifth of 1 per cent, a fraction so small the Swedes rounded it down to the nearest whole number, which was zero.

Weapons of mass destruction did 'come from the West' in a sense – West Germany, whose companies provided Saddam with one of the largest chemical weapons manufacturing industries in the world. (In a revolting example of Cold War cooperation, the East German communists gave Saddam's forces training on how to use them.) Meanwhile France built the Tammuz nuclear reactor, which might have given Saddam the bomb if the Israeli air force had not infuriated Jacques Chirac by blowing it up.

These figures appear to exonerate Britain and America, but they are not as kind as they look. The people in power in both countries did not want to know about the Iraq *Republic of Fear* described, and one of the few remarks of Henry Kissinger's that is worth remembering explains why. 'It's a pity they can't both lose,' he said of the Iran–Iraq War. When Khomeini's revolutionary armies looked as if they would win, and seize Iraq's oil fields and go on to control a large chunk of the world's oil by seizing the Saudi Arabian oil fields as well, the United States intervened. It helped the Baathists with facts rather than arms sales. What Saddam got out of the approaches first from the Carter administration and then from Donald Rumsfeld for the Reagan administration was an intelligence-sharing agreement. AWACS spy planes recorded Iranian troop deployments so the Iraqi army could concentrate its fire. American jets brought down Iranian civilian and military flights to deter the Ayatollah Khomeini from destroying the Iraqi war economy by sinking Iraqi tankers in the Persian Gulf.

As valuable to Saddam as the intelligence was the silence. Instead of fighting the Islamic revolution themselves, Britain and America were happy for a fascistic despot to do its fighting for them. So there was no complaint when Saddam acquired between 2,000 and 4,000 tons of chemical agents; no real protest beyond mealy-mouthed mutterings when he used them to kill about 50,000 Iranian soldiers. Donald Rumsfeld went to Baghdad in 1984 to assure the Baathists that what condemnations there had been were for form's sake and should not be taken personally. To stop the Islamic revolution spreading, the West was prepared to hold its tongue.

From 1987, it had to bite it. Saddam was about to sink lower than his worst enemies had imagined possible and organize the first genocide since Pol Pot's slaughter of the Cambodians. The victims were the Kurds, the largest people on earth without a state of their own. They never received the attention given to the Palestinians or even the Basques and the Catalans. In part, it was Moynihan's Law: the Kurds were trapped in the closed or semi-closed societies of nationalist Turkey, Islamist Iran and Baathist Syria and Iraq. To make matters worse, you could not really blame 'capitalism' or 'Western imperialism' for their suffering unless you went back to the failure of the great powers to establish a Kurdish state at the end of the First World War. The Kurds were an uncomfortable people who could not be tidied away into neat boxes.

In all their occupied territories, they fought guerrilla wars against enemies who regarded them as racial inferiors. With the Baath Party diverted by the Iran–Iraq War, they allied with Iranian forces and went on the advance. In 1987, Saddam determined to punish them by exterminating all Kurds who weren't under his direct control. He made his cousin, Ali Hassan al-Majid ('Chemical Ali') secretary-general of the Northern Bureau, the administrative centre that covered Iraqi Kurdistan, and gave him complete discretion. 'Comrade al-Majid's decisions shall be mandatory for all state agencies,' Saddam told his underlings. Al-Majid had free rein to 'solve the Kurdish problem and slaughter the saboteurs'.

The echo of Adolf Hitler's Final Solution was prophetic. On his arrival, al-Majid promised the staff of the Northern Bureau: 'I will kill them all with chemical weapons! Who is going to say anything? The international community? Fuck them!'

It always comes to this. They always say the same thing when they think outsiders aren't listening. When the pretensions of the workers' state or the thousand-year Reich or the glorious union of Arabs are stripped away, when the differences between communism and fascism are forgotten, what remains is the sneer of the psychopathic gangster who knows he's got the cops in his pocket.

When he ordered the Great Purge of 1936, Stalin said: 'Who's going to remember this riffraff in ten or twenty years time? No one. Who remembers the *boyars* Ivan the Terrible got rid of?'

When he ordered the massacre of the Polish intelligentsia, Hitler said: 'After all, who today speaks of the massacre of the Armenians?'

When tens of millions starved in the Great Leap Forward, the single greatest political crime of the twentieth century, Mao Tse-tung told the few brave officials who condemned themselves to death by speaking out: 'A few children die in the kindergarten, a few old men die in the Happiness Court. If there's no death people can't exist. From Confucius to now it would be disastrous if people didn't die.'

Hitler committed suicide and Italian partisans hung Mussolini from a meat hook, but Lenin, Stalin, Mao, Pol Pot, Franco and Amin died in their beds. Because of the American and British armies, I'm glad to say that at the time of writing Saddam Hussein and Comrade al-Majid are on trial in Baghdad. Unfortunately, it seems likely that the 'realism' of the UN route in Darfur has allowed the Islamist government of Sudan to get away with genocide.

Al-Majid had sound historical grounds for thinking that he could 'fuck' the international community and that there would be many among its statespersons and foreign policy analysts who would lie back and enjoy the experience. He launched the *Anfal* ('spoils') campaign to solve the Kurdish 'problem' with the reasonable expectation that he would never be held to account. Waves of Iraqi troops plundered and destroyed 4,000 Kurdish villages. Any man, woman or child who lived in the 'prohibited zone' outside the government's authorized centres was a legitimate target.

The Kurds' initial attempts to rally international support got nowhere. They would have been a total failure had it not been for Peter Galbraith, son of John Kenneth, and a staff member for the US Senate Foreign Relations Committee. He used his pull to persuade the Baathists to allow him to travel into Kurdistan. He drove north with mounting confusion. Kurdish villages that appeared on his maps weren't there on the ground. He would stop at what should have been a busy settlement and see nothing but rubble. Galbraith made a stink when he returned to Washington and got an international campaign going. Despite his efforts, the massacre of the Kurds would have meant as little to the world as the massacres of the Armenians and *boyars* had not al-Majid ordered the bombing of Halabja with a mixture of VX gas, mustard gas and sarin.

Like Makiya, I've tried to avoid the pornography of violence. Atrocity stories are a species of blackmail. The writer – or more often broadcaster these days – is in effect saying 'agree with me or you are guilty by association'. It is too easy.

I have therefore spared you the sacks filled with starving cats, the rape rooms and the plastic-shredding machines. In the case of the *Anfal* campaign, however, you cannot understand it without understanding the thoroughness with which the Baath slaughtered a minimum of 100,000 Kurds. All over northern Iraq, staggered bewildered people with stories of the utmost poignancy. Abdel-Qadir al-Askari will serve for all of them. He was on a hill above his village of Guptapa when he saw planes flying in low over the rooftops. He ran down and found his mother collapsed by the river, her mouth biting the mud bank. 'I wanted to kiss her but I knew that if I did, the chemicals would be passed on. Even now I deeply regret not kissing my beloved mother.' He continued along the river and found the bodies of his children, his brother, his father, his nieces and his nephews. 'At this point I lost my feelings. I didn't know who to cry to anymore.'

No one outside Kurdistan would know what you meant if you talked about Guptapa. Halabja's name flew round the world, not because it was the apogee of the genocide, but because the Baathists blundered by wiping out civilians fifteen miles from the Iranian border. Journalists were able to get in without permission from Baghdad and see the poisoned corpses for themselves: the husband holding the hand of the wife; the father flattened against a wall with his arms round his infant son; the mother caught with her back arched to protect her child . . . hundreds of bodies frozen at the moment of death, as if fossilized in the ash of a new Vesuvius.

Moynihan's Law had no jurisdiction, and Halabja joined

Guernica, Katyn and My Lai in that eccentric but necessary list of comparatively small twentieth-century massacres which act as shorthand notes for atrocities that are too colossal to comprehend. There was a media storm, but that quickly passed as media storms do. Galbraith persuaded the US Senate to pass a bill to impose sanctions on Iraq, but the House of Representatives blocked it. George Shultz, Ronald Reagan's Secretary of State, condemned Iraq, but the State Department was a true friend to dictators in adversity and his officials calmed him down.

To its enormous credit, the only political faction to stand up consistently against fascism and genocide was the liberal-left. Human Rights Watch established itself as an alternative to Amnesty International on the strength of its investigations in Iraq. The book that was to become *Republic of Fear* didn't originate in discussions with a major publishing house but with debates Makiya had with fellow Trotskyists. They gathered around *New Left Review*, a journal for socialist intellectuals that was based in Soho and edited by Perry Anderson, an English Marxist of the upper class. Before Makiya published, Tariq Ali, a Pakistani Marxist of the upper class and *New Left Review* board member, made a documentary with him about Iraq's suffering. The most left-wing MPs in the Labour Party lined up to denounce Saddam as a 'fascist', while the racial persecution of the Kurds in Iraq and Turkey moved Harold Pinter, the left-wing playwright, poet and future winner of the Nobel Prize for Literature, to produce *Mountain Language*.

'Your language is forbidden,' a concentration camp officer bellows at a Kurdish woman. 'It is dead. No one is allowed to speak your language. Your language no longer exists. Any questions?'

The play's conceit was all too realistic: the world would never know of the suffering of the Kurds because the Kurds would never be allowed to speak.

The Left, which had thrown the accusation of 'fascism' around so freely, still had the sense to fight the real thing and offer fraternal support to its victims.

Their struggle was our struggle. Truly, it was.

There was one exception. The Tories who made excuses for the judicial murder of Farzad Bazoft and the other crimes of Saddam Hussein did have their counterparts in a small group on the Left in the Seventies and Eighties. It barely seemed worth bothering about at the time, but in retrospect you can see that it beat the path from the Left to far right that was to turn into a six-lane highway in the twenty-first century.

The Workers' Revolutionary Party was one of the ugliest political movements the British left has produced. It was a cult of the personality that venerated the squat, bald figure of Gerry Healy. According to his account of his life, Healy was a poor Irishman who began work on a ship at the age of 14. Disgusted by the poverty and the hardships he and his contemporaries endured, he became a communist in the Thirties. He switched to Trotskyism because of the Hitler–Stalin pact and spent the rest of his life fighting the sectarian wars of the far left, whose hatreds were in inverse proportion to their impact on British society. Officially, the WRP programme was to seize power in Britain, as the Bolsheviks had seized power in Russia, and establish a dictatorship of the proletariat on behalf of the British working class. Because it knew how Stalin had corrupted the Russian Revolution, there would be no mistake this time. The errors of the past would be avoided, and Healy would follow the shining path of Leon Trotsky and create a communist Utopia in the Britain of the Seventies.

Maybe Healy believed it could be done, he certainly never lacked self-confidence, but the sole practical effect of his life was to exercise a dictatorship over his party's members.

There are plenty of personality cults in mainstream politics. The adulation accorded to Margaret Thatcher and Tony Blair in their prime and pomp by moist-eyed journalists destroyed any sentimental notions of the cussedness of the freeborn Englishman and the fearlessness of the British press. Public scrutiny and the chance of removing a leader at a democratic election keep the cultism under control, however. In the little universes of the late twentieth-century totalitarian sects, it flourished without restraint. Lenin and Trotsky had driven the far left round the bend by proving that a minuscule party governed by fanatical leaders could change the course of history, if, and only if, it followed the correct strategy. For almost a century, other would-be dictators sought to find the magic formula. From the Sixties through to the Nineties the Socialist Workers' Party had Tony Cliff – a noisy and dense man, who believed his followers could seize power if they understood where the Russian Revolution had gone wrong. The Militant Tendency had Ted Grant who believed that his Trotskyists could infiltrate and take over the Labour Party of the Eighties, and complained furiously when it refused to accommodate him.

Healy was the best, however: the perfect example of the politician as cult guru. Like Saddam, he combined megalomania and paranoia as he offered a part of the 1968 generation of middle-class Marxists a Manichaean ideology. On the one hand, he said, British society had decayed to such a point it was possible to imagine that a great revolutionary could storm the citadels of the state, a point he emphasized to 10,000 supporters at a 1973 rally at Wembley while standing beneath a 40-foot image of himself. On the other, he warned that all might be lost. The ruling class was planning 'massive state repressions against the working class and the Marxist movement'. It would rather turn Britain into a fascist state than allow him to take over.

Like many another cult leader, Healy created an ideology of longing and fear. There would be socialism or fascism: heaven or hell. The stakes were so high, there was so much to gain or lose, his followers had no choice but to hurl themselves into the struggle, and obey his commands.

Initially, serious people on the Left gave credence to Healy's claims that a British Bolshevik revolution was possible. The post-war social democratic consensus fell apart in the early Seventies, and Britain for a moment did feel like a country on the edge of pre-revolutionary chaos. In 1973, Arab members of the Organization of Petroleum Exporting Countries said they would not trade with the North American and European countries that had supported Israel in the Yom Kippur War. The price of oil shot up and unemployment and inflation went up with it. Central bankers decided not to worry about inflation and to cut interest rates to prevent unemployment rising. In defiance of every law of economics they thought they knew, they got the worst of both worlds: stagflation with unemployment and inflation increasing together. For the first time since the Thirties – and the last time until the present day – the extremes prospered. Neo-Nazi parties did well in British elections as anti-immigrant sentiment grew, and the far left became a significant force in industry as strikes swept through it and the public services.

In 1973, the National Theatre reflected the apocalyptic mood by staging *The Party*, by Trevor Griffiths. It is a hard text to wade through now, and I doubt if a producer will ever revive it as anything other than a curiosity piece. Everything about the play feels ridiculous because the drama, such as it is, consists of characters representing various shades of Marxist opinion arguing about when and how socialist revolution will come to Britain.

At the time, though, Griffiths' work did not seem peculiar. Makiya's comrades on the far left were not alone in believing that the system was about to break down. A glum A. J. P. Taylor predicted that the end was nigh. 'I've been expecting the collapse of capitalism all my life, but now that it comes I am rather annoyed,' he said. 'There's no future for this country and not much for anywhere else...Revolution is knocking at the door.' Geoffrey Rippon, a minister in the 1970 Tory government, agreed: 'We are on the same course as the Weimar government with runaway inflation and ultra-high unemployment.' When Labour took over in 1974, its ministers were as glum. One warned Harold Wilson that the private sector was facing 'wholesale domestic liquidation'. Should inflation accelerate further, 'a deep constitutional crisis can no longer be treated as fanciful speculation'.

The rise of the far right and far left, the strikes, the power cuts, the inflation, the slump and a civil war in Northern Ireland pushed Sir William Armstrong, the head of the Home Civil Service, into a spectacular nervous breakdown. He was 'really quite mad at the end', said one Conservative minister, who described how he stumbled on Sir William at a Chekhovian summit of British and American leaders in a country house outside Oxford. As rain lashed the windows, the minister found the supposedly cool-headed civil servant 'lying on the floor and talking about moving the Red army from here and the Blue army from there'.

If Trevor Griffiths' Marxist delusions now seem like the fantasies of a fruitcake, he was no fruitier than the mandarins.

The Party is set during the student riots in Paris in 1968. Healy appears as John Tagg, a character played at the National Theatre by Sir Laurence Olivier, no less. Beyond Griffiths' assumption that a Marxist revolution was possible in Britain, the play isn't as didactic as the worst of the agit-prop of the Seventies. Griffiths allows his characters to put forward competing points of view. One who has seen Tagg at close quarters warns that life in his party was one of demeaning subservience. He illustrates the debasement by quoting the dismal speech the cornered Leon Trotsky made when he realized Stalin was using his own theory of revolutionary dictatorship to destroy him.

> Comrades, none of us wishes or is able to be right against the party. The party in the last analysis is *always* right, because the party is the sole historical instrument given to the proletariat for the solution of its basic problems. I know one cannot be right against the party. It is only possible to be right with the party and through the party, for history has not created other ways for the realisation of what is right.

Clearly, Griffiths didn't buy the Workers' Revolutionary Party sales pitch in every detail. Nevertheless, John Tagg is the centre of his play. It is his views on the chances of revolution everyone else argues about; it is his criticism of dilettante middle-class students the rest of the cast debate. Griffiths does not say he is right, but treats him with respect as a substantial figure who is worth hearing.

Healy had a hold over theatrical types. Vanessa and Corin Redgrave were among his most devoted supporters, while the actor members of Equity were the only workers to give him a toehold in the trade union movement – always a bad sign for an aspiring leader of a proletarian revolution. Actors have a professional predilection for extreme emotion, which the thundering Healy satisfied with his bombast. They obeyed him because he was also an authentic member of the working class, who 'realized early in his political career that many middle class people desperately wanted to be abused and humiliated by a self-appointed representative of the proletariat'.

Radicalism in Britain was to come from the free-market right not the far left. When what revolutionary fervour there was faded, the presence of the Redgraves turned the WRP from the subject of grave consideration on the South Bank to a running joke in Fleet Street. Poor little rich girls playing at revolution, actors who lose the plot when they speak without a script...these were butts for satire from central casting.

Vastly enjoyable it was, too, for the chortling newspaper readers. Yet it was also the case that if Healy had seized power the gutters would have bubbled with blood. Britain is not Iraq, and Healy's grandiose ambitions to be Britain's proletarian dictator made the press find him funnier still. The laughter missed the point that while he could not rule globally he could terrorize locally.

Healy convinced his followers that their enemies were everywhere, and probably believed it himself. Outsiders visiting the party headquarters in Clapham, south London, were surprised to see a sheet of polished steel along one wall of his office. He explained it was 'to frustrate the listening devices trained on him day and night by MI5'. A fleet of vehicles waited in the car park outside so that WRP militants could make their escape if the fascist coup came.

In September 1975, the first of many scandals to hit the party broke when a young actress and WRP member called Irene Gorst told the *Observer* how obsessive terrors haunted a redbrick Edwardian mansion that Corin Redgrave had bought for the WRP in the Derbyshire countryside. Healy changed its name from the pastoral 'White Meadows' to the insurgent 'Red House', and made it the party's residential training centre. The rules for members and their families were strict, Gorst said. The party banned fraternization with villagers over beers in the local pub. If your children cried outside the lecture hall, you had to wait until the lecture had finished before finding and comforting them. Nothing was to stand in the way of the preparations for revolution.

The hierarchy ordered her to go to its Clapham headquarters and board a minibus that was to take members to the Red House. She missed it because an IRA bomb had exploded near her home in Kensington the night before. She couldn't get into her flat until the small hours, and waited behind the police cordon drinking tea with the ambulance drivers. The next morning an old boyfriend called to make sure she was all right. He insisted on taking her to lunch and tried to talk her out of her infatuation with revolutionary politics. She thanked him for the meal, then ignored his advice and struggled to Derbyshire under her own steam to apologize for being late.

She described how an inquisition consisting of Vanessa and Corin Redgrave and two party officials ordered her into a room.

'Then they started on me. How long had I been working for Special Branch? Where had I planted the bombs and the drugs? Why did I miss the coach?

'At first I was very flippant. I would say things like, "Let's see *where* did I put the bombs? Was it in the loo? Was it under my bed?"'

After an hour, she tried to leave. They pushed her back into a chair. 'Don't you dare,' cried a party official. 'You're not leaving until we've found out what we want to know.'

He was particularly angry that she had drunk tea with the ambulance crews. 'Didn't I realize that the police planted those bombs and would have been delighted to find a WRP member on the spot.'

So it went on, all day. They searched her luggage. They examined her address book and stripped down her transistor radio. They imagined fantastical links between her brother and the CIA. They treated as highly suspicious the fact that her father's drinks company bought cork from Portugal – then under the same right-wing dictatorship whose oranges so repelled my mother. 'Ahaa,' they said in a knowing way.

'Even if you discover I am what you think I am, what are you going to do?' she asked. 'Put me up against a wall and shoot me?'

Gorst said she was 'quite hysterical by this time' and told her interrogators, 'You're all mad, let me go.'

They did in the end, and she went to the *Observer*. The WRP said it had not held her against her will, sued for libel and lost. In answers to questions from the judge, the jury said that although it did not necessarily believe every word of Irene Gorst's testimony it did believe the main thrust of it. What mistakes the jury suspected did not alter its decision to find against the WRP because they did not 'materially injure' the accusations against the party.

The *Observer* may not have got every last detail right, but I think it is reasonable to conclude that Gorst was accurately describing a sect in the grip of raging paranoia.

Fear has its uses. Political cults create their own reality as effectively as the Scientologists or the Exclusive Brethren. Their leaders cannot allow members to take at face value evidence that contradicts their teachings. It has to be the result of a capitalist plot or a Jewish conspiracy or the machinations of Freemasons or a disinformation campaign by the security services. To maintain control the cult must blacken the world beyond its walls. Families are the most credible source of dissonant information. Parents, husbands, wives, lovers and children are the people whose cries of 'Get a grip!' or 'Don't be daft' are most likely to hit home. Nazi Germany, communist Russia, Maoist China and Baathist Iraq all worked to weaken family influence. So too did those tiny mirrors in Britain and America, those fragments of totalitarianism, which winked and sparkled as they reflected the dream of Utopia.

Right-wing militia groups in the United States encouraged their members to abandon their homes for 'retreats' in the wilderness. The far-left cults matched their determination to hide their members from the malign influences of unreliable relatives. Corin Redgrave's first wife, Deirdre, described how Healy reacted when she refused to join the party:

> I was suddenly commanded into Healy's presence. Two rather grim looking henchmen took me by the arms, albeit gently. He looked at me with a steady, even gaze and demanded, 'Why don't you join the party? Why won't you support your husband?'
>
> I told Healy quite clearly that I had two young children to bring up – and I didn't want them to grow up disturbed. I wanted them to be normal kids. If you are a member of the WRP – a real dedicated member, that is – you would seldom see your children. You are travelling everywhere. Bradford one day. Cardiff the next.

She refused to accept the party line, and the marriage broke up.

In her almost charmingly naïve autobiography, Vanessa Redgrave describes sitting on the bed of her young daughter,

Natasha Richardson. 'Natasha appealed to me to spend more time with her. I tried to explain that our political struggle was for her future, and that of all the children of her generation. She looked at me with a serious, sweet smile. "But I need you *now*. I won't need you so much then".'

Cult leaders know they must exhaust their followers as well as isolate them. The harder the party or the church forces them to work, the less time they have to think for themselves. As important, the harder they work, the greater their investment and the tougher it becomes to accept that the years of labour have been an expense of spirit in a waste of shame. Overly rational historians wonder why supporters of causes from Bolshevism through to Islamism don't give up when they realize that the death and suffering will never bring the workers' paradise or new Caliphate; why they fight on for decades, only to achieve more death and suffering? They forget the emotional outlay and the lost lives of dead comrades and martyrs. For immense and minute revolutionary movements alike, more suffering is easier to accept than the admission that all the previous suffering was in vain. Macbeth explained messianic politics better than most historians when he said:

> *I am in blood*
> *Stepped in so far that, should I wade no more,*
> *Returning were as tedious as go o'er.*

Trying to find rational explanations for the irrational sects of the far left and far right is like trying to find 'the root causes' of Islamism or trying to explain Saddam Hussein by looking at the 'realism' of Iraqi foreign policy. It is more profitable to look at persecution fantasies, group loyalty, the strongman's will to power and the feeble personality's willingness to obey.

Once the sect has its claws dug in, it takes a tremendous jolt to shake devotees free. In *On the Edge*, their study of cultish politics, Dennis Tourish and Tim Wohlforth describe how Kate Blakeney, a mother of four, threw herself into organizing meetings and making collections for the WRP. She distributed its leaflets in the streets of Oxford and sold its newspaper at factory gates. The more newspapers she sold the more copies the party sent her to sell. If she couldn't sell them, the party didn't mind. She had to pay for them whether she sold them or not. The more money she collected, the more Healy demanded. Blakeney finally allowed him to debit funds direct from her account so he could take what he wanted at will. She borrowed from her friends until she ran out of ones she could tap. Once she had met the party's demands, she barely had enough left over to feed her children.

Still she kept on working herself into the ground. 'We were too busy, always busy, and could hope only to catch a few hours' sleep.' Still she carried on believing that the party would either triumph and be a beacon to the human race or go down as the first victim of a British fascist dictatorship.

One day Healy asked to meet her in his London flat. She went hoping to convince him to give her and her comrades in Oxford a respite from his demands:

> [He] opened the door for me. He had been drinking. Something was all wrong. I pushed by his large body, sat down in the chair and started to make my report. Healy came towards me, was hovering over me. He was not listening to a word I was saying.
>
> He wanted only one thing from me, my sexual submission. For a moment, I just stared at him: fat, ugly, red-faced. Was this the price I was supposed to pay for some respite for my area?

Something snapped in me. I guess it was my faith, my belief. The dream that drove me forward now seemed unreal, and reality entered, tawdry, petty, dirty, seamy reality. It wasn't a matter of morality or some special virtue on my part. It was as if everything I believed in was proved, in one revealing second, to be false, lies. I, my husband, my children, my comrades had sacrificed so much, had worked so hard for this . . . animal.

At the next meeting of the central committee, Healy duly denounced her for political crimes. When a friend interceded, he was beaten. Healy enjoyed the beatings. Party members who crossed him described how he would hit them while his goons held them down. When he had finished, he would stand back and savour his victims' pain. 'It's Christmas,' he would gloat as he rubbed his hands together.

It was only a matter of time before Gerry Healy and Saddam Hussein became friends.

The party always had money, and it did not all come from its weary members. The WRP ran a head office and flats in Clapham, regional offices and Corin Redgrave's Derbyshire mansion. It also produced a daily newspaper *News Line* – a Herculean undertaking and a constant drain on resources for a small group of Trotskyists. Healy kept insolvency at bay by soliciting funds from the Arab tyrants of twenty-five years ago. Dictatorial regimes will reward any group that supports their cause unequivocally, however obscure it may be, because they want to be able to show their subject peoples that foreigners beyond the reach of their security services freely choose to flatter them. Lucrative printing contracts arrived at the *News Line* offices. Perhaps because they in turn wanted to show what they could do for their new friends, the party's propagandists descended into the fascist conspiracy theory that the Jews controlled Britain.

'A powerful Zionist connection runs from the so called Left of the Labour Party right into the centre of Thatcher's government in Downing Street,' *News Line* told its readers. 'Top of the list we have Mr Stuart Young, a director of the *Jewish Chronicle*, as youngest-ever chairman of the BBC... He is the brother of Mr David Young, another Thatcher appointee, who is chairman of the Manpower Services Commission.'

Jews controlled the Labour Party, the Conservative Party... every party except the Workers' Revolutionary Party. They were everywhere.

Charlie Pottins joined *News Line* as a young journalist in 1976 and later described its subservience to Saddam. 'To my shame, I accepted a report that the Baathist regime was conceding autonomy to the Kurds, but I was shocked when Healy denied the Kurds were a nation entitled to rights.'

Pottins was fired, but he continued to hear more about the strange relationship between the dictator of a large country and the dictator of a tiny party.

Hostilities between Iraqi intelligence services and the PLO put the *News Line* in a spot, as did the later outbreak of war between Iraq and Iran, but, when Saddam Hussein was attacking his own people, Healy had no problem deciding whom to support. This one-time 'revolutionary' had enjoyed VIP treatment and a motorcycle escort on his trip to Baghdad! The WRP came up with excuses for the execution of Iraqi Communist Party members, even calling a mass meeting to back the Iraqi regime. But that was not all. *News Line* photographers took pictures of a student demonstration outside the Iraqi embassy, probably assuming it was just a normal reporting task. But, when Healy asked them to make blow-ups to deliver to the embassy, one at least had the temerity to refuse, and she quit.

A debased part of the British left was spying on the left-wing Iraqi exiles whose stories Kanan Makiya was collecting. Typical of the propaganda the WRP put out was a special issue of *News Line* in 1980 entitled *Iraq Under Leadership of the Arab Baath Party.* Its journalist gazed with awe at the plans for the Baghdad Saddam wanted to create – possibly from the designs of Makiya Associates. The Baath building boom was a sign of a 'great march forward,' he cried. Baath propagandists assured him the march would take Iraqis to a new form of society that would see 'the elimination of all forms of exploitation'.

The WRP blew apart in October 1985 when a delighted Fleet Street broke the sensational news of the 'Reds in the Bed' scandal. The papers revealed that Healy was not only a paranoid bully and megalomaniac but a rapist near as dammit. Kate Blakeney was not the only object of his unwelcome attentions. Twenty-six women members accused him of 'cruel and systematic debauchery' on party premises. One of them was the daughter of two of Healy's oldest friends. She told how he had rewarded her parents' loyalty by sleeping with her and beating her. She had been hurt so often she was close to being a cripple. Many more women came forward. The *Sunday Mirror* described how Healy's seduction technique included chat-up lines Leon Trotsky would have recognized. 'He would throw his arms around women and tell them to submit. If they protested – and some of them did – he would say, "You are doing this for the party and I AM THE PARTY".'

As his rivals moved against him, Healy took off with as many documents as he could grab. One he left behind showed that the WRP had taken about £20,000 from Iraq.

Unabashed by the revelations, about 150 members of the WRP stuck by Healy and formed an even tinier party for him to lead. Vanessa and Corin Redgrave were among them. Like Cordelia and the Fool, they stayed with their Lear to the end, dismissing the abuse of women and the money from dictatorships as the black propaganda of MI5. When he died in 1990, their funeral orations predicted that one day he would be recognized as a great thinker.

As an example of how the Left is not a happy family of decent people, the story of the WRP is hard to beat. Dostoevsky said that revolutionaries were attracted to causes that gave them 'the right to dishonour' under the cover of high-sounding ideals, and Healy certainly enjoyed the pretext to dishonour women revolutionary socialism gave him. Despite communism, people still need reminding that the far left can be just as thuggish and perverted as the far right. As I said above, the tale is also an example of how the far left can be more cultish than the worst religious sects – like the Moonies, but without the smiles.

Looking back, what is interesting is not that Healy chose to go along with totalitarianism – there were plenty of fellow travellers in Western democracies in the twentieth century – but the nature of the Iraqi regime he chose to follow. He had very few other options because Trotskyists were the loneliest of political animals in the twentieth century. They couldn't tolerate Western democracy, but they couldn't become the fellow travellers of the communist tyrannies because all the communist regimes and parties accepted the legacy of Stalin, Trotsky's enemy, to varying degrees. Healy had to look elsewhere and ended up with Saddam Hussein for want of better. The totalitarianism of the Baathist ultra-right was preferable to the real enemy – the liberal version of democracy that permitted him to organize a party and argue his case. His choice anticipated the choices of the twenty-first century. After the collapse of the Berlin Wall, hardly any communist tyrannies survived. When people wanted to go from justifiable democratic opposition into fellow travelling with totalitarianism, what else was there to travel with other than the regimes and movements of the ultra-right?

I write this with the benefit of hindsight. In 1985, the collapse of the WRP didn't seem significant to me or anyone else. It delighted the newspapers, but if the Redgraves had not brought their celebrity to the party, few journalists would have been interested. Everyone else on the Left of the day thought the WRP was a party of nutcases. An exception was Ken Livingstone, the future Mayor of London. At Healy's funeral, he praised the quality of *News Line*'s journalism and said that Healy was a victim rather than a victimizer. 'I haven't the slightest doubt that the upheavals that split apart the Workers' Revolutionary Party were not some accident or some clash of personalities. They were a sustained and deliberate decision by MI5 to smash the organisation because they feared it was going to become too pivotal in terms of domestic politics.'

The public image of Livingstone as a lovable Londoner was as wrong-headed as most other public images. None the less, the WRP's support for Baathism was a one-off, which no other left-wing group imitated. Even the WRP abandoned Saddam after the start of the Iran–Iraq War in 1980. It met its bills by taking the shilling of Colonel Gaddafi's Libya instead – a little more than a shilling, to be precise, more like £500,000. Leftists of the period would have dismissed as absurd the idea that 23 years on, the greatest demonstration in the history of the Left would be led by Saddam's avowed apologists without so much as a squeak of protest coming from the morally earnest and intellectually respectable voices of liberal England.

CHAPTER THREE

Leftists Without a Left

I pondered all these things, and how men fight and lose the battle, and the thing that they fought for comes about in spite of their defeat, and when it comes turns out not to be what they meant, and other men have to fight for what they meant under another name.

William Morris, 1888

ON 2 AUGUST 1990, Saddam Hussein invaded Kuwait and Kanan Makiya awoke to find himself famous – and infamous. *Republic of Fear* sold out within days. The publishers ordered second editions, but this time with print runs in the tens of thousands. Senators, MPs, diplomats and journalists belatedly realized that they needed to know about the new menace. They had looked the other way because they worried the demented Ayatollah Khomeini would invade Iraq and be in a position to move into Kuwait and Saudi Arabia and control most of the world's oil. Now the demented Saddam Hussein had invaded Kuwait and could move into Saudi Arabia and control most of the world's oil.

In *1984*, George Orwell's Winston Smith says:

At this moment, for example, in 1984 (if it was 1984), Oceania was at war with Eurasia and in alliance with Eastasia. In no

70

public or private utterance was it ever admitted that the three powers had at any time been grouped along different lines. Actually, as Winston well knew, it was only four years since Oceania had been at war with Eastasia and in alliance with Eurasia.

It was like that with Saddam. You could hear the screech as the world's leaders stamped on the brakes and wrenched the gear stick into reverse.

Makiya knew he had to speak plainly. News anchors wanted his face on their shows; editors wanted his words in their comment pages. He threw away his wig and pseudonym and used his celebrity to help his country. Much of what he said pleased leftish audiences. He lacerated the United Nations forces for bombing civilian targets, and tore into the refusal of George Bush senior's State Department to meet Saddam's opponents. So far so good, governments in general and America in particular were killing the innocent and betraying democrats. What hypocrites.

Then Makiya went too far by saying the war had not gone far enough. Instead of stopping at the border when they had defeated the Iraqi armies and thrown them out of Kuwait, the UN forces should help the Iraqi Kurds and Shia Arabs who had taken their chance to rise up. The world must know by now that Saddam wasn't another tin-pot dictator. Baathism was a rolling programme of war and genocide – first Iran, then the Kurds, then Kuwait, while all the time the mutilation of Iraq continued. Saddam had to be stopped and the only way to stop him was to march on to Baghdad.

Iraqi exiles cheered Makiya, but Britain, America, the European Union, China, the Soviet Union and, predictably, the Arab dictatorships were adamant that Iraq had to stay a dictatorship. When *Hajiz al-khwaf inksier* – the barrier of fear – was broken and Iraqi *intifada* began, Brent Scowcroft, Bush senior's National Security Adviser, bluntly told ABC News: 'We clearly would have preferred a coup. There's no question of that.'

In the ceasefire negotiations, the United States forces specifically allowed Saddam Hussein to keep helicopter gunships, which he duly used to slaughter the revolutionaries. The great powers wanted a palace revolution that would bring a reliable autocrat to the fore, not a popular uprising. After the humiliating defeat in Kuwait, they assumed the Iraqi army would seize the radio stations and install a sensible general. They waited, and kept on waiting because once a totalitarian regime is secure its totalitarian methods prevent its overthrow.

With Saddam clearly going nowhere, the US, UK and France tried other remedies. No-fly zones were established. They helped the Kurds in the north escape Baathist rule, but brought no good to the rest of the country. Sanctions were imposed which wiped out legitimate businesses while allowing black marketeers to flourish. The United Nations tried to relieve the suffering by establishing an 'oil-for-food' programme. This lavishly corrupt affair allowed the Baath to engage in smuggling on a gargantuan scale and bribe foreign supporters with money meant for the destitute. As General Tommy Franks said when the US Army finally invaded Iraq in 2003, it was more 'oil for palaces' than 'oil for food'. The United Nations secured Saddam's position because he decided who could and could not receive international aid.

The Nineties in Iraq were strange beyond measure. The Baathists had committed one of the last genocides of the twentieth century. They had started the longest conventional war of the whole twentieth century. They had invaded Kuwait and been defeated in battle. They had harboured international terrorists and organized terrorism themselves. They had developed weapons of mass destruction and used them against domestic and foreign opponents alike. Yet while George Bush senior, Margaret Thatcher, the Ayatollah Khomeini and all his other enemies lost power or died, Saddam Hussein stayed on, a victor of sorts.

Nothing, though, was stranger and less discussed than the behaviour of the Left. The initial reaction of Makiya's friends to Saddam's invasion of Kuwait was to allow him to keep it. 'Everyone I respected – anyone who was a friend, it seemed, immediately gravitated towards the peace position. And with almost every fibre of my being I longed to be there with them. Only, in this instance, it couldn't be. It was an incredibly painful time.'

When he insisted on harping on about the Baathists' crimes after Saddam became America's enemy, Makiya's friends turned on him. Writing of his former comrade in the *New Statesman*, Alexander Cockburn, an American leftist, said, 'out of despair comes mental pandemonium'. Tariq Ali was like a teacher patting a little boy on the head. There were aspects of his former friend's work which he 'respected enormously, but I'm afraid he's an innocent, a complete babe'. The Americans 'were never going to support democracy in Iraq', he concluded somewhat rashly. Edward Said, a *New Left Review* contributor and the most fluent defender of the Palestinian cause in the Western universities, was almost lost for words, and spluttered: 'He suddenly discovers he's got to do something, and what does he do? He appeals to the United States to come to rescue him! It's astonishing.'

It wasn't only Makiya who was being excommunicated from the church of the Left. The bell was being tolled and the book closed on the peoples of Iraq. In leftish circles and among the Arab intelligentsia, an instantaneous change took place. The screeching of brakes and the crunching gears weren't only heard in the foreign ministries of the great powers. A tyrant the Left had happily characterized as a 'fascist' poured fire on a rebellious population from helicopter gunships. To punish the Marsh Arabs he unleashed an ecological catastrophe by blocking the flow of water into the Tigris-Euphrates flood plain. The angry condemnations that had once flowed as freely as the rivers of Mesopotamia dried up. From then on, the loudest voices on the Left were raised in favour of the causes of Saddam Hussein, not necessarily in favour of Saddam Hussein, although we were to hear that eventually, but in support of his demands. As the mood shifted, the liberal-left began to make novel arguments.

From the emergence of the pacifist movement in the mid-nineteenth century, the liberal-left had generally preferred the peaceful coercion of sanctions to war. As the Nineties wore on, however, sanctions against Saddam's Iraq fell out of favour. At a meeting chaired by the Labour MP George Galloway in 1998, Harold Pinter said the deaths that resulted in Iraq were 'Tony Blair's legacy of corpses'. Labour MPs and Green Party activists agreed. The demands for a change of policy weren't confined to the far left. In 2000 Sir Menzies Campbell – the then foreign affairs spokesman for the Liberal Democrats who was to go on to be the party's leader – demanded that all sanctions except the ban on the sale of military equipment be lifted because they were being 'used by the regime in Iraq to justify the systematic degradation of the Iraqi people'.

So they were, but none of those who called for the lifting of sanctions in whole or in part went on to say that troops should be sent in to remove the dictator from power. The option they supported, but rarely stated explicitly, was close to the option Saddam wanted: no sanctions and greater freedom for his dictatorship to perpetuate its rule.

Makiya saw at once that many on the liberal-left were prepared to turn their eyes from fascistic totalitarianism and realized the dismal consequences for the future. In 1993, he published *Cruelty and Silence*, which dissected the Arab intelligentsia's unwillingness to confront its monsters. He took on Edward Said, whose *Orientalism* was and is a hugely influential account of how the West shaped the Middle East. *Orientalism* is a narrative of victimhood that finds in racist outsiders a comforting explanation for Arab backwardness. Makiya replied that if you placed all the blame for the region's disasters on Western imperialism and racism, you ignored the home-grown disasters of Arab nationalism and Islamism. The unintended consequence was an inverted racism that denied the autonomy of Arabs and let local oppressors off the hook. Tyrants could always claim that the woes that afflicted their peoples came from America or Israel, and divert the anger that should have been directed against them.

Makiya said that for all their radical rhetoric, Said and those like him made 'Arabs feel contented with the way they are, instead of making them rethink fundamental assumptions which so clearly haven't worked'. India had been occupied by the British for several centuries, and Indians had far more reason to be angry than the Arab states, which had been occupied by the British and French for a few decades. Yet Indians got on with the struggle to build a successful democracy and economy, while Arab intellectuals were crippled by their resentments.

Said greeted the challenge with incontinent abuse. He sounded more like a Soviet prosecutor than an academic when he denounced Makiya as a 'guinea pig witness' and 'native informant' for the Americans. His former comrade was now 'a man of vanity who has no compassion, no demonstrable awareness of human suffering'. His work was 'revolting', and based 'on cowardly innuendo and false interpretation'. Westerners respected Makiya only because he 'confirmed the view in the West that Arabs were villainous and shabby conformists'.

Said was a Palestinian and in a small way his viciousness and betrayals of principle were excusable. For the early Zionists to say that Palestine was 'a land without a people for a people without a land' was not so much to look down on Palestinians from a position of colonial superiority, as to look through them and deny their existence. You can see why Makiya's comparison of the thousands killed by the Israelis with the millions killed by the Baathists horrified him. Said had an urgent interest in keeping anger and attention directed at the Israeli occupation of Palestine. If it turned to other horrors, which had little to do with the West, the Palestinian cause might suffer.

Yet to use this excuse is to sink into the racism of low expectations – he's a Palestinian and so we can't expect too high a moral and intellectual standard. Said summed up his own failure to confront totalitarianism, and with it the failure of a large section of the Arab intelligentsia, just before the war in Iraq and his own death.

He said the war was all the fault of . . . oh, go on, guess.

Iraq 'was the one Arab country with the human and natural resources, as well as the infrastructure, to take on Israel's arrogant brutality', he explained. 'That is why Begin bombed Iraq pre-emptively in 1981, supplying a model for the United States in its own pre-emptive war.' (He meant the Israelis' destruction of the Tammuz nuclear reactor, which was going to give Saddam the bomb.) Because Said believed Saddam could one day have the men and munitions to take on Israel, the war against him had to be the result of a sinister plot by Jewish puppet masters who pulled the strings of American policy. The Jews operated with impunity, he explained, because corporate media covered up their crimes by failing 'to elucidate the Likud's slow takeover of US military and political thinking about the Arab world'.

Although the Israeli government was far more worried about Iran than Iraq, there were supporters of Israel in Washington who believed that a democratic Iraq would inspire revolutions across the Arab world. If they resulted in democratic governments, they reasoned, the pressure on Israel to cut a deal with the Palestinians would be reduced. The wacky and frankly insulting assumption behind their thinking was that Arabs would abandon the Palestinians if they were given a free choice in democratic societies.

Said's underlying assumptions weren't so different from the friends of Israel on Capitol Hill. He saw Saddam's Iraq only as a potentially powerful enemy of Israel with 'the human and natural resources' to take Jerusalem on. The Americans must not overthrow Saddam because the toppling of the dictatorship would weaken the Palestinians' hand. Said's line of reasoning led to the conclusion that Iraqis must live under tyranny so that Palestinians might be spared the Israeli occupation – some Arabs must be in bondage so that others might be free. This was a counsel of despair and a scandalous one at that. What was wrong with supporting freedom for Palestinians and Iraqis and Syrians, Saudis and Egyptians for that matter?

Writing in 1997, Makiya tried to be generous. He saw that he and Said shared a common delusion. Campaigners against oppression have a temptation to identify with its victims because 'one needs some kind of moral assurance, some handle on the hellishness of the world, in circumstances where God and religion are undeniably absent (at least for me)'. The alternative was 'a descent into the nausea and misanthropy and self-hatred about whose destructive possibilities this century has taught us everything we need to know'. However, Makiya conceded that support for victims could lead to an idiotic myopia. There were Arab intellectuals 'who so idolised Palestinian victimhood that they became blinded to the nature of the regime in Iraq'. He admitted, the same could be said of his idolization of Iraqi victimhood. Both Palestinians and Iraqis were:

> allowing ourselves to believe that there is something morally redeeming in the quality of victimhood itself. There isn't. The very opposite is likely to be the case: the victims of cruelty or injustice are not only no better than their tormentors; they are more often than not just wanting to change places with them. That has been the experience of Israelis, particularly since they became an occupying power in 1967, and it has been the experience of Palestinians and Kurds under self-rule in recent years.

The Bertrand Russell whom his mother had dragged his father to hear in the Forties was more succinct when he mocked 'The Fallacy of the Superior Virtue of the Oppressed'. Russell said that for too many right-thinking, left-leaning people it wasn't enough to assert that oppression was an evil which destroyed its victims. The oppressed's experience of oppression had to ennoble them. Their leaders had to become titans, their poets geniuses and their fighters heroes. The point of honest politics is to end oppression and allow its victims to be like everyone else. The Fallacy of the Superior Virtue implied that victimhood was morally invigorating, so the more of it there was the better.

You only have to glance at a newspaper or turn on the television to learn that Russell's fallacy has spread like bindweed through a well-manured flowerbed.

Both Makiya and the British and American forces would have done well to think about it before the invasion of Iraq – so would I and other supporters of the war. Makiya realized it wouldn't be easy. 'Iraq was a state whose legitimacy was derived from impossibly intertwined circles of complicity and victimhood,' he wrote long before the invasion. The post-Baathist future was 'going to be like walking a tightrope, balancing the legitimate grievances of all those who have suffered against the knowledge that if everyone is held accountable who is in fact guilty, the country will be torn apart'.

In the Nineties, however, the ranks of those outside Iraq who wanted to overthrow the Baath Party were thin. The Berlin Wall was down and the terrors of the twentieth century appeared to be over. Consumers dedicated their lives to getting and spending, and the liberal-minded among them relaxed and enjoyed their world music and GM-free organic food. Makiya cut a lonely figure as he toured American universities and think tanks trying to prick consciences. In his speeches he declared that it was foolish to regard Iraq as a sovereign nation whose internal affairs were its own business, and not only because of the crimes against humanity the Baathists had committed. Iraq's political system was now the responsibility of the international community, he argued. The United Nations had imposed sanctions and no-fly zones but had left Saddam Hussein in power. Iraqis were ruled by the Baathists, and punished because the Baathists ruled them.

His audiences tut-tutted and offered what sympathy they could. Few had the faintest idea what to do. At the end of a talk in Washington DC, a well-dressed middle-aged man with a lined face and an intense gaze approached Makiya and offered him an apology. He in particular and the United States in general had let the people of Iraq down in 1991, he said. We should never have allowed Saddam to crush the rebellion. The massacre and his own failure to act haunted him.

'I was impressed,' Makiya told me. 'It was an unsolicited gesture. There was no audience watching, no possible political gain. He said his name was Paul Wolfowitz. It meant nothing to me.'

Within a decade Wolfowitz's name would be a swear word. As the conservative journalist Mark Steyn noted, the first half reminded his enemies of a scary predator and the second of a scary Jew. At the time, Wolfowitz was just another Republican out of office during the Clinton years. His last government job was as under-secretary of state at the Pentagon from where he watched in 1991 as Bush senior ordered American troops to pull back from helping the Iraqi revolutionaries for fear of upsetting a Saudi Arabian monarchy that most definitely did not want to see democracy in the Middle East. A character based on Wolfowitz appears in Saul Bellow's *Ravelstein* fulminating at the cowardice of it all. 'They send out a terrific army and give a demonstration of up-to-date high-tech warfare that flesh and blood can't stand up to. But then they leave the dictatorship in place and steal away.'

Bellow didn't get it right, Wolfowitz wasn't shouting 'forward to Baghdad' in 1991, but he agonized over the failure to remove the Baath Party and the tens of thousands of Iraqis who had died in the attempted revolution. Wolfowitz's academic parents brought him up on George Orwell and other writers from the democratic left. His father's family had survived European fascism by fleeing Poland before the Nazis invaded. Other relatives weren't as fortunate. He did not find a policy which left fascist dictatorships in power easy to live with. According to the conventional measures of the time, Wolfowitz was on the Right and Makiya on the Left, but they weren't so different in beliefs and background, and in any case, conventional measures were no longer as reliable as they once had been.

George Packer, a historian of America's involvement with Iraq, presents Wolfowitz as a tortured man who wanted to remove Saddam but accepted the reasons for stopping at the Iraqi border in 1991. If the Americans were to go in, of course, 'the obvious question would have been: What then? It's a question that Wolfowitz never managed to answer.'

If this makes Wolfowitz sound a tad more likeable than the standard portrait of a blood-crazed lackey of imperialist oil corporations, then that is because he was. True he had been a Cold Warrior and produced ludicrous overestimates of Soviet strength in the Seventies. But as communism fell apart, democracy began to follow Wolfowitz around. He argued that America should back the revolution against Ferdinand Marcos, its Cold War dictator of the Philippines, and was a supporter of the democratic movement against the pro-American tyranny in Indonesia and the feminist cause in Iran.

I saw him at a press briefing in London in 2004. It was a disconcerting occasion. His adviser told me to meet him in a Mayfair nightclub more usually associated with minor royals than shabby journalists. To make matters worse, the bulk of Wolfowitz's audience consisted of Conservative pundits I'd attacked over the years – occasionally fairly. This wasn't my world and I found the only other leftie in the room and huddled next to him for warmth. We listened to Wolfowitz present a coherent case for helping the democratic movement in Iran fight the priests. It was hard not to be impressed by his seriousness of purpose.

On the way out, I asked my friend, 'What's wrong with supporting the overthrow of a theocracy?'

'Well, it may not work, but apart from that nothing.'

That was the nub of it. The Wolfowitz who introduced himself to Makiya in the mid-Nineties, and the other neo-conservatives who were to take up the anti-Saddam cause, were hated because of their espousal of causes the liberal-left had once owned but no longer had the moral self-confidence to defend. Freud's narcissism of small differences played its part in widening the divide that opened up as the second Iraq war approached; as did the subconscious acknowledgement that the devil had stolen the best tunes. 'The neo-conservatives were fighting the Left's battles for them,' said Makiya pithily, and no one likes a plagiarist.

Like many other political labels from Tory to suffragette, 'neo-conservative' began as an insult. Michael Harrington, a left-wing American activist in the Seventies, invented it to describe liberals who retained their support for the New Deal and welfare state but wanted a hard line against the Soviet Union. The Republican neo-conservatives of the Nineties were different. They had no affection for social democracy. They didn't support the welfare state but said they wanted to 'reform' welfare – i.e. cut it – while simultaneously stuffing the pockets of the wealthy. After 9/11, the Republican priority was to give a huge tax cut to the rich – in contravention of the old and honourable policy that in time of war soldiers and their families should be the first to be compensated. The British Liberals and Conservatives who sent hundreds of thousands to die in the trenches of the First World War gave working-class men the vote when it was over. In 1944, Franklin D. Roosevelt's Democrats passed the Serviceman's Readjustment Act that guaranteed the troops help with finding jobs or a good education when the Second World War was over. When American soldiers came back from Afghanistan and Iraq, they found the Republicans had acknowledged their sacrifice by giving the boss class a tax break for staying at home. Neo-conservatives were as much in favour of privatization and executives bloating themselves at the expense of workers and taxpayers, and just as willing to make excuses for know-nothing creationists, as any other American conservative. In domestic policy, there was no 'neo' about them.

Their difference with other conservatives was their opposition to 'realism' in foreign policy. Or rather, the neo-conservatives held that they were the true realists, as everyone in politics does. The interests of the United States lay in spreading democracy, they said, because democracies did not go to war with each other. This was an idealistic, almost Utopian foreign policy which looked as if it would have no influence in Washington. George W. Bush wasn't a convert. He won power in the 2000 Presidential election on an isolationist ticket and said he had no time for the 'liberal' wars of his predecessor, Bill Clinton. Wolfowitz and his friends had limited influence until Mohamed Atta and his fellow martyrs proved on 11 September 2001 that oppression in the Middle East was not producing virtue, superior or otherwise. Tyrannies were pushing the disaffected into a psychopathic cult of death. For all the interminable arguments about the origins of the second Iraq war, the simple truth remains that it would never have been possible without the atrocities in New York and Washington.

* * *

The friendless Iraqi opposition had been befriended by the neo-conservatives long before. I remember listening in wonderment to socialist Kurds just back from Washington after Bush's election in 2000. They were full of praise for the determination of Wolfowitz and the other neo-conservatives in the Pentagon to overthrow Saddam. Makiya shared their admiration. By 2002, he had had enough of writing about victimhood and the treason of the intellectuals. The Baathists had been in power for all of his adult life and he wanted them out. *Republic of Fear* became a part of the case for war. When no weapons of mass destruction were found beyond odds and ends, you could say it became the whole case for war. Makiya too became a partisan. He argued in favour of going in, and threw himself into the intense and vicious debates within the US administration. Afterwards as he looked on the bloodbath that followed the invasion, he explained that he sided with Wolfowitz against the CIA and the State Department because Wolfowitz and the neo-conservative Pentagon believed that:

US foreign policy towards the Middle East had rested for 50 years on support of autocratic regimes (like Saudi Arabia, like Saddam in the 1980s, like Mubarak's Egypt) in the interests of securing oil supplies. This policy had led to a level of anger at the United States inside the Arab world that provided fertile breeding ground for organisations like Al-Qaeda...The United States should reach out to peoples not governments, to focus on democratisation as opposed to stability. That school of thought emerged in the Pentagon, led by people like Paul Wolfowitz. It ran headlong against the State Department's traditional accommodationist policies. The conflict was between those agencies that were wedded to the policies of the past and those breaking new ground. The former were often in the State Department – people who knew that part of the world in a very particular way. They had been Ambassadors, they had hobnobbed with the Saudi ruling families, and they had developed certain preconceptions about how the Arab world worked. By contrast those who were pushing for a dramatically new policy, like Paul Wolfowitz, were not shackled by such a past, nor burdened by the weight of those prejudices. But they did not necessarily know the Middle East as well.

Intellectuals in politics are occasionally dangerous and invariably disappointed. George Packer, who had known Makiya for years, said his friend didn't understand that for all their tough talk the neo-conservatives were far less worldly than they appeared. The Republicans had been out of the White House in the Nineties. Most of the party's senior figures had treated the decade's debates on humanitarian intervention and failed states with derision, and opposed the wars to stop ethnic cleansing in the former Yugoslavia as bleeding heart indulgences. They hadn't thought about the mass migration of refugees, chemical weapons in the hands of terrorists and global crime. They hadn't come to terms with the new age of warfare where the infantry had to be soldiers one minute and police officers the next. Makiya's last, best hope was George W. Bush, who as Packer said, came to power with 'no curiosity about the world, only a suspicion that his predecessor had entangled America in far too many obscure places of no importance to national interests'.

Needs must when the Devil drives, but the Republicans weren't the best generals to follow into battle. The charge from his old comrades that Makiya had travelled to the right when he went along with them seemed proved beyond reasonable doubt. In conventional political terms, there was truth in it. Yet the purpose of his life was how to end the subjection of his people by a genocidal warmonger, and from that Makiya never faltered. While all around rushed by, he kept his feet on the ground and his eyes fixed on the face of fascism. If he had gone from left to right, he had crossed the political spectrum by standing still.

And what of our friends on the Left, where were they going as they heaped abuse on their former comrade? A long way from where they came from was the kindest answer.

By chance, Makiya's family found asylum in London rather than Paris, New York or Kuwait City. Perhaps more predictably, Kanan Makiya fell in with leftists who were like him: refined revolutionaries, many with family money in trust funds to keep them in style while they fought the workers' cause. With Saddam's Iraq throwing millions of refugees into dozens of countries the initial confrontation between the Western and Iraqi lefts might have been in a different city with a different group of leftists, but I doubt that the outcome would have been very different.

As it was, the workings of chance had it that Iraq's foremost dissident fell in with intellectuals from the English-speaking academic left of the Eighties. They were among the first to face the challenge of coping with the ultra-right after the end of the Cold War, and among the first to flunk it. Two decades on, the brazenness of their behaviour remains astonishing. The U-turns of this part of the Left precisely matched the U-turns of the powerful. When Saddam was America's ally, Iraqis received fraternal sympathy; when he was America's enemy, they got the cold shoulder.

The virulence with which they tore into Makiya is telling. The Eighties leftists made no expressions of regret for the

Iraqis who must continue to live under Saddam; delivered no arguments more in sorrow than in anger. They didn't conclude with a remorseful shake of the head that on the balance of the available evidence it was better to leave Saddam in power, but turned on their former friend and screamed that he was 'a man of vanity who has no compassion', a 'guinea pig witness' and a sufferer from 'mental pandemonium'.

They were flipping and flopping in a crucial year. The world's decision to pull back from Baghdad in 1991 coincided with the final collapse of the Soviet Union. Crowds had torn down statues of tyrants in Europe, but in the Middle East, the United Nations ruled that they should remain in place. For the Left of all shades, the collapse of communism presented both an opportunity and a potential crisis. Most seized the opportunity to remove the faint hint of association with totalitarianism. The victories of centre-left parties in Britain and Western Europe, and Bill Clinton's far more equivocal successes in the United States, seemed to foretell a world that took universal human rights seriously.

The crisis began on the far left that needed the Soviet Union, although it pretended it didn't. Many of the revolutionaries of the 1968 generation called themselves Trotskyists rather than communists to avoid taking responsibility for Stalin, a transparent manoeuvre to keep communism alive by pretending that the one-party state would have been fine if only Lenin or Trotsky had stayed in charge of the secret police. While the Soviet Union was there, they could dream that it would transform itself and its occupied territories into true socialist societies, and be flattered by the knowledge that its existence forced important people to take their ideas seriously. Diplomats and spies had to learn the language of Marxism to understand the code of the Soviet Union. Once it was gone,

Marx became just another economist. Parts of his analysis of capitalism still stand up in my view, but I wouldn't argue if you said you could find better elsewhere.

Makiya abandoned his Marxism because it couldn't explain Baathism or Islamism or why the Palestinian groups he and Said had supported when they were young degenerated into criminal gangs in the Lebanese civil war. So, too, did millions of other socialists. Everywhere in the late twentieth century, communist and socialist parties dissolved or transformed themselves. If Iraqis had overthrown Saddam in 1991, and turned to people in the rich world who called themselves Marxists and said, 'Tell us how to govern our country, teach us how to build the good society' they would not have heard an articulate reply. The failures and massacres of communism were too fresh and the success of market economics was too great.

The old double standard whereby the Right tended to support the victims of communism and Soviet-sponsored dictatorships while the Left tended to support the victims of fascism and right-wing dictatorships went with the Cold War. The single standard that most on the liberal-left and moderate right said they accepted was universal human rights. But in the rubble of the far left, among the irreconcilables who could not stand the turn history had taken, a rival standard developed that was anything but a principled call for universal freedom.

On the contrary, its adherents used the end of the Cold War to embrace a kind of nihilism. They could break the old taboos that had stopped them supporting the ideas and movements of the extreme right, and endorse or excuse any foreign force as long as it was the enemy of Western democracy. Naturally, they found that many of those enemies were in the Middle East whose power structures were unaltered by the collapse of Soviet power and the Gulf War of 1991.

You have to have been on the Left to understand the extraordinary nature of the shift. The reason why communism doesn't seem all bad to me is the same reason the BBC gives airtime to Trotskyist comedians but not to neo-Nazi raconteurs: the far left was meant to be solidly against the extreme right. In reality, the anti-fascist left was a bit of a myth. Communists and fascists worked together against liberalism many times in the Twenties and Thirties. Rationally, I know it was a natural partnership because the similarities between communism and fascism were more important than the differences. But viscerally to anyone brought up on the Left after the Second World War, an unwavering opposition to fascism was the trait in which we could take the greatest pride. There was a hierarchy. The best society was some form of socialism that varied according to taste, and like the kingdom of God never came. The runner-up was what we had: a liberal democracy with a mixed economy. The lowest of the low was fascism or some other kind of chauvinism.

After the Cold War, the hierarchy began to crumble. Apologists began to pop up for dictatorships and religious fundamentalists so far to the right it was impossible to out-flank them. As long as they were anti-Western, nothing else mattered. Makiya was among the first to suffer the consequences of the new ideas because Iraq raised the awkward problem of what happened to people whose miseries could not be blamed on 'the West'. Suppose, he said, the Americans had marched on to Baghdad. Suppose they had the worst of imperialist motives, to get their hands on Iraqi oil, for instance. Iraq would still be a better place because they would have to dismantle the apparatus of the genocidal state. He looked at his comrades and asked, 'Do you want to keep that apparatus in place?'

His former friends did not want to defend Saddam passionately in the way that the communists of the Thirties passionately defended the Soviet Union; rather they treated his continued rule with an indifferent nonchalance because the survival of the Baath was against American interests. To their mind, the worst form of government, the power which was responsible for the world's crimes, was 'the West' or liberal democracy or 'capitalism' or America. Bubbling underneath, I suspect, was a fear that freedom from tyranny anywhere in the world would lead in the long run to societies rather like the societies they lived in – and that was intolerable.

Makiya's awkward questions did not go away in the years that followed. What were the leftists of the rich world going to do when confronted by not only Iraqi socialists, but Iranian feminists and Zimbabwean liberals telling them very loudly that there were worse ideas than modern democracy? Betray them? Pretend they didn't exist?

If they did, they would reveal their emptiness. With the exception of religious fundamentalism and extreme nationalism, political ideas are universal. A believer in the free market has to believe it can work as well in Bahrain as Boston and offer intellectual support to his fellow advocates of capitalism. If a Western feminist were to turn her back on persecuted Afghan women, you could call her a hypocrite. If the majority of Western feminists were to do the same, you could conclude that feminism was not a serious political force. The oppression of women is as wrong in London as Kabul. If Western feminists say it isn't, then they unwittingly parrot the imperialists of the nineteenth century who believed God gave rights to free-born Englishmen but not dark-skinned natives. In these circumstances, feminist beliefs wouldn't be a philosophy but a lifestyle choice or a way of obtaining advantage in the Western job market.

So it was with the Marxists Makiya confronted. If they couldn't talk to others who called themselves socialists, and who had suffered far more than wealthy intellectuals could imagine, they were in the absurd position of being socialists without comrades.

When that kind of sickness is abroad, the smell that hits your nostrils is not the whiff of hypocrisy but the stench of death.

CHAPTER FOUR

Academic Scribblers and a Defunct Economist

ENLIGHTENMENT: *Sinister, destructive period of history which had a 'project' to dominate nature, prefer reason to superstition and stop people going to church. All a big mistake, but postmodernism will fix it.*

Ophelia Benson and Jeremy Stangroom, 2004

GOING BACK over the far left's arguments of the last century felt a fool's errand. A historian friend dug out yellowing pamphlets from thirty years ago. He collects them as passionately as men with sheds collect model trains, and can talk for hours on the ferocious rivalries and extravagant ambitions of the rival Marxist sects. It is his hobby, but he accepts that general readers can take only so many manifestos for a revolution that never came before their mouths gape and eyelids droop. Why should they care when humanity has waved goodbye to all that?

I said that Kanan Makiya became an intellectual celebrity, and so he was for a while. None the less, most educated people lived through the Nineties without reading him. Palestinians will remember Edward Said's name, as Iraqis will remember Kanan Makiya's, but Said's influence in the West seemed to be confined to the cultural studies departments of the universities where jargon-spouting post-modern theorists perplexed their students – and each other. Like Makiya, he could walk down most streets without being recognized.

Said, Tariq Ali and the Marxists who first backed then abandoned Makiya gathered around *New Left Review*, the world's foremost journal of Marxist theory for academic leftists. In 2000, on the journal's fortieth birthday, its Old Etonian editor Perry Anderson let out a piercing howl of regret for the lost world of his youth. Like Karl Marx, he had expected so much for history, only for history to leave him beached.

When he was a young man in the Sixties, Marxism had seemed a good bet. Communist tyrants ruled one-third of the world from Berlin to Shanghai. Mass Marxist movements in Western Europe and Japan threatened to overturn the status quo. The Red Guards were preparing to terrorize China. In Vietnam and Cambodia, communist guerrillas led by Ho Chi Minh and Pol Pot were fighting for power. In Latin America, Che Guevara and Fidel Castro were thrilling him and his comrades with their revolutionary élan. Marxism never got anywhere in Britain where the Left generally meant a Labour Party that true Marxists despised for its boringly 'reformist' attempts to make most people's lives a little bit better. But given the success of Marxism elsewhere, they could dream that a true revolutionary socialist party would supplant Labour.

And forty years on, what was left of his Left? Socialism had vanished in the Eighties. Long before the Berlin Wall came down people had stopped thinking about it or seeing it as a plausible answer to the problems of organizing societies. It wasn't just that communism was clearly finished. In the free world, trade union membership fell, and all left-wing parties with a chance of winning an election stopped pretending that they could and should nationalize the commanding heights of the economy. All around Anderson, the movements that had given purpose to his life were dying or dead, going or gone.

He cleared his throat with a few words about the 'enormities of Stalin's rule' and 'the lack of democracy in any of the countries that described themselves as socialist', then bewailed the loss of his youthful love. The Soviet Union had fallen, China was embracing market economics and American capitalism had 'resoundingly re-asserted its primacy in all fields – economic, political, military [and] cultural'. No one cared about him and his kind any more. The names of the Marxist philosophers who had inspired him to fight for revolutionary socialism in the lecture halls and drawing rooms of Bloomsbury were as unfamiliar to modern students as 'a list of Arian bishops'. Neo-liberalism had triumphed and become 'the most successful ideology in world history'. Like the Roman Catholic Church in pre-Reformation Christendom, it had no credible competitor, no rival creed that might mount a plausible challenge. 'To say that these changes are enormous would be an under-statement,' he concluded.

If you can stomach his lament for the passing of the communist slave empires, you must grant that Anderson's analysis was an honest recognition of defeat.

The political chasm that separates the twenty-first century from the twentieth is that socialism is no longer credible. The loss of Anderson's Marxism is no loss at all, but the enfeeblement of the humane and generous forces of social democracy in Europe, India and North America has been a disaster. There were plenty of leftists at the millennium, but no radical left with a practical plan to transform society.

James Buchan picked up the sound of the creaking joints in *High Latitudes*, his 1996 novel about the Britain Margaret Thatcher helped to create. Jane Haddon, his heroine, is an aristocratic banker, who is not only successful, beautiful and rich, but thoughtful and kind with it. She confronts Sean McVie, the leader of the Workers' Party, whose resemblance to Gerry Healy Buchan makes no effort to disguise. He is everything she is not: ugly, irrelevant and boring beyond measure. McVie's timid secretary, Sheila, takes Jane to his office. The dirty old man tries to terrify her. For a moment it seems as if she will suffer the same fate as 'all those girls in charity shop jackets, those extras from the Gaiety, those orphans from Sidon and Beit Jennine; so many girls, so many girls; brought round by Sheila in tightly buttoned rage and up the stairs and to the sofa'.

But the communist is no match for the capitalist. She escapes unscathed, leaving him wounded by the parting shot:

> There's so much hatred in you Sean McVie. What happened to you? What did they do to you, Sean McVie, over all those years? And it's nearly over, and where is your revolution: just fifteen hundred members, six hundred in arrears, some odd jobs for the Iraqis and an old man and a terrorised woman in a dingy office off Streatham High Street.

'Where is your revolution?' was a good question, and in trying to explain why the chance of his revolution succeeding had vanished, Anderson blamed the style of the far left as much as the slow death of revolutionary politics in the dingy offices of socialist parties. Anderson said that he and Edward Said had noticed that intellectuals who supported market economics wrote in 'a fluent popular style, designed not for an academic readership but a broad international public'. It should be 'a matter of honour on the Left to write at least as well, without redundancy or clutter, as its adversaries'.

He didn't admit it, but few who had tried to read *New Left Review* could pretend that its intellectuals who called themselves left wing did that. Many were post-modern academics employed by the states they presumably wanted to topple to teach 'theory' in Western universities. Anderson did not realize that their infamous obscurantism was a sign of their cowardice as well as their political isolation.

Writers write badly when they have something to hide. Clarity makes their shaky assumptions plain to the readers – and to themselves. By keeping it foggy they save themselves the trouble of spelling out their beliefs and recommendations for the future. For academics, of all people, this is a disreputable way of going about business, but one that has many uses. Obscurantism spared the theorists who emerged from the grave of Marxism the pain of testing dearly held beliefs and prejudices, as well as the inevitable accusations of selling out from friends and colleagues a clear-headed revision of their ideas would bring.

In defence of academics, jokes about incomprehensible intellectuals are as old as Aristophanes' digs at Socrates. In any case, they hardly formed a monolithic bloc. The best critics of the post-modern academics were not golf course wags who found P. J. O'Rourke a riot, but other academics, particularly philosophers, scientists and historians, who insisted on clear logic and reliable evidence, and psychiatrists exploring the arts of manipulation. A psychiatric team led by Donald H. Naftulin, a professor at the University of Southern California School of Medicine, suggested why students would take the theorists seriously when it showed how easily educated people can be seduced into believing gobbledegook with the marvellous 'Dr Fox' experiment of 1972.

Dr Myron L. Fox inspired confidence. He was an imposing figure: tall, poised and well spoken; silver of hair and sober of dress...every inch the authoritative scholar. As his curriculum vitae proved, he was an expert in the newly fashionable field of 'game theory', a branch of mathematics that calculated how game players try to maximize their returns. The Cold War had made game theory a subject of urgent interest – if America drops an H bomb, will the Soviet Union respond and both sides carry on until the destruction of the world? Or will there be a point where it would be in the best interests of both sides to pull back? The *Scientific American* had published an article on this vital new area of knowledge, and the educated public was keen to hear more. Dr Fox seemed the man to tell them. He attracted audiences of graduates to a series of lectures entitled *Mathematical Game Theory as Applied to Physical Education*. Afterwards the listeners filled in questionnaires on his performance. They were overwhelmingly positive. Eighty per cent rated him 'an outstanding psychiatrist' who had used 'well organized' material and 'stimulated their thinking'. One said that 'he was certainly captivating'. Another reported that 'his relaxed manner of presentation was a large factor in holding my interest'.

They didn't know it but Dr Myron L. Fox had blinded them with the illusion of intellectual authority. He was an actor, of course. Naftulin and his colleagues had rearranged sentences from the *Scientific American*'s article into a meaningless muddle and hired Dr Fox to read them. 'Excessive use of double talk, neologisms, non sequiturs, and contradictory statements' filled the lecture, said a proud Naftulin as he reported the results of the experiment. A minority was unimpressed, but Naftulin said that no one had 'a competent crap detector' to warn them the speaker was a fraud. Dr Fox seduced all his listeners into believing he was an expert.

Dr Fox was addressing educated people who weren't specialists in game theory. In 1980, J. Scott Armstrong, from the University of Pennsylvania, examined which writing styles seduced specialists. He sent articles from the business press to thirty-two professors in North American business schools. They all covered the same story and conveyed the same accurate information. Armstrong discovered that the harder an article was to read, the more trustworthy the professors found it. His method of distinguishing good writing from bad was questionable. He said a clear piece of writing was composed of short sentences. Like this. But many clear writers don't use short sentences. They carry the reader with them by building up clause after clause until they reach the conclusion. As business writers rarely deliver perorations, Armstrong was probably still right to conclude that 'overall, the evidence is consistent with a common suspicion: clear communication of one's research is not appreciated'.

Jargon-mongers certainly stuffed the business schools and used convoluted language to make banalities appear profound. However, no academics could come close to matching the obfuscation and murkiness of post-modern specialists in 'theory' – feminist theory, postcolonial theory, 'other' theory, critical race theory, queer theory, communicative action theory, structuration theory, neo-Marxian theory...any kind of theory, every kind of theory.

In 1996 'theory' was the victim of the Sokal hoax, the academic sting of the decade. Naftulin and his team had shown that a plausible conman could convince an educated audience to believe rubbish if they weren't experts in the field. Armstrong had suggested that authentic experts preferred true but unnecessarily convoluted writing about their field. Alan Sokal, a New York University physics professor, showed that experts in the field of 'theory' beat them all: they believed unnecessarily convoluted writing which was also rubbish. He strung together bizarre claims from Jacques Lacan, Jacques Derrida, Luce Irigaray and many another star of the humanities departments into a gibbering argument that reality was a bourgeois illusion. (Irigaray was my favourite. She denounced Einstein's $E = mc^2$ as a sexist equation which 'privileges the speed of light' over more feminine speeds 'which are vitally necessary to us'. Presumably, light might have appeased her if it had shown its feminine side by slowing down to 30 m.p.h. in built-up areas.) Sokal stacked up the idiocies and then concluded that the laws of mathematics were instruments of capitalist repression. He sent his spoof to the editors of *Social Text*, a leading postmodernist journal, which published it in a special edition that promised to 'uncover the gender-laden and racist assumptions built into the Euro-American scientific method'.

Sokal was a man of the Left and his hoax proved that not every left-wing intellectual was a theorist. But 'theory' was the dominant form of thought in arts and social studies departments, particularly in American universities, and what the theorists were trying to say appalled academics who wanted to uphold basic intellectual standards. In 1996 Denis Dutton, the editor of *Philosophy and Literature*, fought back by opening the annual Bad Writing Contest. 'No one denies the need for a specialized vocabulary in biochemistry or physics or in technical areas of the humanities like linguistics,' he said. 'But among literature professors who do what they now call "theory" – mostly inept philosophy applied to literature and culture – jargon has become the emperor's clothing of choice.' Dutton invited readers to send him egregious examples of academic prose from the English-speaking world. The winner of his 1999 Bad Writing Contest was a piece by Judith Butler, a Marxist and feminist acclaimed by her fellow theorists as one of the most significant thinkers in America. She informed the reader that:

> The move from a structuralist account in which capital is understood to structure social relations in relatively homologous ways to a view of hegemony in which power relations are subject to repetition, convergence, and rearticulation brought the question of temporality into the thinking of structure, and marked a shift from a form of Althusserian theory that takes structural totalities as theoretical objects to one in which the insights into the contingent possibility of structure inaugurate a renewed conception of hegemony as bound up with the contingent sites and strategies of the rearticulation of power.

To ask what Butler means is to miss the point, said Dutton. 'This sentence beats readers into submission and instructs them that they are in the presence of a great and deep mind. Actual communication has nothing to do with it.'

The response of the theorists was instructive. Instead of accepting that they were going badly wrong, they produced books in defence of bad writing. The authors of *Critical Terms for Literary Study* turned on opponents who claimed their 'artificially difficult style' hid the truth that the theorists had 'nothing to say'. The fault was in our readers not in ourselves, the authors replied. 'The project of theory is unsettling' because 'it brings assumptions into question'. They admitted that some theorists could be self-indulgent on occasion, but said that the writing of others was difficult for 'compelling reasons'. They went into dangerous territories and questioned the preconceptions of the thoughtless. Conservative readers were 'frightened off' and 'dismissed' theory with a defensive horror because they couldn't handle the red-raw radicalism on the page.

Such supercilious self-regard led Ophelia Benson of *The Philosophers' Magazine* to remark acidly:

> Ah – so that's it. It's not that the writing is bad, it's that the readers who think it's bad are 98-pound weaklings who turn pale and sick at unsettling projects. They are 'frightened off', the poor cowardly things, by the 'difficulty' of theory – not the ineptitude, mind you, or the slavish imitativeness, or the endless formulaic repetition of repetition – no, the difficulty. So as a result they 'can dismiss' theory – not laugh at, not hold up to scorn and derision, or set fire to or thrust firmly into the bin or take back to the shop and loudly demand a refund – no, dismiss. And dismiss 'as an effort to cover up in an artificially difficult style the fact that it has nothing to say'. Well – yes, that's right, as a matter of fact. We couldn't have said it better ourselves.

Benson had a chamber of horrors to match Dutton's collection. Her main attraction for lovers of pseudo-leftish academic schlock was a rave review by Azfar Hussain of the snappily titled *Dis/locating Cultures/Identities, Traditions, and Third World Feminism*. It was the work of a fellow theorist, Uma Narayan, who was examining Western feminist condemnations of 'sati' – the Indian widows forced by convention to throw themselves on to their husbands' funeral pyres – and 'dowry murder' – the Indian wives burned alive by husbands and in-laws because their dowries weren't as large as expected. According to Hussain:

Narayan's preoccupations with the problematics of the representations of sati in Western feminist discourse indeed remain intimately connected to other representationalist discursive areas, namely dowry-murders in India and domestic violence-murders in the United States – issues that she takes up in the third chapter of her book. Narayan takes a hard, critical look at the ways in which dowry-murders in India are framed, focused, and even formulated in US academic feminist discourse, while pointing up the dangerous problems kept alive by Western culturalist epistemological approaches to Third-World subjects, identities, traditions, and cultures. She argues that while crossing 'borders' in the age of globalization, images, narratives, and the entire chain of events pertaining to the Third World lose their national and historical differentia specifica under the homogenizing epistemic logic of some readily available connection-making apparatuses. As Narayan further argues, such apparatuses – informational, ideological, and mediatic as they are – continue to provide visibility to dowry-murders in India and relative invisibility to domestic-violence murders in the United States, thereby serving the hegemonic.

Who could deny that after a lifetime of hanging round the fringes of totalitarianism, Makiya's old comrades at last seemed to have got one big thing right? Such writing appeared the death rattle of an exhausted revolutionary tradition. If university administrators had transported the Arian bishops of the fourth century to modern lecture halls to deny that Jesus and the Holy Spirit were on a par with God, they could not have given a worse performance.

But ideas don't die. They metamorphose into outlandish shapes and can on occasion become their opposites. When he tried to explain why Marxism and its variants had entranced so many members of the intelligentsia in the twentieth century, Robert Conquest gave up on social and economic root causes and instead concentrated on quotes that illuminated an emotional need for total opposition to all aspects of the status quo. The Russian communist Pavel Axelrod said his real objection to peaceful revolution was that it 'would be exceedingly boring'. Simone de Beauvoir said that she and Jean-Paul Sartre were 'temperamentally opposed to the idea of reform'. When the British communist historian Eric Hobsbawm was asked if Soviet communism had lived up to its promise of a radiant tomorrow, would the loss of fifteen, twenty million people been justifiable, he replied at once, 'Yes'.

The Utopian, the irreconcilable, the hate-filled and the grandiose are abiding types. They don't disappear with changes in geo-politics. Combine their persistence with the injustices of the global economy of the Nineties, the growth of corporations and money markets whose size was beyond comprehension, the survival of America as the only superpower in a lopsided world and the acquiescence of moderate centre-left politicians to the new order, and you can see that a revived radicalism was inevitable and potentially desirable.

Yet the death of socialism meant that what followed was a devious radicalism; one that sounded left wing as it charged past the 'Stop!' signs that had constrained the old left from embracing the philosophies of the far right. You catch glimpses of what was coming in the theories that were baffling students in the university lecture halls of the Eighties and Nineties. To understand how the Left's notion of solidarity with the oppressed metamorphosed into a new creed – how not only the heirs of Gerry Healy but otherwise decent people could shun the victims of Islamist and Baathist fascism – we should ignore the well-deserved gags made at their expense, and pay the theorists the compliment of taking what they said seriously.

It wasn't only claptrap. They were appalling writers to be sure, but you could make a stab at translating what they wrote into straightforward English. Take the theorist's musings on the politics of setting women alight. I cannot put my hand on my heart and say I know exactly what Azfar Hussain meant – I doubt if he could tell us exactly what he meant – but this translation is as close to the original as I can get:

> The author rightly denounces the double standards of interfering American feminists. They protest when news reaches them from India ['*crossing "borders" in the age of globalization*'] of an extreme sexist culture. They don't understand the background ['*national and historical differentia specifica*'] and twist the already crude stories of the media to suit their prejudices ['*dowry-murders in India are framed, focused, and even formulated in US academic feminist discourse*']. The feminists think that no woman anywhere should be condemned to an early and horrible death. But their lofty talk of universal women's rights is a smoke screen that hides their determination to force their values on others ['*homogenizing epistemic logic of some readily available connection-making apparatuses*']. What cheek and what hypocrites! They're no better than they ought to be. Wife beating goes on under their noses in America, and they keep very quiet about that, don't they? Feminists are targeting India and ignoring America because they are the lackeys of the world's only superpower and its imperialist values ['*serving the hegemonic*']. It is racist to oppose sexists.

Leave aside for the moment that what he was saying was a slur – feminists in America and around the world had turned domestic violence from a private torment to a public crime – and marvel at the transformation.

The theorists' obscurantism marked the conclusion of the strange story of the 1968 generation of radicals, many of whom ended up standing on their heads and using the language of the Left to justify the far right. When they were young, of course, nothing could have been further from their minds. Their real achievements had little to do with the socialism so many of them espoused. If anything, they anticipated Margaret Thatcher and Ronald Reagan by breaking down old communal bonds and prejudices and affirming the primacy of the individual. They liberated women, gays and blacks by rethinking roles and challenging every custom from housework to racist language. And jolly good much of what they did was, too. (It was the Sixties generation in Russia and Eastern Europe that brought down the Soviet Empire, after all.)

But as many radical intellectuals in the West retreated into the lecture halls before the tide of conservatism they had in part inspired, they fled from universal values. To generalize, the idea that a homosexual black woman should have the same rights as a heterosexual white man was replaced by a relativism which took the original and hopeful challenge of the early feminist, gay and anti-racist movements and flipped it over. Homosexuality, blackness and womanhood became separate cultures that couldn't be criticized or understood by outsiders applying universal criteria. Nor, by extension, could any other culture, even if it was the culture of fascism, religious tyranny, wife burning or suicide bombing. Each separate cultural group was playing its own 'language game', to use the phrase the postmodernists took from Wittgenstein, and only players in the game, whether feminists or Holocaust deniers, could determine whether what was being said was right or wrong. As epistemic relativism infected leftish intellectual life, all the old universal criteria, including human rights, the search for truth and the scientific method, became suspect instruments of elite oppression and Western cultural imperialism.

Joseph de Maistre, an eighteenth-century reactionary philosopher, who hated the Enlightenment and its revolutions, dismissed the rights of man by saying: 'There is no such thing in the world as *man*. In my life I have seen Frenchmen, Italians, Russians…But as for *man*, I declare I've never encountered him.'

Perversely, theorists who boasted that they were the most transgressively radical thinkers in the West, agreed with the diehards of the *Ancien Régime*, and denied the central tenet of the Enlightenment that men and women have the ability to transcend their circumstances and culture.

The story of how political defeat took the radical Sixties left into the wilderness of post-modernism has been told many times. Still, it was astonishing to see a nominally left-wing theorist using radical language to claim that the separate culture of wife burners could not be condemned unequivocally, and concentrate instead on condemning as hypocrites outsiders who poured cold water, as it were, on the killers' ideology. Our theorist stops just short of supporting wife burning, he still calls murder 'murder', but what matters to him, what stirs his anger and prompts his derision, is the sight of American feminists opposing it.

You have to judge people by the bulk of the evidence they present: the burden of the proof they offer by way of explanation. If they say, 'Of course I oppose burning women/the "enormities" of communism/ Saddam Hussein/ Guantánamo Bay', and then spend the rest of their time in passionate polemics against feminists, democracy, the American invasion of Iraq or the gullibility of critics of the US administration, you can reasonably doubt the strength of their opposition and convict them of rhetorical throat clearing. You certainly cannot expect them to be at the forefront of campaigns to end the abuses they dismiss with a splutter.

They don't support, but they don't oppose either.

The old left believed in socialism and was prepared to argue for it. The excuse-makers for totalitarianism who came after may have been better than those on the Left who took the worst position of supporting Stalin and Mao, and those on the Right who supported Hitler and Mussolini. Rationally, I know it was an advance but their moral outlook was almost as bad: a free-floating, gutless state of frantic evasiveness that preferred to twist and temporize rather than take a stand which required commitment to defend.

The big daddy of French theory, Michel Foucault, was braver in his way than many of his imitators in that he was prepared to make a commitment to the Ayatollah Khomeini. He went to Iran in 1978 to support the Islamists and drooled that 'an Islamic movement can set the entire region afire, overturn the most unstable regimes, and disturb the most solid. Islam – which is not simply a religion, but an entire way of life, an adherence to a history and a civilization – has a good chance to become a gigantic powder keg, at the level of hundreds of millions of men.'

With socialist revolutions gone, he was desperate for something new to set the world afire. If that something new was a vicious clerical reaction, then so be it. Notice, though, that the Iranian revolution was a vicious clerical reaction whose persecutions others had to suffer. If the bishops of the French Catholic Church had achieved the theocratic power of the ayatollahs and used it to prescribe what Foucault and his colleagues could teach at the Collège de France in Paris, I'm sure Foucault and all his admirers in the Anglo-American academe would have gone ape and shouted 'fascism'. As it was, the victims of the Ayatollah Khomeini's theocracy had brown skins and lived in a faraway country. When an interviewer asked him about the fate of the secular Iranian friends of Afsaneh Najmabadi, who might have expected the sympathy and support of French philosophers, Foucault justified their persecution by saying that Iran 'did not have the same regime of truth as ours'.

Foucault had many successors in the decades after the Iranian revolution, but the song was always the same: they're not like us, they've got a different regime of truth, you can't apply the same standards. If 'they' told you differently, then 'they' were denounced or ignored. The indifference was a sign of the degeneration of revolutionary thought. In the early twentieth century, intellectuals who called themselves revolutionaries believed that their own proletariats in the advanced countries would rise up as Marx predicted. When the rich world's working class failed to do as it was told, intellectual revolutionaries invested their hopes in the socialist revolutions in Russia, China and other backward countries. By the Eighties socialism was dying even in the poor world, and there was nothing left to do for those who hated the status quo but embrace the programme of the anti-democratic far right, as Foucault had done, or more usually, just refuse to come out against radical reactionary forces on the grounds that any movement that was against the West couldn't be all bad.

To get to the almost racist state in which philosophers revelled in the denial of rights to Iranian women required a little more than cultural relativism, however. Our theorist of wife burning provided the missing ingredient when he indicted American feminists on the charge of 'serving the hegemonic'. It sounds as if he thinks feminists were the tools of the CIA, but the 'hegemonic' did not mean the policies of this or that US administration but the liberal order of markets, intellectual freedom, democracy and human rights per se.

This was not just the view of one little-read academic reviewing the work of another. Foucault himself argued that liberal democracy was the worst form of tyranny. The Enlightenment that Westerners imagined had freed them had in fact enslaved them in insidious ways that Westerners were too stupid to see – with the exception of French philosophers. In Naomi Klein's *No Logo*, the best-selling leftish book of the millennium, modern 'capitalism' was an almost supernatural force. 'In ways both insidious and overt,' she wrote, 'this corporate obsession with brand identity is waging a war on public and individual space: on public institutions such as schools, on youthful identities, on the concept of nationality and on the possibilities for unmarketed space.' The idea that, with the exception of impressionable children, most self-confident citizens in free societies can cope with advertising was beyond her. Freedom was as nothing when set against the sinister power of the marketing departments. Michael Hardt and Antonio Negri, a university lecturer, whom the Italian courts jailed on flimsy evidence for inspiring the Red Brigade attacks in the Seventies, produced *Empire*, the most successful work of Marxisant 'theory' of the time. The Harvard University Press released it in 2001, and the *New York Times* reviewer speculated that it might supply the next 'master theory' and become the *Das Kapital* of the twenty-first century. Unlike Marx, however, Hardt and Negri had no idea how they might build a better future. All they could do was support anyone who opposed the hegemonic 'empire', whoever they were and whatever they believed. In characteristically painful prose, they explained that religious fundamentalists were the inheritors of the socialists and should not be condemned as vicious bigots from the traditionalist right. 'It is more accurate and more useful . . . to understand the various fundamentalism [sic] not as the re-creation of a pre-modern world, but rather as a powerful refusal of the contemporary historical passage in course.'

The religious right was against 'the empire' of liberal democracy and globalization ('*the contemporary historical passage*'), so it had to be progressive.

Jean Baudrillard, an overrated French theorist, was no different. To him the hegemonic empire was represented by American mass culture that had the terrifying power to make manufactured images more real than reality. It had brainwashed US citizens – although not, once again, French philosophers – into believing that lies were true and the truth was a lie. 'Disneyland is presented as imaginary in order to make us believe that the rest is real,' he declared. 'When in fact all of Los Angeles and America surrounding it are no longer real, but of the order of the hyperreal and of simulation.' It goes without saying that Monsieur Baudrillard didn't talk to the citizens of Los Angeles and produce evidence that Disneyland was more real to them than their work, loves, sicknesses and pleasures. America wasn't the world's oldest democratic country with virtues as well as vices, but an arid nightmare – the 'desert of the real'.

Meanwhile the Bad Writing Contest's judges could be forgiven for not noticing it, but the acclaimed Marxist-feminist's blathering about power relations being 'subject to repetition, convergence, and rearticulation' was also about the overwhelming might of the neo-liberal order. What Judith Butler meant was that hegemonic structures were so powerful they guaranteed the inequality of women and marginalization of gay men and lesbians. Nothing could change. There was no way out, no point in collective action to remedy the unhappiness of women or homosexuals. The power structure was just too strong. All that women (and men) could do was deploy irony to mock their oppressors.

As Martha Nussbaum (a genuine American feminist, who really did have as little time for wife beaters as wife burners) said, the conjuring up of a hegemonic leviathan had the pleasing consequence of freeing middle-class graduates from the hard grind of going out and fighting for change.

> In Butler, resistance is always imagined as personal, more or less private, involving no unironic, organized public action for legal or institutional change...Butlerian feminism is in many ways easier than the old feminism. It tells scores of talented young women that they need not work on changing the law, or feeding the hungry, or assailing power through theory harnessed to material politics. They can do politics in the safety of their campuses, remaining on the symbolic level, making subversive gestures at power through speech and gesture. This, the theory says, is pretty much all that is available to us anyway, by way of political action, and isn't it exciting and sexy?

It is beyond me how anyone could think that change was impossible when the previous generation had seen the second wave of feminism come crashing into shore and the supporters of gay rights force their enemies to retreat from an apparently impregnable position, but there you are, Butler did.

It wasn't just the undoubted miseries and inequalities of wealth and power the liberal order brought with it that were being condemned by the theorists. The victories of the Enlightenment, the vote, welfare, bills of rights, the separation of church and state and the emancipation of women, homosexuals and blacks, which previous generations had fought and on occasion died to achieve, were all now treated as parts of 'the hegemonic' and included in condemnations of a monolithic world order that made no distinctions. The theorists could not and did not want to discriminate, because discrimination would force them to admit that not everything was rotten in their societies and some victories had been worth winning. In the past people who believed in total opposition would offer a revolutionary programme to overthrow the established order. With no revolutionary programme available, the theorists offered a quasi-satirical attack on double standards of the democracies instead.

The most telling part of our theorist's musings on wife burning is that he has no suggestions on how to protect Indian or American women threatened with murder or abuse, no practical proposals to improve their wretched lot. All he gives the reader is a feeble satire. It is a style of denigration so commonplace today we forget how impoverished our predecessors would have found it. His main complaint is about the alleged hypocrisy of American feminists who pick on the misogyny of a poor culture while ignoring domestic violence that is going on in their own backyard. Even if the accusation of double standards had been true, which it wasn't, so what? Even if feminists were the dupes of the CIA or hegemonic US corporations, and engaged in a conspiracy to cover up wife beating in America, their hypocrisy could not make wife burning in India right.

I don't want to sound too high-minded. Everyone in politics has always believed their enemies are hypocrites. Liberals expect to find the moralizing conservative in bed with a live man or a dead woman. Conservatives expect the liberal news-paper editor to sack his staff on Christmas Eve. From the 1880s to the 1980s, however, the liberal-left did not leave it there. A Roosevelt Democrat or Labour MP in Clement Attlee's 1945 Labour government or a communist anywhere in the world believed that the Right's version of market economics was demonstrably wrong. They would win power and show that their programme of collective provision and public ownership was more efficient and productive than free enterprise. The reliance on quasi-satirical attacks on your opponents' hypo-crisy comes when you think you are losing and don't know how to escape defeat.

Conservatives have always done satire best because although their certainties may be absurd, they are sanctified by tradition. Those who want change should get used to being laughed at because new ways of ordering society inevitably bring with them fads and novelties that look ridiculous at first glance, and often at second glance as well. However, no one on the Left should have envied conservatives for their ability to produce satire in the first half of the twentieth century, because satire is the art of the anxious. The brilliance of the mockery of humourless lefties that Evelyn Waugh, Anthony Powell and other conservative novelists produced came from their despair at the disintegration of their established order as social democ-racy grew in confidence. Given the choice, they would rather have kept their established order and lost the satire.

By the end of the twentieth century, the roles were reversed and lefties turned comical all of a sudden. Comedians satirized the management-speak from the business schools and tore into the depredations of the global corporations with savage indignation. Americans had P. J. O'Rourke and others who mocked political correctness – another novel idea, which was often ridiculous, but still triumphed – but in Britain it was hard to find a political comedian who wasn't left wing. The condemnations of hypocrisy were far better than anything the theorists produced, but Margaret Thatcher and Tony Blair kept winning elections. Leftists were on the defensive now, and mockery was their only weapon. They were the new conservatives whose sanctified certainties were being destroyed by disconcerting forces.

The theorists' bad writing hid questions which intellectual clarity would have made obvious to reader and writer alike. All right, we accept there are iniquities and double standards, but what is your plan to end them? You seem to think that the democratic countries, for all their ills and hypocrisies, are incapable of reform. Do you mean that? And do you seriously suggest that they are the root cause of all that is wrong with the world?

The best question of all, however, was the bluntest. When it comes to burning women, are you for it or against it?

'The ideas of economists and political philosophers, both when they are right and when they are wrong, are more powerful than is commonly understood,' wrote John Maynard Keynes in 1936 as he tried to explain how ideologies seeped through society. 'Indeed the world is ruled by little else. Practical men, who believe themselves to be quite exempt from any intellectual influence, are usually the slaves of some defunct economist. Madmen in authority, who hear voices in the air, are distilling their frenzy from some academic scribbler of a few years back.'

The theorists may have been obscure scribblers, but middle-class arts students heard their ideas before moving on to journalism, publishing, teaching and politics. As their philosophies trickled down from the universities, the theorists chimed with millions of people who had never heard of Michel Foucault or enrolled in a cultural studies course. The contempt for universal standards of judgement suited the liberalism of the late twentieth century which placed an inordinate emphasis on respecting cultural difference and opposing integration even if the culture in question was anti-liberal and integration would bring new freedoms and prosperity. It fitted neatly with a form of postcolonial guilt that held that not only were we 'wrong to force western rationality or western science down other people's throats, but that their rationality or their science was every bit as good as ours'. For the sexually voracious it had the further advantage of suiting those who enjoyed to excess the permissive freedoms the Sixties and Seventies had brought, and most definitely did not want others to think that they could be 'judgemental' about their behaviour.

As an example of theory being turned into practice, however, the anti-globalization movement of the Nineties was hard to beat. In the rowdy demonstrations outside the summits of the World Trade Organization and in the chaotic meetings of the European Social Forum and World Social Forum, you could see all the theorists' frenzies laid out.

In the movement's early days, it felt beastly to be too hard on the demonstrators, or it felt that way to me in any event. If America was the world's only superpower, a little anti-Americanism was surely justified. If pundits were strutting through the lobbies of Washington think tanks saying that 'history was over' and liberal democracy was all that was left, then it was reasonable to hold the neo-liberal order to account. And if roughly a billion people lived in abject poverty, nearly half of them in such utter destitution that they daily faced death by starvation and disease; if access to adequate sanitation was unknown to 2.4 billion; if malaria, measles, tetanus, syphilis and AIDS were ravaging Africa while being controlled in the rich countries; if in the United States, the richest of the rich world's countries, 40 million had no health insurance and 20 per cent were functionally illiterate; if the differential between the richest and poorest countries was around 3:1 200 years ago, and 75:1 today (and rising); and if that differential meant more corruption, prostitution, child soldiers and crime; then yes and by all means, a vigorous campaign aimed at the people at the top of the heap was in order.

But as the ideas the anti-globalization movement represented spread into the mainstream of the liberal-left, they began to look ever more threadbare. What fuelled the anti-globalization movement was a passionate and often well-merited hatred of the rich world in which its supporters lived. Like the theorists, the protesters believed their rich countries in general and America in particular constituted a global hegemon which oppressed suffering humanity. The psychological pressures behind the error were easy to explain. Contrary to the fashionable post-modern theory of the time, people don't always hate the alien 'other'; more often they hate what they know. British left-wingers were likely to have a deeper loathing for British Tories than for Saddam Hussein or Kim Jong-Il because they had seen them up close all their lives and learned to find the thought of a victorious smirk on their enemies' faces intolerable. The contempt bred by familiarity meant you had to go to the Balkans to find irrational hatreds to match those of American Republicans for Democrats and vice versa. (And if the Balkans wouldn't do, you could always try studying the hatreds in your own family or office.)

Because of their parochialism, however, the anti-globalizers could not see large parts of the planet. Communist China should have been the nightmare for a principled left, but because it wasn't a Western power, leftists didn't storm Chinese embassies as the one-party state sent the leaders of free trade unions to camps to be 'reformed through labour', while giving corporations a freedom to exploit workers that they could never enjoy in the allegedly 'capitalist' West. Nor was the movement's commitment to reducing poverty in Africa as high-minded as it seemed. Its supporters could think only about the 'capitalism' of the World Trade Organization and the International Monetary Fund. They sobbed and sighed for Africa, and then shamefully refused to demonstrate against the massacre of the peoples of Darfur by the Islamist Sudanese government and the rape of Zimbabwe by Robert Mugabe. It was not that they positively supported Islamists or loopy African nationalists – that would have taken guts. They just looked away, and when others protested, their sole contribution was to say that Westerners had no right to criticize.

In 2005 the Environment Editor of the *Guardian* produced a near-perfect example of how the ideas of the theorists had flooded the mainstream when he castigated those who 'demonised' Mugabe. He cleared his throat with a quick declaration that he didn't actually support the tyrant, then bellowed that what Mugabe was doing was nothing new. 'Forced evictions, brutal land grabs and slum clearances were all used by Britain's own rulers in the past to enlarge their estates, build bigger, more modern cities, construct reservoirs, make way for railways and lay out fine parks and fashionable areas for the newly rich to live.'

This one clumsy sentence revealed all the symptoms of the sickness of the radical left at the millennium. When Britain's rulers cleared the peasants from the Scottish Highlands in the eighteenth and nineteenth centuries, radicals of the day opposed them. You might have thought that their successors would have believed that if it was wrong then, it was wrong now. Not so. Because you could not blame Mugabe on the West, you had to attack his opponents. The crimes of 200 years ago diminished the crimes of today and made anyone who showed solidarity with Zimbabweans a hypocrite, even though they weren't alive when the Highlands were cleared, and even if they would have opposed the evictions if they had been around at the time. Hypocrisy had gone from being the compliment that vice pays to virtue to the first of the cardinal sins.

Such defiance of the basic assumptions of rational argument wasn't criticized with the vigour it deserved because most of the anti-globalizers were at once furious about politics and above the normal scrutiny of political life. With the exception of the green parties, they refused to stand for election on a programme for power – not least because they would have lost – and their combination of fury and disengagement emphatically separated them from what had gone before.

The concentration on America and the mixed economies they mistook for 'capitalist' makes them sound like a continuation of the twentieth-century left. But the old left, whether social democratic or totalitarian communist, had parties with manifestos and leaders who wanted to put programmes into practice when they came to power. The anti-globalization, global justice or anti-capitalism movement (the failure to agree on a name was symptomatic of a wider confusion) eschewed participation in favour of a simple and insular lament for the ills of their own governments and societies.

The British Labour thinker John Lloyd said that the failure to get involved in practical politics had the advantage of keeping the movement pure and away from the inevitable compromises and questions from the media participation in democratic life brings. 'They operate on an idealist plane, far above the political world they oppose. Consciously or unconsciously, this separation of ideals from any coherent arrangements that might further them acts as a prophylactic for the movements: their approach cannot be opposed, because to do so is to oppose virtue. Unlike communism, which sought power, the core of the global movements' narrative is oppositional, and must remain so.'

Occasionally, anti-capitalists would realize that their friends were in danger of becoming poseurs. George Monbiot, a leader of the British Green movement, described how he addressed one of the debates at the meeting of 50,000 anti-globalizers at the 2003 European Social Forum in Paris. It was entitled 'Life after Capitalism', but Monbiot said that as he mounted the stage and began to put forward his prospectus for a new order for humanity:

the words died in my mouth, as it struck me with horrible clarity that as long as incentives to cheat exist (and they always will) none of our alternatives could be applied universally without totalitarianism. The only coherent programme presented in the meeting was the one proposed by the man from the 'League for the Fifth International', who called for the destruction of the capitalist class and the establishment of a command economy. I searched the pamphlet he gave me for any recognition of the fact that something like this had been tried before and hadn't worked out very well, but without success . . . It seems to me that the questions we urgently need to ask ourselves are these: is totalitarianism the only means of eliminating capitalism? If so, and if, as almost all of us profess to do, we abhor totalitarianism, can we continue to call ourselves anti-capitalists? If there is no humane and democratic answer to the question of what a world without capitalism would look like, then should we not abandon the pursuit of unicorns, and concentrate on capturing and taming the beast whose den we already inhabit?

These were honest questions. The only honest answer was that Marxism had not only destroyed itself and the lives and liberties of hundreds of millions of people, but crippled those who sought to overthrow the status quo thereafter. Democratic reform was the only way. It had always been the only way, and the only good and true way at that. But most of Monbiot's comrades prided themselves on their total opposition to everything about their societies, and as a matter of principle and point of pride were unable to say a good word about them. They were incapable of supporting reform at home because if they did they would have to admit that democracy was not broken beyond repair. More seriously, their provincialism risked betraying the very foreigners they affected to support.

India has a vigorous feminist movement that fights ancient cultural and religious prejudices. Like all strong political campaigns, it does not believe that an omnipotent 'hegemon' makes resistance futile. It wants Indian women to enjoy the same rights as Western women, and regards those rights as universal rather than Western. It would no more accept that freedom from murderous violence was an imperialist demand from the all-powerful empire than that the right to vote was for whites only.

It has been illegal to demand dowries in India since 1961. In practice, many parents do not value their daughters and pay prospective husbands and in-laws to take them off their hands. Women and girls can become disposable goods. If they are unlucky, the husband can throw them away if they don't provide satisfaction, and go back into the market for a better model. Indian government statisticians reported that husbands and in-laws killed nearly 7,000 women in 2001 because they did not bring enough money with them. Everyone agrees the figure is an underestimate. So heavy is the burden of daughters, parents kill them before they are born. The sex testing of foetuses has left India with 933 women for every 1,000 men.

Indian feminists have battled to stop the police pretending that charred corpses of wives were the result of 'accidental kitchen deaths'. They won the partial victory of persuading the authorities to create special divisions of women police officers who treat all inquiries into the mysterious deaths of wives as murder investigations until proven otherwise. The suffering continues, however. In 2003 Ranjana Kumari, who ran seven women's refuges in Delhi, described how her clients were victims of an ascending scale of violence. 'Sometimes women are tortured to squeeze more money out of their families and in extreme cases they're killed,' she said. 'Then the husband is free to remarry and get another dowry.' The Vimochana women's group in Bangalore said that the city hospital's burns unit admitted between three to five women a week. Lucy Ash of the BBC paid it a visit and found a young woman called Sundurahma with 70 per cent burns. 'She screams for her mother as the doctor forces her to sit up so he can examine the raw flesh on her back. The only part of her body which is not badly burned are her feet. I notice a silver ring on one of her toes and immaculate nail polish. Sundurahma said her husband poured kerosene over her and told her to die. Doctors told me she would not last the week.'

Now try a thought experiment and suppose that the organizers of refuges in Delhi and Bangalore were to combine with like-minded women across the subcontinent and appeal to Western feminists for support. India is a democracy, but democratic politicians can be wary about tackling traditional prejudices and losing conservative votes. Foreign pressure can force them to face abuses they would rather ignore. It is embarrassing to have dirty linen washed in front of the world's public and for fellow prime ministers to take them to one side at a state dinner and mutter that questions in parliament and the press have forced them to raise an unpleasant subject.

Foreign sympathizers would have to endure a long slog before they could compel their politicians to intervene. When W. H. Auden was trying to build support in Britain for the Spanish Republic as fascism's forces overwhelmed it in 1937, he wrote of the necessary but wearisome duty of putting aside his poetry and friendships for tomorrow. Today was for

> *the expending of powers*
> *On the flat ephemeral pamphlet and the boring meeting.*

And that's not the half of it. Powers must also be expended on letters to newspapers, resolutions at party and trade union conferences, and pickets of embassies. Time must be wasted begging for funds for the rents for offices and on maintaining the morale of fellow activists, whose children ask why mummy is never home. Every now and again, it can be worth it, as the success of the campaign against apartheid proved.

Realizing the advantages of appealing to sisterhood, suppose the Indian refuge organizers plead with Western feminists to show solidarity, the oldest and noblest virtue of the Left, and begin the long march to turn lethal misogyny into an international outrage.

I doubt if they would be treated any differently from the way the Iraqi left, the Iranian secularists, the Chinese trade unionists, the Darfurian peasants and the slum dwellers of Zimbabwe were treated. A minority on the Left would be sympathetic, but most would either ignore them or say that the persecution of Indian women was a part of Indian culture and it would be a hypocritical act of 'cultural imperialism' for outsiders to interfere. If Western governments or – heaven forfend – the American government gave them a sympathetic hearing, they would be denounced as turncoats.

There's something to be said for keeping your nose out of other people's business, although it wasn't until the late twentieth century that the Left started saying it. Many of the people who campaigned against apartheid did not have the faintest idea about divisions within black South African society, which were as deep as the chasm between black and white. They were interfering in a country whose subtleties and tensions were beyond them and idolizing an African National Congress that had its grim side. For that matter, the Auden generation's understanding of the Spanish Civil War was naïve, to put it kindly.

Equally, a world where there is no revolution worth striving for can feel a disenchanted and dreary place. There is admittedly something a little boring and wholesome about striving for reform and democracy. Suicide bombers and wife burners, whatever else they are, are not boring and wholesome: not sensible shoes, wholemeal bread and composite resolutions.

But it is one thing to bewail conformism in the lecture halls of Berkeley and the London School of Economics, quite another to ignore Spanish Republicans, black South Africans, Indian feminists or Iraqi democrats who ask for your support. At that moment, you must choose, and the choice of neutrality is the choice to keep the funeral pyres burning.

For if those who expend powers on the ephemeral pamphlet and the boring meeting are the hypocritical agents of the 'hegemon' then true radicalism rests with those who turn away and refuse to get involved. Traditionally, the apathetic do nothing because they are lazy or because they reason that nothing they can do could make the world better. Regarding all ideologies as equally useless, they sink into the gentle consolations of idleness. What was brewing in the Nineties could not have been more different: a raging apathy, a righteous refusal to commit to Iraqis, Darfurians, Zimbabweans, the Chinese . . . to anyone who was not a victim of Western governments and business. It assured believers that activism was passivity and isolationism was commitment.

Making people interested in any version of politics seemed an awesomely difficult task at the time. In all democratic countries, turnouts fell after the Berlin Wall came down and politics mattered less. Global institutions and money markets sapped the power of national governments. Judges and international courts sapped the power of parliaments. The media sapped the confidence of democratic politicians by making them look ridiculous, or, more usually, by taking their electorates off into an entertainment supermarket where multichannel television and the Internet provided hundreds of rival amusements to politics. The 2004 British comedy-horror *Shaun of the Dead* caught the ease with which citizens slipped away from political debate when it opened with the all-too-plausible scene of Shaun missing the pressing news that flesh-eating zombies were ravaging London because he switched to one of hundreds of other channels whenever a bulletin began.

As the stock of politics fell, so did good reasons to become involved in it. Social scientists wrote learned books on the reasons for 'post-democracy', 'the market state' or 'bowling alone'. They shared a vision of a dystopian future in which all forms of communal life – running charities, joining political parties, staying in a marriage – would shrivel. People would retreat into the private universes of gated villages with homes where bedrooms were individually equipped with en-suite bathrooms and entertainment centres that spared them the necessity of talking even to their family.

However much they overdid it, there was truth in the idea that isolation and self-satisfaction were growing in the rich world at the end of the twentieth century. It was a future about as far from the dreams of the Left as it was possible to get.

What no-one asked was what would happen when the apathetic citizens revolted for what they took to be a left-wing cause; I don't suppose anyone ever thought that they would. When modern consumers flocked to the new left's banner during the years of mayhem brought by al-Qaeda and George W. Bush, they found it had a new ideology which accommodated them very nicely. Ian McEwan noticed it in *Saturday*, his novel set on the Saturday of the million-strong anti-war march in London in February 2003. His hero Henry Perowne is a surgeon who has treated Saddam's victims and knows that the debate is about whether or not to keep a genocidal regime as well as whether to have war or peace. The doctor looks at the banners bearing the self-centred slogan 'Not in My Name' and is repelled. 'Its cloying self-regard suggests a bright new world of protest, with the fussy consumers of shampoos and soft drinks demanding to feel good, or nice.'

The Left is by ideology and taste austerely anti-commercial, but consumers could now appreciate its message. You owe nothing to anyone, the new ideology implied. There is no need to make a commitment to Darfurian peasants or Iraqi democrats, no need to talk to them and temper your demands to suit their needs. You no more have to think of what they have suffered than an angry customer has to think of the hard life of a shop girl. You no more have to suggest how to improve their lives, than an angry customer has to suggest ways to repair faulty goods. We no longer believe in internationalism and fraternity. Sticking by your comrades is as absurd a notion as staying loyal to Microsoft when Apple has a better product. Join us, and revel in the righteousness of your solipsistic anger.

Nothing the neo-liberal world order produced suited the consumer society as well as the thinkers who purported to oppose it.

It took one more war and one more professor for protest's new brand to go global.

CHAPTER FIVE

Tories Against the War

Douglas, Douglas, you would make Neville Chamberlain look like a warmonger.

Margaret Thatcher, 1993

BY THE WINTER OF 1991, the Baath's slaughters of the Kurds and the Shia Arabs had ended – not least because there was hardly anyone left standing who could fight back. After the briefest of pauses for breath, the politics of racial purity moved to the borders of a European Union that lectured the rest of the world on the need to uphold civilized standards. In the states of the former Yugoslavia, Franjo Tudjman's Croatian nationalist movement committed atrocities against Serb civilians, and, much later in Bosnia, so did Muslim mujahideen. But the primary aggressor was Slobodan Milosevic, a former communist bureaucrat who employed a familiar combination of nationalism and socialism to destroy Bosnia's Muslims and Croats and create a Serb statelet on as much Bosnian territory as his proxies could conquer.

Despite the obfuscation that followed, Milosevic's desire for an uncontaminated homeland caused the Bosnian war. The Bosnian government was multi-national and had the support of many Bosnian Serbs and Croats. It was never just a Muslim government and its citizens were never simply 'the Muslims', as a slapdash Europe insisted on calling them. By contrast, only Serbs served in the militias of Radovan Karadzic and Ratko Mladic – Milosevic's sidekicks. While they destroyed or desecrated nearly every mosque in the Serb-held districts of Bosnia, nearly all the Orthodox and Roman Catholic churches in the zone controlled by the Bosnian government survived, as did nearly all of the Serbian and Croatian non-combatants. The massacres were the result not of an escalation of a long and bitter war between racially segregated armies but of a deliberate policy decision taken calmly and without provocation by the Serb nationalists.

They came up with a pretty euphemism for the dictionary of late twentieth-century totalitarianism: *etničko čišćenje*, 'ethnic cleansing', which carried an echo – perhaps unconscious, perhaps as homage – of the Nazis' *Säuberung* – 'cleansing' – of the Jews. The Serb nationalists did not want simply to drive the Muslims and Croats out. To stop their enemies ever returning, ethnic cleansing sought to rub out all honourable connections between people and place. Hence the destruction of the mosques, the pounding of Sarajevo and the ripping-up of birth certificates and title deeds; hence the tactic of raping girls or forcing fathers to castrate their sons and molest their daughters. The Bosnian conflict produced hundreds of books and millions of newspaper articles. Journalists and politicians emphasized how hellishly complicated the Balkan 'quagmire' was and how mind-achingly difficult it was to know what to do. The historian of genocide, Samantha Power, cut through the double-talk when she encapsulated Serb strategy in a sentence: 'This was a deliberate policy of destruction and degradation: destruction so that this avowed enemy race would have no homes to which to return; degradation so the former inhabitants would not stand tall – and thus would not dare again stand – in Serb-held territory.'

It is all you need to know, and the great powers knew it at the time. Moynihan's Law did not apply in the Balkan conflict. American satellites plotted the advance of the Serb rapists mile by mile. Journalists risked and sometimes lost their lives to tell Europe what was happening on its doorstep.

As early as August 1992, British reporters revealed the true nature of the conflict. Ed Vulliamy of the *Guardian*, Penny Marshall of Independent Television News and Ian Williams of Channel 4 News, along with Jeremy Irvin, a freelance cameraman, broke the news that the savagry Europe thought had died with Nazism and communism was back. They found it at the Omarska and Trnopolje prison camps in the Prijedor region of north-western Bosnia after receiving an invitation to visit from a surprising source. That summer, as Serb militias swept through the country, the Bosnian government alleged that they had herded Bosnian Muslims and Croats into fifty-seven concentration camps. Radovan Karadzic, the leader of the Bosnian Serb nationalists, denied the allegation vehemently. So confident was he that the Serbs were the victims of a baseless propaganda campaign, he boasted that Western reporters could inspect any prison they wished. The British journalists took him up on his generous offer and asked to see the Prijedor camps.

Their first stop was Omarska. It was a concentration rather than an extermination camp: a Belsen rather than an Auschwitz. Although they were to kill thousands of Croats and Bosnians, the Serb nationalists weren't killing every Croat and Bosnian they arrested. In Omarska and elsewhere, the Serbs murdered many but degraded and then expelled many more. The United Nations defines genocide as the massacre of a people 'in whole or in part'. The International Criminal Tribunal for the Former Yugoslavia later convicted a Serb thug of aiding and abetting genocide in the town of Srebrenica, where Muslim men and boys were massacred wholesale by Serb militias. Elsewhere, Milosevic and his allies slaughtered their enemies 'in part', and used the example of mass murder and mass rape as a means of driving the survivors away. It was closer to Hitler's treatment of the Poles and Ukrainians than the Jews and gypsies – an attempted genocide rather than a holocaust.

This does not make Serb nationalism 'better' than German fascism. This is not a competition.

Serb police and paramilitaries took over former mine buildings at Omarska after seizing control of the nearby town of Prijedor at the start of the war. In a pattern repeated across the country, the Serb leadership first restricted the movements of Bosnian Muslims and Croats, then sent gangs of drunken arsonists to attack their homes and march the survivors to the camp. According to the International Criminal Tribunal indictment, 'The camp guards and frequent visitors who came to the camps used all types of weapons and instruments to beat and otherwise physically abuse the detainees. In particular, Bosnian Muslim and Bosnian Croat political and civic leaders, teachers, the wealthy, and non-Serbs who were considered as extremists or to have resisted the Bosnian Serbs were subjected to beatings and mistreatment which often resulted in death.' Like Hitler, Stalin and Pol Pot, the Serb commanders understood that it is always a smart move to knock out the natural leaders so the masses become a body without a head.

The British journalists did not know about the decapitation of Bosnian civic society. They had their suspicions, but they needed evidence. The chances of getting it were slim. Naturally, Vulliamy and his colleagues weren't allowed full access. War criminals do not parade their crimes; even Hitler did not parade his crimes. Karadzic's invitation to inspect the camps seems incredibly reckless in retrospect, but he must have thought that he could afford to go through the motions of openness. When the journalists arrived, the camp guards did not allow them into the rusty sheds where the real business of Omarska went on. The inmates of Karadzic's Potemkin prison kept their heads down and their mouths shut. The ghastly knowledge of what would happen to them if they spoke out meant that most refused to say a word. Those who talked were wisely circumspect. 'I don't want to tell any lies, but I cannot tell the truth,' a young man with a wasted body and trembling hands told Vulliamy.

If the day had ended there, Karadzic's gamble would have paid off handsomely. When people complained that he was denying access to the International Red Cross he would be able to say that sceptical representatives of the British press had been to Omarska and found nothing beyond a normal PoW camp.

Feeling they had been within yards of the real story, the disconsolate reporters left for the next stop on the official tour.

Trnopolje was a transit camp for prisoners awaiting either deportation out of the 'cleansed' areas or a move to another camp for more punishment. It was not a concentration camp, but a holding centre. I don't want to make it sound too cosy a place. Here is the testimony of one 15-year-old Bosnian girl collected by the US State Department for the United Nations. It is worth repeating the pornographic details for once because of the denial that was to come later from the Right and the Left.

She was at school when the Serbs moved into her town of Kozarc. She ran into the woods but the paramilitaries caught her and sent her to Trnopolje. Early on in her imprisonment, she went to collect water from a well near the gates. Serb troops blocked her path, and took her and nine other girls to a house beyond the perimeter fence. Some thirty Serbian soldiers were waiting. They taunted the girls, calling them 'Turkish whores' (Turkish because they were Bosnian Muslims). They forced them to undress and parade slowly in a circle for fifteen minutes while the men watched. 'Three soldiers took one girl – one to rape her while two others held her down. The men took turns. A soldier approached the 15-year-old and mocked her, saying he had seen her before. He pulled out a photo of her 19-year-old Muslim boyfriend, and cursed him for being in the Bosnian Territorial Defense Forces and then raped her.' She fought as best she could, but he bit her and hit her with the butt of his gun. Another rapist ran the blade of his knife across her breasts as if to slice the skin off, leaving bleeding scratches. After that, eight more men raped her and she lost consciousness. A Trnopolje guard who had been at her school came to her rescue and dragged her back to the camp. As they left, he called over his shoulder, 'Remember, you will be accountable for this!'

No they wouldn't, not if the outside world knew nothing about what had happened.

The dejected reporters came down the road to Trnopolje a few days after the gang rapes. Their assignment was turning into a shambles. The Serb guards escorting them were half-drunk, and the Serb authorities had insulted their intelligence by trying to get them to believe propaganda an unusually stupid toddler might have seen through. To make the day more surreal, a team from Serbian television was reporting on the British reporters and filming their every move. The assignment had not been entirely pointless, however. Vulliamy, Williams and Marshall had the Bosnian government's account of Croats and Muslims disappearing into a network of camps. For all the greasy inanities the Serb police had offered them, they had met a few of the emaciated prisoners at Omarska. If they had put together what they had seen with what they had heard, they would have had enough to produce reasonable pieces. There was one hitch: Irvin had little tape worth showing in his camera, and this initially trivial failing grew into an insurmountable obstacle as the day wore on.

I cannot begin to describe to you how deeply sophisticated journalists hate it when some cocksure, hunchbacked, sub-literate snapper – who has failed to confront his personal hygiene crisis for over a decade – turns to us and asserts with an exultant cackle that 'a picture is worth a thousand words'.

We hate it because it is true.

Seeing changes everything. Without pictures, their editors would have buried their stories at the back of the foreign section or way down the TV news running order, and the reporters knew it. They seemed to be stuck, until they reached the perimeter fence of Trnopolje complex, and the grubby god who watches over hacks smiled on them.

As their convoy turned towards the main gate, they caught a glimpse of an extraordinary sight. 'Stop!' they shouted. The reporters jumped out, the Serb TV crew reporting on the reporters jumped out, the half-drunk guards jumped out; everyone went off in different directions except Jeremy Irvin, who hoisted his camera to his shoulder and let it roll.

There, once again in the heart of Europe, were starving men behind barbed wire with ribs pushing at shrunken chests and ravaged eyes gazing out at the land that had once been their home. There, once again, were people who had been listening to the same songs and wearing the same clothes as the rest of Europe, condemned to imprisonment or death for no other reason than they had the wrong name or religion.

One prisoner stood out. Fikret Alic told the British journalists how the Serbs had flattened Muslim homes and brought them to the camp. 'We are not soldiers,' he protested as he searched for an explanation for his imprisonment.

It wasn't what he said that hit people but how he looked. Alic was a young man who would have been handsome if he hadn't been painfully thin. The camera caught him stripped to the waist with his jeans almost falling off his starved body. At one point in the TV footage, two rows of barbed wire perfectly framed his face. Behind him were older men, most half-naked, and all worn and anxious. They huddled around Alic and leaned forward towards the camera on the other side of the wire as if searching for the momentum that might push the world into rescuing them.

The pictures were sensational. They looked like the Holocaust. Hundreds of TV companies ran the footage and hundreds of newspapers and magazines grabbed the still image of Alic's face behind the wire. It uncannily recalled one of the most famous photographs from the Second World War: Margaret Bourke-White's *The Living Dead at Buchenwald, April 1945*. Even US intelligence officers who had intercepted the radio traffic of the Serb march through Bosnia, and knew about atrocities far worse than the British reporters imagined, were stunned. Jon Weston of the State Department said, 'We had all the demonstration we needed before. We knew all we needed to know. But the one thing we didn't have was videotape. We had never *seen* the men emaciated behind barbed wire.'

Only foreign intervention could save them. That was as clear from the beginning as the real nature of the Serb atrocities. A glance at the map told you that the Bosnian Serbs had Serbia proper over one border supplying them with arms and fighters, and the Bosnian Croats had Tudjman's Croatia over another border. Only the Bosnian government was an orphan. She had no neighbours to whom she might turn, no friends to defend her. Poor, ruined Bosnia's last best hope was the international community. As Ali Hassan al-Majid might have predicted, the international community refused its help for the four years when she needed it most.

George Bush senior's administration was no more interested in invading Bosnia than invading Iraq. Brent Scowcroft, who had so bluntly rejected the idea of a democratic Iraq after the Kuwait War, explained that military intervention couldn't be justified 'in terms of the US national interest'. If the Serbs threatened to ignite a regional conflict by taking the war to Kosovo, he would think again. For as long as the war was contained in Bosnia, 'it might have been horrible but did not affect us'. In any case, the Bush family's first administration assured the growing number of appalled American politicians, human rights groups and Muslim and Jewish organizations, the Europeans would bring Milosevic and Tudjman to heel.

They had good reason to think that Europe would be true. The European Union's official ideology was anti-totalitarianism. The case for integration held that European nation-states had created the great evils of the modern age – imperialism, mechanized war, communism and fascism. Since the foundations of European unity were dug in the Fifties, however, Western Europe had been at peace and war and massacre had become impossible to imagine. Borders had gone and the nationalism which so entranced the Serbs and Croats had become a curiosity from a lurid past. Instead of fighting, nations pooled their sovereignty and ceded power to the commissioners, councils of ministers and judges of the European

Union. The European Court of Human Rights upheld liberal standards in the EU and beyond. NATO and a string of arms control pacts guaranteed collective security and openness about the possession of weapons.

Robert Cooper, a foreign policy adviser to Tony Blair, defined Europe as the centre of 'the postmodern world [where] there are no security threats in the traditional sense because its members do not consider invading each other'. The American neo-conservative Robert Kagan picked up the theme and called Europe 'Paradise', a haven where lavish benefits freed citizens from the human race's oldest burden of work while perpetual peace freed them from the human race's oldest fear of violence.

Whenever sceptics asked why taxpayers of modest means had to subsidize agri-business, or worried that there wasn't an honest auditor on the Continent who would certify the EU's accounts, pro-Europeans yelled that the very act of raising questions about corruption and oligarchy risked a return to the horror of the totalitarian past. To their minds, there was no middle way between the Panzer division and the European Commission. So automatic was the anti-totalitarian reflex, that during the 2005 Dutch referendum on the European Constitution the Dutch political establishment admonished the 'No' campaign with a 'Never Again!' TV commercial that used pictures of the massacres at Auschwitz and – shockingly, for reasons we will get to – Srebrenica as a warning of what would happen if the voters rejected plans to rearrange the bureaucrats' chairs in Brussels. (The Dutch voters ignored their leaders. They lived.)

As Milosevic unleashed the demons of totalitarianism, anyone who believed the stories the European Union told about itself must have believed Europe would respond. Jacques Poos gave them hope. The foreign minister of mighty Luxembourg stirred the blood of true believers when he thundered in an indomitable voice, 'The hour of Europe has come!'

The hour of Europe had done nothing of the sort. Post-modern Paradise had a fatal weakness: it wasn't prepared to fight for itself or its values. Indeed, its post-modern condition rested on the belief that it had no absolute values that were not open to negotiation. With conflict unimaginable, the leaders of Paradise felt no need to waste money on preparing for war. After the fall of the Berlin Wall, they cashed in on the peace dividend and reduced military spending from 3 to 2 per cent of gross domestic product while the US kept it at 3 per cent. A difference of 1 per cent doesn't sound a vast gap. But Paradise's welfare state was becoming ever more expensive as its inhabitants lived longer and had fewer children. The enjoyment of Paradise's exquisite regional cuisines and the relaxation brought by long holidays at its innumerable resorts were easier to afford without the costs and inconveniences of raising the young. Without enough new workers, the price of paying for an ageing population could not be borne without bringing in immigrants, many of whom found Paradise's values repugnant. The high cost of social spending would have mattered less if deflationary central bankers who had forgotten every lesson Keynes had taught had not been in charge of Paradise's monetary policy. During the Eighties, the European and American economies were about even. In the Nineties, the brutal American market shot ahead, allowing Washington to build an unassailable lead. That apparently insignificant 1 per cent difference in GDP bought a revolution in American military technology.

More important than the money was the European mentality. With children rare, their parents weren't prepared to risk the lives of the young in battle. They reassured themselves that the lesson of recent history was that fighting got you nowhere. The EU had brought peace to Western Europe for fifty years, while the fall of the Berlin Wall had been a miracle. A terrible ideological conflict between opponents equipped with nuclear weapons that had threatened to destroy the planet had ended with barely a shot fired. Unarmed citizens took to the streets of Prague, Berlin and Dresden and – poof – communism was gone. The residents of Paradise didn't like to think that pressure from the American arms build-up had played a part in finishing the Soviet Union. As far as they were concerned, European integration, the reunification of Germany and the end of the possibility of nuclear annihilation had come without violence or the threat of it. War was the way of the past. Compromises hacked out in interminable meetings in Brussels had bored the old European hatreds to death.

Even when European governments weren't formally committed to keeping their troops within their borders – as Germany's was – the temperament of the European public was pacific and conciliatory. Anti-Americanism was already building in reaction to the infuriating success of the American economy that affronted Paradise's core social democratic beliefs. The Europeans worried that military power made Americans far too willing to barge in with all guns blazing and without a thought for the consequences.

'If you have a hammer, all problems look like a nail,' they said.

'If you don't have a hammer, a nail doesn't look like a nail,' the Americans replied.

The exception to the rule was Britain. Along with France, it possessed one of the European Union's two surviving martial cultures. Unlike the French, and with the exception of the intelligentsia, the British were not instinctively anti-American.

A majority of the population regarded the dominant European culture with suspicion. Euroscepticism ruled the Conservative Party in the Nineties, and many on the liberal-left muttered about the EU's anti-democratic ethos.

More than any other European country, Britain defined itself by its willingness to stand up to totalitarianism. Our finest hour was 1940, the history of which could still make the most unpatriotic of hearts leap. Britain might have coordinated military intervention in Bosnia with Washington while selling it to the Continent.

Unluckily for Bosnia and for Britain and for Europe, Her Majesty's Prime Minister in 1992 was John Major.

Living through the Major administration was like being trapped in a railway carriage with a party of bent accountants. For seven years. The Tories in their decadence managed to be simultaneously sleazy and tedious. Their conventional suits and monotone delivery concealed an intellectual cowardice that preferred the acceptance of millions on the dole in Britain and millions driven from their homes in the Balkans to the political risks of confronting trouble. John Major and his colleagues never faced up to the big questions of the Nineties in domestic or foreign policy. The initiative was always with others, whether they were George Soros and the foreign exchange dealers who destroyed the Conservative Party's reputation for economic competence when they forced the pound out of the European Exchange Rate Mechanism, or Slobodan Milosevic who dragged down an acquiescent Foreign Office to its lowest point since Suez.

London consistently stopped effective political or military action from September 1991, when it stifled a French proposal to send in a Western European force, to 1995, when its opposition to the American policy of lifting an arms embargo on the Bosnian government and hitting the Serb forces from the air collapsed. So vicious and determined was the Tory hostility, the Bosnian government considered charging Britain before the International Criminal Court as an accomplice to genocide. It wasn't a publicity stunt. The Bosnians had a case. As the leaders of other European countries acknowledged, Britain sought to wreck every initiative that might have ended the violence. Tadeusz Mazowiecki, the Prime Minister of Poland in 1993, said, 'Any time there was a likelihood of effective action, a particular Western statesman intervened to prevent it.'

The Western statesman he had in mind was the British Foreign Secretary, Douglas Hurd, an Old Etonian and son of a peer who had graduated to politics from Cambridge University and the Diplomatic Service. Hurd was every inch the English grandee: a calm and measured politician, who proved the breadth of his interests by writing thrillers that weren't at all bad. His ally in government and successor at the Foreign Office was the Defence Secretary, Malcolm Rifkind, an Edinburgh lawyer, whose putdowns were so polite on the rare occasions he was rude it was almost worth being insulted to hear them.

For all the talk of 'the death of deference', the British still tug the forelock. Obsequiousness seemed in order for Hurd and Rifkind, who appeared to preserve the best values of the old British ruling class. They were well-spoken and good-mannered Tories rather than doctrinaire Thatcherites; sound men with gravitas and bottom. A respectful note entered the voices of socially insecure journalists when they interviewed them.

Yet it was these men of taste and breeding who watched as the Balkans burned. They manoeuvred through the United Nations and the foreign ministries of the world to give the ethnic cleansers what they wanted by Balkanizing the Balkans.

Conspiracy theorists speculated that the only plausible explanation for their behaviour was that Hurd and Rifkind were Islamophobes. The accusation was not plausible and the accusers could not find a shred of supporting evidence. By the standards of Conservatives of their time and class, they were remarkably free of prejudice. Nor were they wilfully blind. Every now and then, they looked up like sheep raising their heads from a meadow, and bleated that they knew what was happening around them. As Hurd acknowledged, 'there were clearly close parallels in moral terms between what has happened in Bosnia and what happened in Germany as a result of Nazi policy'.

Their failure to confront it makes the anti-war Tories of the Nineties sound like 'Little Englanders', a label which is not necessarily an insult. Despite the bad press it got because of appeasement, a Little England policy (or isolationist policy in the United States) is often coherent and moral. There is no necessary virtue in wasting other men's blood and other taxpayers' treasure in other nations' conflicts rather than attending to pressing issues at home. Little Englandism, like its continental and American counterparts, is more popular than the strategists who move imaginary armies around maps like to believe. It will become more popular still as the bonds of the nation-state crack under the pressure of globalization. Apathetic, isolated citizens who cannot even commit themselves to participating in an election are unlikely to commit themselves to war.

Unfortunately, as globalization weakens the old bonds of national loyalty, so it brings new threats. Furious voices in Britain, America and Europe said it was foolish for their governments to pretend that Bosnia had nothing to do with them.

The failed states of the former Yugoslavia were spewing refugees and crime gangs across Europe. Very prescient commentators noticed that outlandish groups of Islamist fanatics were springing up everywhere and using the refusal of the West to come to the aid of Bosnia's Muslims as proof that an evil conspiracy of Christians and the Jews wanted to annihilate Islam. Some believed in the conspiracy so fervently, they sent 'warriors' to Bosnia to fight the Serbs and radicalize Europe's Muslims.

The refusal of Hurd and Rifkind to listen to the warning voices did not make them Little Englanders, however. They prided themselves on being men of the world. Like the liberal-left, they looked down their noses at the Conservative Party's anti-Europeans and rejected chauvinism and vulgar nationalism.

Nor were they 'realists' from the same mould as Brent Scowcroft and the other members of Bush senior's administration, although they liked to pretend that they, too, were merely sticking up for the national interest. Scowcroft didn't doubt that the United States *could* have overthrown Saddam Hussein in 1991 or lifted the siege of Sarajevo in 1993, he just did not think it was in America's interests to do so. He readily conceded that he would think about America's interests again if Milosevic took the war to Kosovo and began a regional conflict.

By contrast, Hurd and Rifkind didn't only oppose intervening in the war in Bosnia because they thought it was against Britain's interests to send troops; they didn't just paraphrase Bismarck and say the Balkans were not worth the bones of a single British grenadier. They believed that no one *could* intervene or *should* intervene. They were determined that no troops, whether British or not, should take on the Serbs.

The best explanation for the disaster of Tory foreign policy came from the Cambridge historian Brendan Simms. He defined Hurd and Rifkind – and a large section of Britain's old establishment – as 'conservative pessimists', potentially talented men and women who had been corrupted by defeat. The High Tories' rout was different from the rout of the socialist left but the moral and intellectual consequences were eerily similar. Like Kanan Makiya's former comrades, these were members of the upper class who had seen history grind their expectations to dust. In their lifetime, Britain had fallen from the status of a great power it had enjoyed since the early eighteenth century. Suez had been the defining moment for their generation and had taught them the limits of British strength. The Northern Ireland conflict had taught them the hopelessness of trying to reconcile competing ethnic groups and inculcated a desire to treat with men of violence. Margaret Thatcher had ridiculed their patrician values and undermined their self-confidence, while the end of the Cold War had given new vigour to the threatening doctrine of universal human rights. Hurd and Rifkind never put it like this, but their refusal to help the Bosnian government seems to me to have been a way of slapping down the hopes of the early Nineties for a new world order which would take human rights seriously. Since Edmund Burke fought Tom Paine, a strain of conservative thinking has loathed the notion that what is right in one country must be right in all countries.

The Major government also upheld the exhausted post-imperial elite's belief in the virtues of partition that sprang from Britain's flight from an empire it could neither control nor afford. In Ireland, India, Palestine and Cyprus, Britain took the easy route of partitioning on ethnic lines and running – 'Divide and quit,' Sir Penderel Moon, a British civil servant who saw the horrors of the partition of India, called it.

Behind the unquenchable desire to scorch new lines on the map lay an Establishment version of post-modern cultural relativism which held that different peoples could not live together. The problem was they couldn't live apart either. From Ireland to Kashmir, the legacy of the British scuttle from empire was hot and cold wars over arbitrary borders. Hurd and Rifkind appeared to know nothing about them. Their instinctive reaction against universal human rights and multinational states came from deep within the Tory soul. And just as the nihilists on the Left weren't quiet in their apathy but raging in their defence of righteous laziness, so the Tory pessimists weren't droopy-faced wet blankets who stuttered with fear, but eloquent and full of ardent conviction. They were evangelists for pessimism: surrender's happy-clappies.

To her credit, the behaviour of her former colleagues revolted the deposed Margaret Thatcher. Rejecting Hurd's notion that lifting an arms embargo that hurt only the Bosnian government would create 'a level killing field', she said that Bosnia was 'already a killing field the like of which I thought we would never see in Europe again. [It] was not worthy of Europe, not worthy of the West and not worthy of the United States.' The massacres were happening 'in the heart of Europe, in Europe's sphere of influence. It should be in Europe's sphere of conscience.'

Comparisons with the appeasers of the Thirties spring to mind, but at least Neville Chamberlain's government allowed thousands of Jewish refugees to escape. The Major government sank lower than its Tory predecessors did by closing Britain's borders to Bosnian refugees. As the Balkans erupted, the Home Office pulled the slyest trick in its book and imposed visa restrictions on Bosnia. It assured the public that as long as Bosnians obtained the correct papers from the British embassy, we would welcome them. It kept quiet about two catches: the first was that British embassies refused to give visas to anyone they suspected of being a refugee; second, even if they were generous, there was no British embassy in Bosnia where refugees might make their applications for a visa. Hurd was unapologetic. 'The civilians have an effect on the combatants,' he explained. 'Their interests put pressure on the warring factions to treat for peace.' You had to read this passage several times before you realized that Hurd was denying sanctuary to the victims of the Serbs (and of his refusal to intervene) so he could use their misery to force Bosnia to cut a deal with the ethnic cleansers and accept partition.

I made an angry call to the Home Office the day it announced the closing of the ports, and its civil servants almost laughed at my naïvety. They weren't worried about a scandal. They judged correctly that few people understood the immigration rules. In any case, they were bringing in a token number of Bosnian refugees who could be paraded before the cameras as evidence of the government's compassion. That would do the trick, they thought – and it did.

It wasn't the humanitarian crisis that forced Tory policy to crack, but the growing pressure from America. Very slowly, and with many a false start and act of cowardice of its own, the Clinton White House began to think about bringing the war criminals to justice and organizing air strikes against the Serb positions. Far more important was the American Congress. Senators, most notably Bob Dole, John McCain and Joseph Lieberman, increased the pressure on Clinton and the Europeans. They and others asked: what if the Serb nationalists weren't in a brilliant guerrilla army who would bog Western forces down in a Balkan quagmire like a European Viet Cong. What if they were no more than a bunch of drunken sadists, who could only win battles against unarmed civilians?

Anyone who has been on a Left which has had most of its established truths contradicted by events would have recognized the delirium which then gripped the Tory pessimists as they struggled to find a coherent reply. Your beliefs are a part of your personality: at the heart of your identity. To admit they are wrong is to renounce a part of your life and sense of yourself, along with the hopes and vendettas you have accumulated over the years. For the Major administration, the admission of a mistake would have been an acceptance that tens of thousands had died needlessly. Conservative ministers and their officials had not wanted them to die and had not killed them. They would happily have gone through their careers without hearing the word 'Bosnia'. They had honourable worries about the deaths of British soldiers and the unintended consequences of a war that could drag on for years. As good people, they expected to sleep well at night and greet the face in the mirror in the morning with a smile. They didn't want to think of themselves as accessories to massacre. Yet if they were wrong, the massacres would be due in part to their sins of omission.

Rather than accept the psychological consequences of confessing error, people lose their bearings. They talk only to friends. They imagine conspiracies as they seek the worst possible motives for their critics. They retreat into coteries and speak in code. If they're not sure which side a stranger is on, they look for the verbal clues which reveal whether they are friend or foe. Do they say 'the Balkan quagmire' (friend) or the 'legitimate Bosnian government' (foe)? To cut a long story short, they go a little mad.

When American officials argued for a tougher line, the ferocity of the reaction from London came close to knocking them over. John Fox, an Anglophile State Department official who had been educated at a British private school, described the 'vigour and desperation' with which Hurd's argument was pushed. 'I never saw in my lifetime of dealing with these folks in and out of government...that kind of, I would almost call it passion, except it wasn't passion, it was interest expressed in such a determined way, no holds barred.' British policy 'was not just indifferent, but actively hostile to steps that could prevent...ethnic cleansing'.

John Major's grasp of the English language, which was uncertain at the best of times, lost its hold on reason as he fell into one of his dottiest images. Those who wanted war, he said, were cowards 'grandstanding from the safety of their arm-chairs'.

He and his colleagues became just as anti-American as the emerging new left. The Yanks were naïve fools from a Graham Greene novel who didn't understand the complexities of the world, they implied. Stupid white men – pistol-packing cowboys – who made bad situations worse and left others to clear up the mess. By contrast, British ministers may no longer be the rulers of a great power but they had the wisdom to see the world for what it was. They were shrewd Greeks to the brutish Romans. If only the Americans did what they said, they could order Europe's affairs for the best.

The anti-American mania came to a head in late 1994 when a magnificently macabre anecdote began to do the rounds. Aides to the Republican Senator Bob Dole told of a furious row with Malcolm Rifkind. Dole had pressed Rifkind on the need to stop the massacres. Rifkind replied that Dole did not understand the dangers of intervention. The argument got nastier and nastier until it culminated in Rifkind crying, 'You Americans know nothing about the horrors of war.'

Now, during the Second World War, the young Bob Dole

fought in the Italian campaign as a platoon leader in the 10th Mountain Division of the US Army. He led an attack on a German machine gun nest in the Po Valley. As the platoon advanced, a German bullet hit his radio operator and Dole ran to his rescue. A shell caught him before he got there, shattering his back, paralysing his arms and legs and damaging his lungs and kidneys. It was nine hours before his comrades could get him off the battlefield. His superiors gave him a Purple Heart and shipped him back to Kansas in a full-body cast. They didn't expect him to live. Dole's neighbours rallied round and stuffed notes into a cigar box at his local drug store until they had raised the money to send him to see Dr Hampar Kelikian, an Armenian-American surgeon who practised in Chicago. It took three years for the doctor to piece him back together. While he recovered, Kelikian told him how his family had escaped the Turkish genocide of the Armenians. Dole, for one, remembered the Armenians and took an interest in the politics of Turkey and the Balkans thereafter. Decades on, anyone with ordinary curiosity only had to glance at the Senator to see that Kelikian might have been an excellent doctor but he had his limits. He could not save Dole's right arm.

Malcolm Rifkind was a lawyer from Edinburgh. The closest he had come to combat was the backstabbing of the Major Cabinet.

'Don't talk to me about sacrifice,' Dole snapped back.

Rifkind told Brendan Simms that there had been a difficult meeting but denied he had questioned Dole's knowledge of war's evils. Whatever the detail, the thrust of the story was revealing. Bosnia was turning the world upside down. Dole was a hero of the Second World War, while the North Vietnamese communists had tortured his fellow Senator John McCain in a prisoner-of-war camp. Despite or because of what they knew, they were leading the push for international intervention. Their British and French counterparts had grown up in the Paradise of post-war Western Europe. Despite or because of what they knew, they were unwilling to risk a war to extend peace to their neighbours.

It stopped soon after that. The outrages became too great even for an insouciant world. Bosnians in the territory conquered by Serb forces were holed up in satirically named 'safe havens'. Their protectors were troops from Europe and beyond operating under the authority of the United Nations. The largest enclave was Srebrenica, which was home to 40,000 mainly Muslim men, women and children, who had been ethnically cleansed from the villages of eastern Bosnia. Charged with the duty of protecting them were 600 Dutch troops. They were lightly armed and had no combat experience. To make matters worse, their superiors didn't want them to fight. NATO and the United Nations told them that they were peacekeepers, not soldiers who must be ready to shoot back if necessary.

The Serb forces scented the whiff of fear and licked their lips. They surrounded Srebrenica and cut off its fuel supplies. Nothing happened. Their snipers took pot shots at the Dutch. Again no response: not from NATO, the United Nations or the Dutch government. Having learned all he needed to know, Ratko Mladic led the Serb forces into Srebrenica on 11 July 1995, and began the biggest massacre Europe had seen since the Forties. The gallant Dutch army, whose political masters were to invoke the name of Srebrenica as a justification for their policies, stood back and let them do it. Defenceless and abandoned, some Bosnians fled to the hills. Others gathered around the UN compound, as if it was a cathedral where they might find sanctuary. None was forthcoming. The Serbs took the men and teenage boys, loaded them on to buses, drove them out of town to schools in the surrounding villages and murdered them – about 8,000 in all. They spared the women and children, if 'spared' is the right word. They were loaded on to buses and driven out of Serb territory. From the windows they could see the corpses of their men in the fields. Their buses stopped at checkpoints along the way. The Serb troops who were on sentry duty while their brave friends were murdering the passengers' husbands, sons and brothers, pulled young women off and raped them.

There was no reaction worthy of the name from the British government. John Major made no public commitment that British troops in other 'safe havens' would protect civilians. In a taste of what was to come, metropolitan liberal opinion began to sound like the Hurd wing of the Tory Party. Both the *Independent* and the *Observer* argued against retaliation. London continued to insist that the embargo on the sale of weapons to the Bosnian government could not be lifted and the Serb forces could not be attacked from the air.

Nor was Bill Clinton anxious to punish the aggressors, but the political risks of doing nothing began to dawn on him. Bob Dole was certain to be the Republican challenger to Clinton in 1996. The ghastly images from Srebrenica and his war record could help him paint Clinton as a feeble draft dodger. The American press was furious, so too were the newly freed nations of Eastern Europe, which openly wondered if a West which could not protect civilians in Srebrenica would protect them if the Russians tried to return. The US Congress voted to lift the arms embargo and Jacques Chirac all but laughed in Britain's face as he compared the appeasement of the Serbs to Munich. Rifkind fought back, but Britain was isolated and the game was up.

When Jacques Chirac attacks you from the moral high ground, the game is always up.

What had been impossible in 1991 became possible four years and tens of thousands of lives later. The Serb positions around Sarajevo were attacked by NATO and the siege lifted. In 1999, Milosevic tried to do to Kosovo what he had done in Bosnia and Tony Blair proved why it was worth having a New Labour prime minister when he allied with Clinton and stopped him. An added bonus was that the Kosovo war encouraged the Serbs to overthrow Milosevic.

Before Conservative pessimism fell apart, however, it took one final and maniacal twist and sank into denial of the oldest sort. As the Tories headed towards the bottom of the barrel, a part of the Left cheered them on.

CHAPTER SIX

The Boy on the Edge of the Gang

Thus it will not be found according to the sound rules of pseudology to report of a pious and religious prince that he neglects his devotion, and would introduce heresy; but you may report of a merciful prince, that he has pardoned a criminal who did not deserve it. You will be unsuccessful if you give out of a great man, who is remarkable for his frugality for the public, that he squanders away the nation's money; but you may safely relate that he hoards it... because, though neither may be true, yet the last is credible, the first not.

Dr Arbuthnot, 1712

IN HIS INDISPENSABLE *Treatise on the Art of Political Lying* of 1712, Dr John Arbuthnot, friend of Swift and Pope, physician to Queen Anne and leading Tory pacifist of his day, warned smart political operators to choose their words with care. The good lie must build on assumptions that people take to be true. Your listeners must be able to say to themselves that the accusation makes sense given what they know, and a man they previously regarded as an upright custodian of public money was likely to be a miser who would refuse to allow essential spending.

Arbuthnot was writing at the height of the 'rage of party' in the early eighteenth century when the modern system of party politics was in its mewling infancy. The rages became more furious in the twentieth century, and psychologists began to talk about 'denial' rather than 'lies'. It is a better word to describe people in the grip of a political or emotional frenzy because they may well not be deliberately lying. It doesn't matter if they are or they are not, because the notion the theorists took up that hypocrisy was the greatest vice missed the point that the worst people are often sincere. And so are men and women who aren't usually wicked. An otherwise reasonable politician whose ideology is breaking up will believe any argument that justifies his actions. The rejected husband who screams insults about the wife who left him may well think every smear is true. In both instances, they will believe their untruths when they tell them. In both instances, they are likely to follow Dr Arbuthnot's rule, because if they are not to descend into a deep madness, what they say must make sense to them as well as their audience.

When the briefing from the Tory pessimists of the late twentieth century began about Bosnians staging murders, the most pointless question you could ask was whether the Foreign Office, MI6 and the Conservative Party were lying. What mattered was that they weren't telling the truth.

In February 1994 Alistair Goodlad, a Conservative Foreign Office minister, addressed the Commons on the plight of Sarajevo, the besieged Bosnian capital whose defenders couldn't defend themselves because Britain and the rest of the European Union insisted that no one should sell them arms. 'We are looking for effective action – if necessary, muscular action – to protect the civilian population of Sarajevo,' he said. 'They have been subject to mortar attacks from both Serbian and Bosnian forces.'

Sorry, *Bosnian* forces? Sarajevo was the victim of an un-provoked attack by the Serb nationalists that had 'the primary purpose of spreading terror among the civilian population', as the International Criminal Tribunal put it.

After the allegedly safe area of Gorazde was hit by a massive Serb assault, which killed hundreds of Bosnians, Malcolm Rifkind said, 'The events in Gorazde of the past few days have undoubtedly been the consequence of Serb aggression. But there are still a number of warring factions in Bosnia. One of the British soldiers who lost their lives in the past week was killed by Serbian action; a Bosnian government soldier shot the other one dead.'

Sorry, *warring factions*, does that mean moral equivalence?

Indeed it did. General Sir Michael Rose opined that demands for intervention came from 'the powerful Jewish lobby behind the Bosnian state' and wondered, at a performance of Mozart's *Requiem* in Sarajevo, if Alija Izetbegovic, the cultured Muslim president of Bosnia, understood 'the Christian sentiment behind the words and music'. While his peacekeepers did little worth mentioning in dispatches as the Serbs shelled Sarajevo, he said that 'much of the bad news concerning the situation in Bosnia was Bosnian government propaganda and this was often being repeated by the US State Department'.

Politicians, generals and journalists, not all of them Conservatives, constantly went on about 'ancient hatreds' as if all sides were as bad as each other. By a subtle sleight of hand, the legitimate government of the multi-ethnic Bosnian state, which was recognized by the United Nations and European Union, became 'the Muslims' although the Serbs were never 'the Orthodox' or the Croats 'the Catholics'. Presenting the victims of a campaign of murder and rape in confessional terms made it a little bit simpler for the thought to suggest itself that there was nothing to choose between the slaughtered and the slaughterer. It also made a second charge sound plausible when anonymous Whitehall briefers whispered to reporters. 'What you are seeing is a lie,' they said. 'You think you are witnessing Serb atrocities when the news shows pictures of Bosnians being blown to pieces as they shop in Sarajevo street markets. Sometimes you may be, but sometimes the Bosnians are killing their own to force us to intervene.'

Dr Arbuthnot would have applauded, because the position of the Bosnians was so hopeless and their suffering so remorseless, the notion that they would murder their own families and neighbours to save the rest of their people was plausible. London may have believed it, because the burden of the realization of where its dearly held ideology had led would be too much for anyone but monsters to carry.

It is hard looking back to find a good word to say about the Major administration. The best I can manage is the backhanded compliment that at least the Conservatives admitted that there were massacres. The task of building a conspiracy theory that denied that they had taken place fell to a segment of the Left. To his shame, the most celebrated left-wing thinker of the time gave the deniers respectability. His reputation should have gone the way of Douglas Hurd's and Malcolm Rifkind's. Ominously, his fame only grew.

Noam Chomsky was born in 1928 into an American-Jewish family. He grew up in a working-class district of Philadelphia where the politics of the post-Bolshevik far left weren't curiosities but live debates. Arguments about communism and Nazism, capitalism and anarchism, swirled around him. 'Growing up in the place I did I never was aware of any other option but to question everything,' he remembered. 'The first article I wrote, at the age of 10, was concerned with the Spanish

Civil War and the rise of fascism in Europe. Even as a child I would haunt second-hand bookshops for radical pamphlets.' At 13, he decided he believed in anarchism, an honourable political philosophy that did not implicate itself in any of the criminal ideologies of the twentieth century from colonialism to Islamism, but also a facile one because its supporters could never put its theories into practice.

On 6 August 1945, the teenage Noam had his epiphany. A burst of light from beyond the ocean revealed the true horror of his country and the blindness of its people. *Enola Gay*, a US Air Force B-29 bomber, dropped 'Little Boy' on the Japanese city of Hiroshima, the first of only two nuclear bombs exploded in anger to date. No one bothered to pretend that Hiroshima was a military target and the 80,000 dead were anything other than civilians. Yet all around him the young Chomsky saw Americans celebrating. 'I remember that I literally couldn't talk to anybody,' he said decades later. 'There was nobody. I was at a summer camp and I walked off into the woods and stayed alone for a couple of hours when I heard about it. I could never talk to anyone about it and never understood anyone's reaction. I felt completely isolated.'

His upbringing in revolutionary politics had prepared him to draw two conclusions from his moment of utter loneliness in the forest. He was to cling to them for the rest of his life. The first was that democracy was a sham: the plaything of militarists and corporations. Here was the United States, the greatest democracy on earth, committing a war crime – the deliberate targeting of civilians is always a war crime – with a new weapon of previously unimaginable destructive power in the name of freedom and justice. A quarter of a century on, in his first book on politics, *American Power and the New Mandarins*, he was emphatic on the worthlessness of the US system of government. America was a quasi-fascist state and 'to me it seems that what is needed is a kind of denazification'. The bombs haunted him, as they haunted many others. The Japanese were about to surrender, he maintained. The American military's claim that Japan would have fought on for months or years if it had not dropped the atom bombs was a lie spread by the propagandists of the new nuclear age. The truth was that the bombs were a part of a sordid scramble for money and power. Rather than trying to save the lives of US troops by bringing the war in the Far East to an early end, American militarists had incinerated Hiroshima and Nagasaki to intimidate Stalin so they could grab as much of the post-war world as possible for their friends in the corporations. 'Two atom bombs were used against a beaten and virtually defenceless enemy,' he said, in 'history's most abominable experiment.'

When evidence from the archives in Tokyo and Washington DC contradicted him by showing that the Japanese army had been ready to fight on for months or years until the atom bombs forced a capitulation, Chomsky, characteristically, did not change his mind. He couldn't confine himself to saying that Hiroshima and Nagasaki had been crimes against humanity. There had to be more to them than that.

His second conclusion was that the peoples of the democracies didn't realize that their freedom was a fraud because they were duped by the 'propaganda' of the corporate media. The jubilation of all the Americans around him on the day the news of Hiroshima broke could not be sincere; it had to have been 'manufactured' by the real rulers of the world.

Chomsky was thin-skinned and vituperative, but not without redeeming features. A bored friend of mine who was working through the night as a security guard once emailed him on a whim. To his astonishment, he received a long and careful answer to his off-the-cuff questions – a respect for debate that showed Chomsky didn't mind if his interrogators were professors in a Harvard lecture hall or janitors twiddling their thumbs in an empty office block. An academic colleague who had known him for forty years said that 'when you send him five pages of criticism, he sends 10 pages back, whoever you are. It's not ego, it's the substance of the criticism that's the issue.'

Nor do you become the most feted left-wing pundit of your time – ranked 'with Marx, Shakespeare and the Bible as one of the 10 most quoted sources in the humanities' – by talking complete twaddle.

It is obviously true that much of what appears in the media is nonsense, and on occasion self-serving nonsense. Chomsky's mistake was to confuse corporate interests with political interests. Corporate bias is everywhere. Newspapers and radio and TV stations cover each other with rank dishonesty. Chomsky's notion of media propaganda went way beyond the usual critiques of media folly and bias and revived the old notion of false consciousness that Friedrich Engels invented in 1893 after Karl Marx's death. The Marxists of the early twentieth century took it up to explain away the discomforting fact that the workers of the most advanced societies were not organizing socialist revolutions as Marx had insisted they would. The reason for the failure of Marxist theory could not possibly be that it was wrong and the workers didn't want communism. It had to be that a 'hegemonic' capitalist media befuddled them and stopped them understanding their real interests. At its worst, the theory of false consciousness legitimized tyranny. If the stupid masses swallowed lies, then middle-class intellectuals, who could see through the propaganda because of their superior education, were entitled to seize power in the people's name. By Chomsky's time, the age of socialist revolution was dying. In his hands, false consciousness became less of an excuse for a *coup d'état* than a consoling explanation for defeat. The Left lost because democracies fooled their electorates with subtle media propaganda rather than subjugating them with the tear gas and jackboots of the dictatorships. To Chomsky there was no difference between the two. 'Propaganda is to a democracy what the bludgeon is to a totalitarian state,' he declared.

The theory of false consciousness assumes their rival media owners unite in a political pact to brainwash the masses and keep the elite in power. George Orwell subscribed to it. In his essay on boys' comics he said that their tales of upper-class boarding schools and ripping adventures in the service of the British Empire were part of a plot 'by capitalist newspaper proprietors' to indoctrinate the young 'in the interest [of maintaining] the class structure of society'. An amused Evelyn Waugh replied that 'a study of those noblemen's more important papers reveals a reckless disregard of any such obligation'.

The same applies today. The majority of British newspaper proprietors are as right wing as they were in the Forties. Yet they turned on John Major's Conservative government when its popularity vanished and allowed their reporters to reveal as many of the sexual secrets of its members as they could find. They based their treachery on the sound commercial grounds that their readers had had enough of the Tories and sex sold. Owners and editors, including the senior management of the publicly funded BBC, are true capitalists because they will put the interests of increasing market share before the interests of their class. If that entails turning on the governing elite, so be it.

A study for the *Columbia Journalism Review* of why American reporters censor themselves said that the third most common reason reporters gave for ignoring newsworthy stories was the one many would have put first: important information conflicted with the commercial interests of their organization or its advertisers. The second surprised the researchers: peer pressure and the 'fear of embarrassment or potential career damage' the decision to step out of line with other reporters would bring. It wasn't so surprising a finding. What matters to most people in work is the status accumulated by the approval of colleagues. If the pack is howling off in one direction, very few journalists want to break ranks and head off on their own. Peer pressure isn't always bad. One reason reporters go to places such as Omarska is that war reporting is a form of journalism other journalists admire. Their colleagues will applaud their bravery, even if the public doesn't care about crimes in faraway countries. That it may well be more interested in the sex tips of celebrities and sex lives of sportsmen was suggested by the most popular reason journalists gave for self-censorship. Eight out of ten said they came across stories they knew were newsworthy and believed should be told but dropped them because they thought the audience would find them 'boring' or 'complicated'.

The report made dismal reading but remained a rebuke to all those who thought the masses would embrace the radical left if it wasn't for those darned media magnates uniting to manufacture consent for the powerful. Chomsky was determined, however, that the messy trade of journalism with its many failings and occasional glories was a propaganda operation that covered up the crimes of the elites of the democratic world. He wasn't all wrong about the crimes. To pretend as many did after the Cold War that the West was always for freedom was to rewrite history. Highlights from the list of Western felonies between 1945 and 1989 include: the British and French imperial wars in Kenya, Malaysia, Algeria and Vietnam; the American takeover of the French war in Indochina and the saturation bombing of Vietnam, Cambodia and Laos; Western backing for the Falangist regimes of Spain and Portugal; simultaneous support for the Greek colonels *and* the Turkish military dictatorship; the American-backed overthrow of the democratic governments of Iran, Guatemala and Chile; acquiescence in the Indonesian invasion of East Timor; and the Israeli occupation of the West Bank and Gaza. The promotion of democracy was not always the first priority in these conflicts, to put it charitably.

I'm not saying there was moral equivalence. You were born lucky in the twentieth century if you were born American rather than Russian, or British rather than Chinese. Nevertheless, it was far from clear if fortune was smiling on you if you were born Timorese rather than Polish during the Cold War.

A few of Chomsky's denunciations of what the West would rather forget stand up well. But it is not a competition, as I said. Chomsky's fault was that he thought it was, and one the American elite must always lose. In this, he was ahead of his time. Rock stars, political activists and students came to adore him because he anticipated the themes of the supposed left of the twenty-first century in the late twentieth. It was all there in his writings. The empty belief that you can be serious about politics without a coherent and practical plan for society. (Neither Chomsky nor his millions of admirers found it remarkable that he deplored the Indonesian invasion of East Timor on America's nod in 1975, but had nothing to say to the East Timorese on what they should do after Australian and British troops infuriated Osama bin Laden by ending the terror in 1999.) The dissection of hypocrisy rather than the promotion of the common good was there as well, as was the over-whelming emphasis on the overweening power of the United States.

His critics on the Right accused him of being a fellow traveller of communism. Chomsky, however, had no time for the Soviet Union, and although he offered gruesome and gormless support to the Chinese and Vietnamese communists, my overall impression is that he wasn't interested in evils which could not be linked to America. In this narrow-mindedness, he was closer to the caricature of the parochial American than he liked to admit. He wasn't an anarchist: a true anarchist is against all governments. Nor was the most influential modern theorist of linguistics a political theorist. If you can't explain why subjugation is worse in East Timor than Poland, you descend into the relativism which Chomsky deplored in his serious work on linguistics.

Your mind is also ready to deny. Not to embrace the outright denial of totalitarianism, but to accept a denial of which Dr Arbuthnot would have approved: plausible denial – deniable denial, if you wish; the denial of a boy on the edge of a gang of bullies who can step back and smile innocently when the teacher storms into the playground.

Every political, national or religious ideology engages in denial in weak forms. The British rarely discuss the millions who died in the famines which ravaged India right up to 1943 but stopped as soon as we left in 1947 and India became a democracy. We don't like to talk about them because they destroy the complacent belief that the Empire always brought efficiency and know-how to benighted corners of the world. In 2005, Turkey was still prosecuting authors such as Orhan Pamuk who remembered the Armenian genocide of 1915. A confrontation with the historical record still threatened Turkish nationalists' self-assurance.

For modern fascists, however, denial is essential. It may seem that the slaughtered innocents of Europe died because of an insane and pointless ideology. Yet their deaths were not entirely futile because they destroyed fascism as an idea in Europe, if not elsewhere. Whenever Europeans were tempted to try it again they ran up against the horror of the gas chambers and shied away. For the remaining fascists there was only one option if they were ever to make ground: they had to deny the horror. Naturally, their denial concentrated on destroying the abiding image of fascism: the gas chambers at the end of the railway line to Auschwitz.

Thirty years ago, a French lecturer called Robert Faurisson was the most fervent of the deniers. In the mid-Seventies he began to propagate the notion that everything you thought you knew about fascism was a lie. The Nazis had not run extermination camps. The judges at Nuremberg coerced the testimony of alleged camp survivors out of them. The *Diary of Anne Frank* was a fake. All accepted history was a gigantic fraud that covered up a plot by scheming Jews to get their hands on German gold and Palestinian land.

> The alleged Hitlerite gas chambers and the alleged genocide of the Jews form one and the same historical lie, which opened the way to a gigantic political-financial swindle, the principal beneficiaries of which are the State of Israel and international Zionism, and the principal victims of which are the German people – but not its leaders – and the entire Palestinian people.

Obsessional racism underpinned the work of Faurisson and the other Holocaust deniers. It is hard to squeeze into their tiny minds, but maybe race hatred mattered more to them than the political calculation that denial was essential if fascism was to be rehabilitated. People throw the charge of 'racist' around far too freely today and fail to separate inconsequential prejudice from all-consuming intolerance. The Frenchman who defines himself by his fixation on Jews or the Serb whose hatred of Bosnian Muslims is at the core of his identity wants to humiliate the objects of his loathing beyond endurance. What could be more degrading to the Jew or Bosnian than to scream that their parents had not been gassed in Auschwitz or their daughter had not been gang-raped at Trnopolje? If they protest, what could be more satisfying than to turn to them and say that they are filthy swindlers exploiting the decency of their credulous audience the better to take its money?

The Left of the Seventies was generally against antisemitism – with the perhaps predictable exception of the terrorist wing of the German far left – and there was uproar in France when Faurisson published. Demonstrators roughed him up, critics brought court actions and the administrators of his University suspended him.

At moments such as these principled people must ask themselves a hard question. Voltaire never said, 'I may disagree with what you have to say, but I shall defend, to the death, your right to say it' – a biographer put the words in his mouth in 1906 – but it remains true. Freedom of speech includes the freedom to lie and defame, and if Noam Chomsky had merely signed a petition that defended Faurisson's freedom there would have been no complaint. What happened, however, was that the admired leftist, the scholar whose first political writings were against fascism, went way beyond a statement of elementary principle and gave comfort to neo-Nazi groups around the world.

The petition Chomsky signed was a work of real propaganda

that painted Faurisson as a seeker of truth who was being unjustly targeted for reputable research. He was 'a respected professor of twentieth century French literature and document criticism', it read, who 'has been conducting extensive research into the "Holocaust" question'.

The scare quotes around 'Holocaust' and the petition's assertion that the Jew-baiter was a historian who had made reputable 'findings' infuriated French leftists. They assumed Chomsky was a busy man who had added his name to the petition without realizing what he was signing. Not so. When pained fans contacted their idol and filled him in on the background, he refused to think again. Despite being given chapter and verse on Faurisson's belief that Europe's greatest crime hadn't happened and that the Jews had declared war on Hitler, Chomsky insisted that as far as he could determine he was 'a relatively apolitical liberal of some sort'.

When the criticism of his dalliances with neo-fascists grew more intense, the world's most acclaimed linguist descended into sophistry. Chomsky opined that not believing in the Holocaust was not in itself proof of antisemitism because 'if a person ignorant of modern history were told of the Holocaust and refused to believe that humans are capable of such monstrous acts, we would not conclude that he is an anti-semite. That suffices to establish the point at issue.'

The hell it does. What of those people who have studied modern history but still prefer poisonous fantasy to fact? A child who has never been to school and says the world is flat isn't a fool. But if she studies geography for years and doesn't change her mind she is.

The French historian Pierre Vidal-Naquet, who had exposed the abuses of French forces in Algeria and thought Chomsky an ally in the struggle against oppression, wrote in disgust:

The simple truth, Noam Chomsky, is that you were unable to abide by the ethical maxim you had imposed. You had the right to say: my worst enemy has the right to be free, on condition that he not ask for my death or that of my brothers. You did not have the right to say: my worst enemy is a comrade, or a 'relatively apolitical sort of liberal'. You did not have the right to take a falsifier of history and to recast him in the colours of truth.

I think I can understand why Chomsky had to do just that. If you believe that America is in need of 'denazification' and that a corrupted corporate media covers up this truth with lies, you are bound to have difficulties with real fascism. All around you, mainstream defenders of America say that she has fought the worst systems the human race has produced and point to the evidence in the media and elsewhere which proves the moral superiority of democracy. The danger when you reject the mainstream is that you defend anyone else who is against the mainstream and challenges its version of history.

Maybe I'm trying too hard on his behalf. Maybe Chomsky was just a shallow dogmatist who could never own up to a mistake. He certainly wasn't a fascist. Like his successors in the twenty-first century who made excuses for Islamism, Baathism and wife burning, he couldn't join the gang but couldn't denounce it either for fear of the psychic consequences the admission there were worse ideas in the world than Western democracy would bring.

So he dabbled on the fringes of the totalitarian right, and the fringes of the totalitarian left as well. When America pulled out of Indochina and Pol Pot's armies took over Cambodia, Chomsky and his collaborator Edward S. Herman poured scorn on the journalists who pointed out that there were even worse ideas than the disastrous American campaign in Southeast Asia.

It took most outside observers a few months to grasp that they were right because the reports of what the Paris-educated Marxists who led the Khmer Rouge were doing to Cambodia were incredible. The communists emptied the cities and killed anyone who excited the smallest paranoid suspicion. They murdered the literate and the numerate for being danger-ous intellectuals and town dwellers for being bourgeois reac-tionaries. They went on to wipe out Vietnamese, Chinese and Laotian ethnic minorities for being agents of foreign powers, Buddhists and Muslims for being religious subversives and the old and the frail for failing to work hard enough on the collective farms. Overall, they killed about one-fifth of the population.

Exposing the terror was a ferociously hard task as the com-munists sealed Cambodia's borders and made it a giant prison. François Ponchaud, a French priest, painstakingly assembled the first reliable account by interviewing thousands of refugees who had made it over the border. Ponchaud was hardly a conservative. He was a Khmer-speaking man of the Left who had initially welcomed Pol Pot's victory. What he heard forced him to change his mind. He came up with a book whose title has entered the language, *Cambodia: Year Zero*. If there was any doubt, his findings were supported by the reports of Jon Swain of the London *Times* and Sydney Schanberg of the *New York Times*, who saw the Khmer Rouge force the sick to crawl out of hospitals to the collectivized countryside. Once again, neither Swain nor Schanberg was a supporter of the American war effort.

Chomsky found the patient uncovering of an uncomfortable truth intolerable. While conceding that *Year Zero* was a 'serious' book, he and Edward Herman accused the priest of playing 'fast and loose with quotes and with numbers' and of having 'an anti-communist bias and message'. The *New York Review of Books*, which had given Ponchaud deserved praise, was guilty of 'extreme anti-Khmer Rouge distortions'. Its articles were a living example of how history was 'manufactured' to lull the masses into accepting capitalist propaganda as fact. By contrast, Chomsky and Herman hailed as brave dissidents two authors who reprinted the propaganda broadcasts of Pol Pot's radio station. Chomsky concluded that if there were crimes in Cambodia, they were a reaction to the US saturation bombing campaign. That Marxism had proved over the decades that it had a genocidal life of its own was an idea Chomsky couldn't contemplate.

It was too much to hope that such a man could allow the dead of the Balkans to rest in peace.

Most liberal-minded people couldn't bring themselves to oppose the wars against Milosevic, and many were strong supporters of the interventions in Bosnia and Kosovo. The job of endorsing the Major government's appeasement fell to a motley collection of splenetic Trots, ageing Stalinists, older Quakers, anti-capitalists who forgot about global justice in Bosnia's case, and Greens more interested in saving the whale than saving the Bosnians. Bringing up the rear was Harold Pinter, the future Nobel Laureate. He wept buckets for the 'Mountain People' of Kurdistan, and then joined the International Committee to Defend Slobodan Milosevic, the murderer of the 'Mountain People' of the Balkans.

The Tories' friends on the Left made a rickety bridge between the old and the new protest movements. On the one hand, they bellowed the last hurrah of the Marxists of the twentieth century. Milosevic said he was a socialist, and they took him at his word, and insisted that capitalists were using crimes manufactured by the media to justify the break-up of Yugoslavia because it was the last corner of Europe holding out against market economics after the fall of the Berlin Wall.

Their conspiracy theory didn't make the slightest sense. The published diaries of Milosevic lieutenants show that they, not the 'capitalist' West, planned the break-up of Yugoslavia. The idea that Serb nationalists were the last socialists in Europe fighting a desperate rearguard action against the forces of the 'hegemonic' market was dished by the fact that the Conservative administration of John Major and the equally right-wing Republican administration of George Bush senior refused to stop their ethnic cleansing. In any case, Karadzic's Serb Democratic Party in Bosnia identified with the monarchist and Nazi-collaborationist Chetnik movement of the Second World War rather than the Left. In its own way, so did Milosevic's 'socialist' Serbia, which was, in reality, a gangsters' paradise where pimps and profiteers flourished, the gap between rich and poor widened and free health care vanished.

The most telling comment on the true nature of the 'socialist' regime the anti-war movement of the Nineties was so anxious to defend came from Douglas Hurd. After leaving office, he accepted a large retainer from the NatWest Bank, and flew to meet Milosevic in Belgrade and negotiate the privatization of the Serb telecommunications network. I doubt if the theory and practice of workers' power topped the agenda when those two gentlemen got down to business. Those who pretended otherwise were lost in a late-socialist delusion.

On the other hand, much of what dominates left and liberal thought today was breaking out all over the anti-war movement of the Nineties. Marko Attila Hoare, a Cambridge

Balkan specialist, looked at its fantasies and apologias and noticed a new indifference on the Left. As well as talking about solidarity with our 'Serbian comrades' or praising the glorious socialists of Belgrade, the anti-war movement huffed and puffed about international law and UN approval. Once these would have been strange subjects for revolutionaries, but the defenders of Slobodan Milosevic were as stranded by the collapse of socialism as the post-modern theorists and the former friends of Kanan Makiya. Once again, there was the signature absence of any principled practical policy. They offered nothing to the Bosnians, Croats or, as Marko Attila Hoare noticed, the Serbs.

> More striking even than the defence or denial of crimes against humanity carried out by the Left revisionists is their sheer lack of any positive vision for the future or political *raison d'être* whatsoever. They should not be seen as 'pro-Serb', for the Serb people are unlikely to benefit from their actions. They are offering precisely nothing to the long-suffering people of Serbia in return for suffering sanctions and isolation. Rather, they appear to view 'resistance to Western imperialism' as something worthwhile for its own sake, no matter how much self-destruction it results in for Serbia and how much misery it inflicts.

Nor, as Chomsky proved, could they provide a guide to their own countries' foreign ministers. After their Cambodian triumph, he and Edward S. Herman teamed up again to condemn the hypocrisy of the Kosovo war of 1999. Turkey was guilty of 'massive atrocities' against the Kurds, they said. Indonesia had perpetrated 'aggression and massacre' of 'near-genocidal levels' in East Timor, while Israel had organized 'murderous and destructive' operations in Lebanon. Typically, words failed the linguist when he came to discussing the Serb nationalist crimes in Kosovo – they weren't 'massive atrocities' at 'near-genocidal' levels but a 'response', as he cutely put it, to attacks by the Muslim Kosovo Liberation Army. Like Pol Pot's alleged 'response' to the American bombing of Indochina, the massacres were, by implication, not the responsibility of the put-upon Serb nationalists. Yet for all his circumlocutions and double standards, what Chomsky said about the treatment of the Kurds, Lebanese and Timorese was true, and prompted the question: what should the West do instead?

Answer came there none, for in Chomsky's universe the West was at fault whatever it did. If it intervened in Bosnia and Kosovo, it was wrong. If it imposed sanctions against Saddam's Iraq, it was wrong. And if it colluded with Turkish, Israeli or Indonesian oppression, it was wrong again. A dazzled Attila Hoare said such freewheeling denunciation left foreign ministers with no options, as 'it is clear that ultimately the West cannot easily reject military intervention, sanctions, and appeasement all at the same time'.

The ignoble and inevitable terminus of the reasoning of Chomsky and his comrades was denial. It had to be. Without denial, they would have to admit that liberal democracies weren't solely motivated by the dictates of the corporations but had on occasion a reasonable desire to end conflicts. As with the Holocaust deniers, the anti-war revisionists went for the abiding memories. The Yugoslav equivalents of the gas chambers at Auschwitz were Srebrenica and the pictures of the wild-eyed starving men behind the barbed wire at Trnopolje. Both had to be denied if the project of blackening the belated interventions in the Balkans was to stand a chance of succeeding.

Its prime movers weren't Western leftists but their Serbian

allies. Bosnia was partitioned, as the Foreign Office wanted, and partition held out the prospect of a new conflict, as it always did. If Serb nationalists could deny the crimes of the previous war successfully, the crimes of the next would be easier to contemplate.

In 2004, Nerma Jelacic went up the mine roads to Omarska and found that a protective scab had covered the old wounds. She was a stranger in her own country. In 1991, when she was 15 years old, she had celebrated New Year's Eve with Muslim and Orthodox friends in her home town of Višegrad. As a bright teenager from a secular family, she watched the party-goers and assumed that religious differences were the least important thing about them and her. Three months later she woke up and learned a basic lesson of totalitarian politics: you are who your assassins say you are.

In the deep of a warm spring night, a light and a crackling sound awoke me. Through a blind, I saw dozens of houses belonging to my Muslim neighbours on fire, male inhabitants rounded up by men in uniforms. Some would come back beaten and bruised; others were never heard from again. Checkpoints sprang up across town, manned by a mix of drunken paramilitaries and regular army units. The war was not official yet – but in Višegrad it had started, with murders in surrounding villages and beatings of influential Muslims from the town.

Many among her family and friends were raped or murdered or both. Jelacic and her parents got out and into Britain as part of the Major government's token attempt at refugee relief. She learned English fast and well, and my employers at the *Guardian* and *Observer* took her on. I thought she would surely stay but she returned home because she had to know what happened next to the survivors.

She went to Omarska with Vulliamy. Bosnian children shyly thanked him for saving their parents' lives, but local Serb nationalists were in furious denial. 'There was no camp here,' security guards at the entrance to Omarska told them. 'It was all lies, Muslim lies, and forgery by the journalists.' A Bosnian Muslim woman told them no one had apologized or even admitted that crimes against humanity had taken place. 'They say they know nothing about the camps. There are 145 mass graves and hundreds of individual graves in this region, and we invite the local authorities to our commemorations, but they never come.'

Denial in the rich world began with the British Revolutionary Communist Party. It was once the most ultra of the ultra-left groups, which attracted wealthy but not very bright recruits who provided the funds to allow the party to operate in some style. What the RCP hated was reform that would prolong the 'capitalist' system and avert the glorious day when communism came. RCP activists would disrupt demonstrations to protect the National Health Service or against apartheid and cry that saving hospitals from closure and ending white rule in South Africa were distractions from the revolution. In the Nineties, they belatedly gave up on communism and accepted market economics. Nothing unusual in that, you might think, except that the party moved as a disciplined unit. The politburo instructed the rank and file to abandon Leninism, and as good Leninists, the rank and file obeyed and U-turned as one. The comrades regrouped first around the magazine *LM* (previously *Living Marxism*) and then a successful think tank called the Institute of Ideas. The British media loved the *LM* crowd because they were 'contrarians' who could be relied on to fill space and generate controversy by saying the opposite of what everyone else was saying – an affectation most people get over around puberty. If the majority of progressive opinion was against genetically modified foods, the RCP was for them. If the majority of progressive opinion was against the Rwandan and Balkan genocides, the RCP denied them. It hadn't really changed.

To deny the Bosnian camps the RCP reached for classic technique of the conspiracy theorist. Professor Werner Cohn defined it as the Method of the Critical Source. It is a 'favourite among cranks', he explained, and 'consists of seizing upon a phrase or sentence or sometimes a longer passage from no matter where, without regard to its provenance or reliability to "prove" a whole novel theory of history or the universe'.

The crank *LM* welcomed was one Thomas Deichmann, a German leftist and apologist for Serb irredentism who tried and failed to discredit the testimony of camp survivors when he helped the defence team for Dusko Tadic, one of the organizers of the Omarska and Trnopolje atrocities, during the war crimes trials at The Hague.

One night as he was sitting at home, he had a Chomskyan epiphany of his own. For the umpteenth time he was poring over the pictures that had convinced the public that Bosnia had seen real crimes against humanity. They stood like a lion in the path of all who wanted to enjoy denial. Deichmann's wife glanced at the familiar faces of Fikret Alic and his fellow prisoners and asked: 'Why was this wire fixed to poles on the side of the fence where they were standing? As any gardener knows, fences are, as a rule, fixed to the poles from outside, so that the area to be enclosed is fenced-in.'

That was it. That was enough to produce Deichmann's eureka moment. If Deichmann had wanted to test his wife's theory, he might have examined the evidence collected by the International Criminal Court, talked to refugees or tracked down Fikret Alic, who was living in exile. Alic no longer looked a handsome young Bosnian after camp goons had broken six of his ribs, his jaw and nose, kicked out all his teeth and left his body with around a hundred scars from stab and burn wounds, but he was available for interview. Deichmann saw no need to talk to survivors. He had his key to all the mythologies: an old wives' tale from his own wife about how gardeners fixed wire to fences. The truth flooded in on him and he realized how the cunning reporters had produced one of the most outrageous lies in the history of journalism with the aid of trick photography.

In a piece *LM* ran under the headline, 'The Picture that Fooled the World', he explained the significance of the fixing of the barbed wire on the posts. The prisoners weren't prisoners at all, but free men standing outside the camp's perimeter fence. The double-dealing journalists had gone into the camp and filmed them from the inside looking out, then pretended that their cameras were on the outside looking in. They had made black white and free men captives with camera angles so they could 'manufacture consent' for a war of free-market aggression. He double-checked with Serb guards who assured him that Trnopolje was a 'collection centre for refugees, many of whom went there seeking safety and could leave again if they wished'. A few of the reports of rapes and murders may not have been invented, he conceded, but the truth was that without the protection of selfless Serb soldiers there would have been many more.

Such was the critical source for *LM*. ITN sued and the jury awarded punitive damages for malicious libel. There is no disgrace about fighting a libel case in London and going down with all guns blazing. The High Court has on occasion ignored honestly collected evidence and awarded enormous damages to Robert Maxwell, Jeffrey Archer and many another brazen crook. However, in his study of the Trnopolje case Professor David Campbell of Durham University, noted that *LM* didn't fight. It couldn't because it had no honest evidence. Once the former Trotskyists were hauled out of the murk of conspiratorial politics and required to justify themselves in open court, Deichmann and Mick Hume, the editor of *LM*, accepted that what they said wasn't true. They agreed that inmates could not come and go as they pleased. When a brave Bosnian doctor who had risked his life to pass film to ITN and the *Guardian* took to the witness box, they and their lawyers sat as quiet as church mice and didn't bother to cross-examine him when he said that far from protecting 'refugees' camp guards murdered and raped their wretched captives.

'Lies have gone faster than a man can ride post,' wrote Dr Arbuthnot, and the new technology of the Internet made them fly faster still. Once the lie about the faked massacres in Bosnia was up and running, the public demonstration of the malice of *LM* had no effect whatsoever. Hate mail flew in at the reporters – one writer told Vulliamy he was a 'piece of shit' who was 'probably a nasty little Jew'. Cries of 'lies' echoed around the Net like screams in a madhouse as hundreds of Serb and leftist websites and magazines claimed the concentration camps had never existed and the Bosnians had murdered themselves.

Meanwhile, leftish publishers denounced the belief that Muslims needed rescuing as a 'humanitarian illusion' and the prosecution of war criminals as nothing more than 'victors' justice'. Among their offerings was *Fools' Crusade* by Diana Johnstone. It carried praise from Chomsky's collaborator Edward S. Herman and purported to show how 'massive deception and self-deception by the media and politicians' allowed the wars against Milosevic to reinforce the 'hegemony' of the United States. It feels superfluous to note that far from dismissing Thomas Deichmann as a loon who preferred his wife's views on the correct hanging of garden fences to the verifiable accounts of survivors, Johnstone accepted without comment his account of the taking of the camp pictures, and treated him as a reliable source whose work 'provided the background to this famous image'.

She then moved on to the second abiding memory – the dead of Srebrenica – and wondered whether they were really dead at all and not living somewhere else and laughing at the stupidity of the idiots who mourned them. Johnstone first put scare quotes around the 'Srebrenica massacre' and then spat it out. There had been no deliberate attempt at genocide, she said, and many of those among the alleged 8,000 Muslim dead 'were presumed to have made it safely into Muslim territory'. As she later explained, the duplicitous 'Muslim authorities never provided information about these men, preferring to let them be counted among the missing, that is, among the massacred'. She was prepared to condemn Serb nationalists for killing only 199 Muslims in Srebrenica. As for the remaining 7,800 or so, 'there is still no clear way to account for the fate of all the Muslim men reported missing in Srebrenica. Insofar as Muslims were actually executed following the fall of Srebrenica, such crimes bear all the signs of spontaneous acts of revenge rather than a project of "genocide".'

Bosnians may have been swapped in prisoner exchanges; maybe they made it to other Yugoslav towns; maybe they moved abroad... who knew?

Lots of people, actually. The court in The Hague had thousands of pages of witness statements, and in 2003 the Bosnian

Serb leadership admitted responsibility and gave a hideous picture of the mechanics of the massacre. Colonel Dragan Obrenovic, the deputy commander of the Srebrenica pogrom, said, 'I'm guilty for what I did and did not do. Thousands of innocent people were killed, only the graves remain.'

His confession had as much effect as the capitulation of *LM*. Evidence had no place in the developing nihilist mentality. When the staff and readers of *Ordfront*, a left-wing Swedish magazine, revolted after its editor gave Johnstone a platform, the heroes of the new left rallied to Johnstone. Tariq Ali – whom we last saw hastily dropping the opponents of Saddam Hussein – Arundhati Roy, the future Nobel Laureate Harold Pinter and – inevitably – Noam Chomsky defended her in an open letter to the Swedish magazine. As with the Faurisson and the Holocaust deniers, Chomsky couldn't confine himself to upholding Johnstone's freedom to write and speak, which no court or police officer was denying her. He and his friends built up her credentials and said they regarded Johnstone's *Fools' Crusade* as 'an outstanding work, dissenting from the mainstream view but doing so by an appeal to fact and reason, in a great tradition'.

When the gang surrounded the Bosnians, the boy was back on the edge again, not denying genocide but darting in with praise for the 'outstanding' Johnstone and then stepping back. The conspiracy theory was kept going, not with outright denial of massacres but with morsels of doubt to whet the appetites of those who would move on to stronger meat.

Srebrenica wasn't the end of it. Chomsky joined the apologists for the Serbs who were saying that the pictures of the Bosnian camp inmates were an outrageous forgery. He told an interviewer from Serb television that, 'there was one famous incident which has completely reshaped Western opinion, and that was the photograph of the thin man behind the barbwire'.

'A fraudulent photograph, as it turned out,' the Serb interrupted.

'You remember!' the pleased Chomsky replied. 'The thin man behind the barbwire, so that was Auschwitz and we can't have Auschwitz again.'

All Holocaust deniers are antisemites, and some might say that those on the far-left who discounted the serb camps were motivated by an Islamophobic hatred of Bosnian Muslims. This view fails to get to what ailed the radical left at the turn of the millennium. They lacked the steadiness of purpose to be consistent, and even racism requires consistency. Their phobia was a fear of America and the West and modernity. If the West had ended up being for the Serbs and against the Bosnians, they would have been for the Bosnians and against the Serbs. Theirs was a rootless affliction.

In November 2005 the readers of *Prospect*, Britain's most intellectually rigorous current affairs magazine, voted Noam Chomsky 'The World's Top Public Intellectual' by a large margin.

A few days later, Ian Mayes, the Readers' Editor of Ed Vulliamy and Nerma Jelacic's own paper, the *Guardian*, responded to complaints from Chomsky and Johnstone about an admittedly poorly subbed piece on leftist denial of crimes against humanity with an apology. Mayes maintained that neither of them had ever denied the Srebrenica massacre. He agreed that Chomsky's support for Johnstone 'related entirely to her right to freedom of speech'. Journalists, survivors of the camps, UN workers in the Balkans and Britain's foremost academic authorities in the former Yugoslavia were appalled and sent Mayes copies of what Chomsky and Johnstone had written. The *Guardian* was one of the world's leading liberal newspapers and Mayes was its ombudsman charged with upholding the highest standards of liberal journalism. He appeared a judicious and well-educated man, whose dry wit and appealing line in self-deprecation seemed to continue the best traditions of middle-class English liberalism.

'None of the material sent to me has convinced me,' he said. He slapped down the survivors and their allies – then the paper's external ombudsman reviewed the case and slapped them down again.

So far, I've been talking as if there were neat dividing lines between mainstream liberals and the far left. But by the early twenty-first century with the Cold War over and the world in flux, it was foolish to think that there were little boxes in which you could plonk different types. People shifted between positions, pushed by fashion and the pressure of events. When what it meant to be on the Left was beset with confusion and disappointment, what immunity genteel liberals had from the fevers of the age collapsed.

CHAPTER SEVEN

What Do We Do Now?

Every time I've run into one of the Bush kids it's been a defeating, debilitating experience. For some reason they always seem to get the upper hand. When I came across George W. in Iowa and tried to ask him a question for my TV show, he shouted at me to 'go find real work.' The entire crowd in the place roared with laughter. I didn't know what to say – he was right, this isn't real work! I had no comeback.

Michael Moore, 2002

IN HIS 1995 NOVEL, *The Information*, Martin Amis sends Richard, a writer who can't find a publisher, to the London mansion of Gwyn Barry, a friend and rival of long standing. Richard is in an envious rage because Gwyn has become a rich man and literary celebrity by producing fey parables that sell by the hundreds of thousands. To make matters worse, Richard walks into the study to find a toadying journalist seeking Gwyn's opinions on the great issues of the day.

Are you a Labour supporter, the interviewer asks Gwyn.

'Obviously.'
'Of course.'
'Of course.'

Of course, thought Richard, yeah of course. Gwyn was Labour. It was obvious. Obvious not from the ripply cornices twenty feet above their heads, not from the brass lamps or the military plumpness of the leather-topped desk. Obvious because Gwyn was what he was, a writer, in England, at the end of the 20th century. There was nothing else for such a person to be. Richard was Labour, equally obviously. It often seemed to him, moving in the circles he moved in and reading what he read, that everyone in the land was Labour, except the Government... All writers, all book people were Labour, which was one of the reasons why they got on so well.

From Malvolio to Gwyn Barry via Mrs Jellyby, the concerned middle classes have been the target of satirists for 400 years, and repeatedly the best have concentrated on the stifling conformity of respectable liberal opinion. Invariably, they have reached for bovine metaphors, for there is a touch of the herd in the unselfconscious manner in which artists, journalists, publishers, writers and academics set off in one direction, mooing as one, and then agree as if by telepathy to wheel round and moo off in another. In 1995, after sixteen years of Tory rule, everyone who was anyone in the liberal intelligentsia was all for Labour. By the general election of 2005, they were all against. As ever, there was little argument about how they had made such an abysmal mistake a decade earlier because public disputation would reveal past faulty thinking and puncture the air of moral and intellectual certainty which is the middle-class left's greatest asset. The herd doesn't do self-criticism but charges this way and that, forward then back as if following a drunken star.

In 1963, Michael Frayn described

The radical middle-classes, the do-gooders; the readers of the *News Chronicle*, the *Guardian*, and the *Observer*; the signers of petitions; the backbone of the BBC. In short, the Herbivores, or gentle ruminants, who look out from the lush pastures which are their natural station in life with eyes full of sorrow for less fortunate creatures, guiltily conscious of their advantages, though not usually ceasing to eat the grass.

Harold Rosenberg, Frayn's American contemporary, put the same thought more succinctly in his gorgeous description of the New York intelligentsia as 'the herd of independent minds'.

Occasionally, and entirely without irony, their targets would prove how right Frayn and Rosenberg had been by bragging about the efficacy of conformist pressures. In 2005, Naomi Wolf, a glamorous feminist of the upper middle class, assured her American readers that Washington society would tame the conservative judges George W. Bush was appointing to the US Supreme Court.

Justices . . . are people who live in and cannot help but respond to the bigger cultural shifts of their time. I believe in the power of this cultural shift around us to move even the judiciary: Institutions are made up of human beings, and no one likes being looked at with contempt at dinner parties.

It is indeed a chilling deterrent, and the question raised by the cruel glances thrown across dinner tables from Bloomsbury to Georgetown was whether they were symptoms of strength or weakness. Regimented opinions can reflect the confidence of a ruling ideology that is certain its ideas are winning, or the laager mentality of an enfeebled creed which fears its opponents are advancing on every front.

The unanimity of Britain's middle-class liberals and their

failure to admit mistakes certainly helped them win propaganda wars. The English Tory historian Geoffrey Wheatcroft tracked how they lost every political battle in the Eighties but still created the impression that they were good while their opponents were wicked. Go back through the great novels of the time and you find that Margaret Thatcher invariably pops up as a malign figure. Even *The Satanic Verses* (1988), remembered for the incitement to murder it produced from the Ayatollah Khomeini, proves on rereading to be just as hard on the Tories as the Islamists. Margaret Thatcher is 'Mrs Torture'. When Saladin Chamcha, the hero, lands in Britain, he is forced to crawl in his own excrement by her immigration officers, who use him as 'guinea pig and as safety valve' when they beat him black and blue. Anti-Thatcherism powered the novels of Jonathan Coe and Ian McEwan; the plays and television dramas of Alan Bleasdale, Sir David Hare, Caryl Churchill and John Mortimer; and the art house films of Mike Leigh and Derek Jarman. Given the malign incompetence that produced mass unemployment in two recessions, what they said about the Thatcherites was not all wrong, but it was always the same, and the artistic agreement was so complete it is hard now to imagine a liberal audience accepting any other treatment of the period. Alan Hollinghurst's 2004 novel, *The Line of Beauty*, proved the point. It won the Booker Prize and was adapted by the BBC after the critics praised Hollinghurst for his exquisite irony. His writing was elegant in all respects but one: his villain, a caddish and treacherous member of Margaret Thatcher's government, was more like a character from pantomime than serious literature.

Wheatcroft had enormous fun dissecting the vanities of the intellectuals of the time. He noted their raging snobbery: Thatcherism was the 'anarchism of the lower middle classes', sniffed the communist historian, Eric Hobsbawm; an 'odious suburban gentility', according to the polymath Jonathan Miller. He reminded us of the naked self-interest of the artists: 'I'm impelled to vote Labour since it's the only party committed to doubling the arts budget,' opined Sir Michael Tippett. But the poor man bathetically concluded that one reason that Britain's Tories lost power was 'those chatterers won the argument'. Millions of people, not all of them selfish members of the middle classes, who voted for Margaret Thatcher in the Eighties ended up by agreeing that they had been supporting an ugly right-wing doctrine. Conservatives couldn't bring themselves to admit that there was truth in the caricature and wiped from their minds the dole queues and the collapse of manufacturing industry, but they were right to suggest that the ideological uniformity of plays, films and novels gradually wore people down, and not only in the Eighties.

Tony Blair was never dafter than when he defined the twentieth century as 'a Conservative century'. Conservative governments may have been in power for most of the time, but liberal ideas triumphed. However far out on the fringe they were to begin with, however viciously the right-wing press attacked them, they always seemed to come through.

A useful thought experiment is to imagine going back 100 years to the London or New York of the early twentieth century and meeting the equivalent of today's intelligentsia. They would have obsessions that you would find baffling – phrenology, teetotalism, spiritualism – but these were no quainter than today's belief in psychotherapy will one day appear. They would admire authors who are close to unread – H. G. Wells, George Bernard Shaw – but oblivion is the fate of 99.9 per cent of writers. Despite their eccentricities, they would still be recognizable types and you would find their professed desires to end oppression and free the human spirit familiar.

If they settled back in their Arts & Crafts chairs and asked you to describe the future, you might say much that would please them.

'Well, all adults will have the vote,' you might begin. 'There will be no more talk of working men needing a stake in the country or of women being too fluffy to be trusted with the franchise, not only here in the rich world, but in dozens of countries. With the exception of China, the empires that oppress the greater part of humanity will be gone. Britain, Russia, France, Belgium, Austria-Hungary, Spain, Portugal, Germany and the Ottomans will lose almost all their foreign possessions. India will be free. Africa will not have one white colony. The pernicious belief in white racial superiority will decline with imperialism. It will take a long time to die, for these are flattering and powerful ideas, but respectable politicians of the Right as well as the Left will abandon stark appeals to racism.

'Monarchs, sultans, tsars and kaisers will be overthrown along with their empires. Germany, Russia, Austria and Turkey will become democratic republics as will the majority of the nations of the world. Where monarchies survive in the West, they will live on as ornaments people stuff into constitutional niches when they can't think of what else to put there. Aristocratic power will expire with the monarchies. The Prussian Junker general and the noble English viceroy will be as remote to us as the age before steam is to you. Christianity will collapse so precipitously that people will talk of a post-Christian Europe. They will be exaggerating, but only by a little. Even the Pope will not be able to compel Western Catholics to follow his teaching on birth control. When the monarchs, aristocrats and priests go, so will deference. The absence of reverence would amaze you, ladies and gentlemen, if you could live long enough to see it. Only the old will admit to respecting titles, and knowledge will be as suspect as noble birth. Scientists will be presumed guilty of trying to murder the public. Teachers will be obliged to make their pupils feel good about themselves rather than force them to memorize lessons. Politicians will have to abase themselves before jeering electorates, judges will take instruction from the victims of crime on what punishments they should deliver and generals will fear risking their troops in battle.

'Everywhere the old rules will break down. Iconoclasts and relativists will attack traditional forms of logic, science, grammar, art, music, architecture, poetry, dress, dance, courting, manners and speech. People who uphold the old standards of courtesy and correctness in the written or spoken word will be mistrusted. Authenticity will be the great god as the ancient art of rhetoric vanishes. The more sentimental and egocentric a writer or speaker is, the better he or she will be received. (And, by the way, everyone will say "he or she" so as not to appear sexist.) There will be no censorship worthy of the name. Your great-grandchildren will be free to read incendiary political pamphlets and the most explicit pornography. Bills of rights will protect them from harassment by the authorities. Armies of lawyers will be on hand to sue those who cause them harm.

'The state will give people you have barely thought about legal equality. By the beginning of the twenty-first century, it will be politically impossible for the leader of the British Conservative Party to condemn equal rights for homosexuals and whole cities will have been adapted to suit the needs of the handicapped.

'Yet society will not fall apart because of these new demands.

Ordinary people will live longer and healthier lives than Roman emperors. About 40 per cent of Britain's national wealth will be spent on welfare. There will be health care free at the point of delivery from cradle to grave, and insurance against unemployment, sickness and old age. Children will be educated until 16 and almost half will go on to universities of varying degrees of academic distinction. European governments will provide more and the United States government will provide less, but in all advanced countries the fear of hunger you can see around you will vanish, and people will go on for ever.

'British babies born in your time can expect to live on average fifty years if they are boys and fifty-seven years if they are girls. Boy babies born in the mid-twentieth century will live for an average of seventy-seven years and girls for eighty-two. By my time, people will be talking of millions reaching 100. Today fourteen out of 100 babies do not make it to their first birthday. By 2001 only one in 100 will die. Smallpox, cholera, polio, measles – diseases which I can see still spread fear – will vanish from the rich world. Machines will clean our clothes, dishes and carpets, freeing women from the drudgery of menial housework. New forms of transport will allow tens of millions to travel around the world in hours. At a push of a few keys, new forms of technology will solve hellishly difficult calculations or allow access to more information than the British Library stores.

'I notice from the pamphlets on your table that you regard marriage as a form of oppression and want adults to express their sexual natures freely. Don't worry, in the next century they will do little else. They will rut like rabbits and it will be the height of bad manners to criticize them. Politicians will make divorce painless from the legal point of view. There will be 27,224 divorces in Britain in 1961 and 167,116 in 2004. There would have been many more if society had forced the young to marry to find sex and children. But marriage will become like a club. Joining it will be a voluntary decision based on personal preference rather than social and legal coercion. If you choose to resign, no one will think the worse of you, with the possible exception of your partner and children. The stigma attached to bastards will disappear sometime around the mid-Seventies. The British Office for National Statistics will report that 42 per cent of births were outside marriage in 2005. We're not there yet, but inevitably there will soon be more "illegitimate" than "legitimate" children, but few will care. True legitimacy will reside with liberalism and liberal ideas. You and your kind will achieve all this by insisting that you know what is right for others and never allowing your self-confidence to crack.'

'We love the sound of the future,' your audience cries. 'It has everything we have always wanted.'

'So it has,' you reply, 'which is why you will hate it.'

If the radical leftists were deformed by defeat, middle-class liberals were depressed by success. They had done the best they could for the working class, really they had, but by the time Margaret Thatcher took power they were having to come to terms with the thought that the masses had let them down badly.

If truth be told, the two had not always got on. Largely thanks to the work of Professor John Carey, we know that intellectuals of the Left were as likely as intellectuals of the Right to detest the teeming masses in the new cities. Walter Bagehot displayed the classic nineteenth-century conservative's prejudices in his *English Constitution* of 1867. Whatever constitution England should have, it should not allow the working class to vote because:

a life of labour, an incomplete education, a monotonous occupation, a career in which the hands are used much and judgement used little cannot create as much flexible thought, as much applicable intelligence as a life of leisure, a long culture, varied experience, and existence by which the judgement is incessantly exercised, and by which it may be incessantly improved.

Like so many wealthy men from his time, Bagehot was a crusty reactionary, but he didn't actually want to kill the poor. You couldn't say the same about the Fabian socialist intellectuals who provided so many of the ideas behind the twentieth-century welfare state. George Bernard Shaw and H. G. Wells were as keen as the European fascists were on eugenics and debated whether birth control, sterilization or outright murder should be used to stop the crude clerks and dirty proles overwhelming civilized society with their hordes of children. 'Extermination must be put on a scientific basis if it is ever to be carried out humanely,' wrote Shaw. 'If we desire a certain type of civilisation and culture, we must exterminate the sort of people who do not fit in.' Wells deplored the 'vicious, helpless and pauper masses' and warned that to 'give them equality is to sink to their level, to protect and cherish them is to be swamped in their fecundity'.

The sheer capriciousness of the loathing of many of the liberal-left intellectuals is as striking as its intensity and criminal ambition. The common people could never win. Here is Virginia Woolf, socialist, pacifist and screaming snob, writing to her sister Vanessa Bell about the Armistice Night celebrations of 1918.

Everyone seemed half drunk – beer bottles were passed round – every wounded soldier was kissed by women; nobody had any

notion where to go or what to do; it poured steadily; crowds
drifted up and down the pavements waving flags and jumping
into omnibuses, but in such a disorganised half hearted sordid
state that I felt more and more melancholy and hopeless of the
human race.

That seems clear. The masses are drunken and licentious
beasts. The sight of their heaving bodies reduces Woolf to
misanthropic despair. But here she is a few years later reporting
on the reception she and her fellow Bloomsbury Bohemians
received when they took a holiday in Wales. Woolf was shocked
that the locals were shocked by the sight of a lady aesthete
smoking a pipe.

What rather appals me . . . is the terrible conventionality of the
workers. That's why – if you want explanations – I don't think
they will be poets or novelists for another hundred years or so.
If they can't face the fact that Lillian smokes a pipe and reads
detective novels, and can't be told that they weigh on average
12 stone – which is largely because they scrub so hard and have
so many children – how can you say that they can face 'reality'
. . . What depresses me is that the workers seem to have taken on
all the middle class respectabilities which we – at any rate if we
are any good at writing or painting – have thrown off.

The workers were damned if they were drunk and damned if
they were sober. If they let rip on Armistice Night, they were
'sordid': if they upheld traditional standards, they displayed
their 'terrible conventionality'.

Woolf was the starkest representative of a liberal elite whose
dislike of the masses conservatives were to exploit mercilessly
for the rest of the century – most notably in George W. Bush's

America. She was born into the Victorian literary aristocracy and much of her political writing consisted of laments that women of the upper class didn't enjoy the same privileges as men of the upper class. Feminist critics of the Seventies greeted her as a sister for the good reason that she was one of the first of English literature's modern women. They did not notice that women (and men) from the lower orders were beneath her contempt. Woolf is usually lumped in with the Fabians because she wrote pamphlets for them, but for all the ravings of Shaw and Wells, other leading Fabians judged work on its merits and published struggling thinkers from modest backgrounds with something to say. Woolf is more important as a representative of the Bloomsbury Group, the fantastically self-regarding clique of artists and intellectuals in pre-war London. Like upper-middle-class cliques in today's Anglo-American liberal-left in publishing, journalism and the arts, the Bloomsbury Group sounded very radical at the same time as it repelled potential working- and middle-class recruits to leftish causes with its insuperable barriers of class and caste. These were – and still are – clubs which outsiders can never join, whatever their talents, and although conservative critics damn Woolf as the intellectual forerunner of today's selfish touchy feely culture, they would be more honest if they thanked her and her kind for doing so much to divide the Left on class lines.

Looking back in 2005 at early twentieth-century intellectuals of Left and Right, Ferdinand Mount noted that charitable historians excused them by saying that although they seemed to anticipate Adolf Hitler, they weren't proto-Nazis because they didn't go on about exterminating Jews. 'This seems to me poor comfort,' he replied. 'The extraordinary thing remains that so many of the finest talents of their generation should have found the mere existence of their fellow countrymen loathsome to the point of being intolerable.'

Fabian ideas helped create the modern welfare state, but they weren't the sole driving force. Ordinary people rarely get help without a fight and across the rich world, the trade unions and the usually middle-class leaders of social democratic parties fought and won the pre-eminent gains of the twentieth century. They had the best of motives. Far from despising the working class, they believed it was the real source of wealth and that the rich were parasites. They wanted decent health care, education and provision against old age and infirmity as fair reward for their toil. For them, protections against poverty and ill health were moral goods in themselves. But it is worth recalling the almost genocidal class hatreds of many leading liberal-left intellectuals, because they show that the motives of a part of the intelligentsia were anything but honourable. They did not want the welfare state to reward their fellow citizens for what they and their ancestors had suffered. They wanted the welfare state to transform them from brutes into men or women whose company Virginia Woolf could tolerate.

It is beyond the scope of this book to examine the changes in Western societies since the early Fabians. What matters more to contemporary attitudes towards totalitarianism and democracy is the middle-class liberal-left's unwarranted disillusionment with the working class. The conventional left-wing argument for dissatisfaction with modern democracy in the twenty-first century was that the parties were all the same and the corporations ran the world. Less flattering to liberal-leftish sensibilities was the thought that if a part of the prejudices of Shaw, Wells and Woolf survived into the modern age, then the liberal middle class was unlikely to be enthusiastic about tackling tyrannical regimes and movements. Democracy requires a minimum of respect for what used to be called the common man. If you don't like him at home, you won't like him abroad or care one way or another about his rights.

Fortunately, you don't hear acclaimed writers dreaming about the mass slaughter of the unwashed today. But it is undeniable that guilt, resentment and indifference colour the attitudes to the working class of the worst leftish intellectuals and professionals in the early twenty-first century as deeply as fear and disgust coloured them in the early twentieth. The guilt comes from the nagging feeling that not all the bourgeois reformers' efforts to improve the lot of the masses had gone as planned. The resentment comes from the failure of the masses to pass muster in Bohemia as anything other than freaks or objects of condescension. The indifference comes from the fact that the working class is no longer the 'class of the future' – the inevitable rulers of the coming society – as they had appeared to be 100 years before.

The one item missing from my list of liberal dreams realized in the twentieth century is some kind of social ownership or control. The mainstream liberal-left never wanted revolutionary socialism, but it believed in public intervention and got it in the years after the Second World War. Status and power in the mid-twentieth century went to men and women in the public sector who were the organizers of society. In the name of acting in the interests of the working class, academics and civil servants designed vast programmes of social relief and planners ordered the destruction of Victorian cities. The elite of the time held the public service ethos to be far superior to the grubby struggle for profit, and so did many others. In 1944 when Friedrich Hayek published what was to be the bible of the free-market right of the Seventies, *The Road to Serfdom*, hardly anyone took him seriously. The Wall Street Crash of 1929 and the Great Depression of the Thirties had made capitalism obsolescent. Everyone, including conservatives, believed central planners should fight the Second World War. George Orwell sympathized with Hayek's fears that centralized regulation would strangle liberty but thought his 'able defence of capitalism' was a waste of time. 'Faced with the choice between serfdom and economic insecurity the masses everywhere would probably choose outright serfdom, at least if it were called by some other name,' he wrote in 1944. Looking back to the America of the early Sixties, two sharp English writers noted that George W. Bush's grandfather was a Republican who would never have described himself a conservative. Meanwhile:

> the Kennedy administration wore its civilised European values on its sleeve (literally so in the case of the haute-coutured first lady). The president liked to point out that he had spent a year at the London School of Economics as a student of a prominent Marxist, Harold Laski. 'These without doubt are the years of the liberal,' John Kenneth Galbraith wrote, somewhat smugly, in 1964. 'Almost everyone now so describes himself.'

Right the way through to the Seventies, the greatest prestige attached to 'experts' in public service. By 2000, entrepreneurs had taken their place.

The British welfare state survived Margaret Thatcher surprisingly well – public spending as a proportion of national wealth actually rose while she was in power in the Eighties. But British culture changed beyond recognition. From then on extraordinary salaries went to executives and bankers as inequality shot up. Social status came with the money as governments abandoned the ideas of professors at the London School of Economics and turned to successful corporations to find the magic formulas to make the state bureaucracies work.

The public sector experts from the liberal middle class had to live with the bitter knowledge that the very people they had tried so selflessly to help were in part responsible for the crumpling of their social status and their relative economic decline. Margaret Thatcher and Ronald Reagan won repeatedly because large numbers of voters from the skilled working class supported them. They were never forgiven for that because from their different points of view Fabians, liberals and Marxists had hoped the working class would take power under their leadership. When it didn't, they despised the working class for its weakness and treachery and condemned its members for their greed and obsession with celebrity.

In liberal-left culture, the contempt was manifested by the replacement of social democracy with identity politics. For good reasons, admirable people championed the causes of women, ethnic minorities and gays. As they did so, the Left became more middle class and more concerned with cultural struggles than economics. The switch in emphasis meant that the white working class was no longer the main object of middle-class reformers' concern. In the twentieth century, the workers had been the exploited producers of wealth whose emancipation would herald a glorious future. By the twenty-first, its male members were sexist, racist homophobes; cultural conservatives suspected of harbouring unsavoury patriotic feelings. They went from being the salt of the earth to the scum of the earth in three generations, and as Thatcher and Reagan had shown, when the liberals despise the working class the opportunities for backlash politics are boundless.

American liberal confidence was blown apart by the racist backlash against equal rights for blacks and the more understandable backlash against the disintegration of families. Along with both came a hatred of the alleged 'dependency culture' of the welfare state that became the guiding ideology of the revived American right.

In Britain, the backlash created the phenomenon of the *Daily Mail*, a newspaper like no other in Europe. It found huge commercial success by operating more like a political party than a conventional purveyor of information and entertainment. Its conformism was beyond anything on the Left Martin Amis mocked. Almost every word in the paper followed the conservative line, and you wouldn't have been surprised to read in the horoscope that 'A full moon in July will mean that Geminis will be mugged by the feral children of a heroin-addled single mother.'

A *Daily Mail* writer put its argument like this. Until the Sixties, the British were famous for their placidity and good manners. The police didn't carry guns because the British policed themselves. We were tastefully rather than flashily dressed and preferred politeness to cleverness. A working-class man could be respectable even if less well off than another worker who was 'rough' and take pride in his 'honesty, industriousness, sobriety and punctuality'. The middle classes used different names for the same virtues. They aspired to be gentlemen or ladies who were 'honest, gracious and considerate to others'.

And now look at us. The work ethic has gone, family values have gone, courtesy has gone and common decency has gone. Crime, child abuse and yobbery have grown like Topsy. The culture is awash with obscenity and the sexual exploitation of women. Universal state education has had the remarkable effect of making today's pupils stupider than their predecessors. The National Health Service cannot treat the sick however much money the taxpayer throws at it. State benefits discourage people from looking after themselves and others. State schools and hospitals destroy the old mutual and charitable ideals which gave the working and middle classes control over institutions. The worst of it is the ludicrous liberal pretence that the traditional family doesn't matter. Divorce and step-parenthood expose girls and boys to rape, while single mothers can't instil discipline in the young. The unhappy children who stagger away from the state-sponsored emotional wreckage are 'responsible for a substantial amount of the dramatically increased level of crime in Britain'.

There were 1,001 objection to *Daily Mail* conservatism – the United States had a weak welfare state but a higher level of crime than Britain to name one – and liberals could always mutter 'they're Tories so they would say that, wouldn't they'. Conservative historians liked telling the story of the early Fabian support for eugenics because they could use it to question by association the motives of hundreds of thousands of decent middle-class and working-class reformers who didn't want to sterilize the poor. American Republicans and British Tories were also very good at condemning the selfish individualism of fathers who ran off and abandoned their children, but couldn't condemn the selfish individualism of an economic system that placed the ability to make money by legal or quasi-legal means above all other virtues.

These were excellent arguments, but, alas, just because conservatives would say what they said didn't make what they said wholly wrong and wholly without appeal to traditional left-wing constituencies.

In 2006, impeccable social democrats from the heart of the Labour tradition looked at the lives of the poor in the East End of London. If you could have asked the twentieth-century

British left to find one mission that defined its purpose, then helping the East End would have been it. The misery of the London slums was a rebuke to the bright lights of the City, Westminster and Mayfair that winked mockingly higher up the Thames. Modern trade unionism was born in its strikes of the 1880s, and the Labour leaders Clement Attlee and George Lansbury represented it in Parliament. East Enders had endured horrific bombing in the war against fascism, and the welfare state of the 1945 Labour government was to be their reward. In 1957, Michael Young, the author of the 1945 Labour manifesto, produced *Family and Kinship in East London* along with his colleague Peter Willmott. Both were inspired by the optimism of the times. East Enders had survived the Blitz because although they were poor and under attack from the Luftwaffe they had a hidden strength: family networks dominated by matriarchs who provided the support and moral and emotional steadfastness that helped them survive adversity. Now was the time for their prize. The welfare state was going to allow them to join the rest of Britain as full and equal citizens.

Half a century on and Young's project was updated by Geoff Dench and Kate Gavron. They retraced his steps but found only bitterness among those old enough to remember the days of hope. Conservatives wouldn't have the courage to acknowledge many of the reasons for their disillusion. Margaret Thatcher had broken the power of the trade unions, the bedrock organizations for the defence of workers' interests. What jobs were on offer weren't in unionized workplaces where East Enders could negotiate their terms and conditions, but included minimum-wage skivvy jobs in the giant towers of Canary Wharf cleaning up after the dealers in its banks and pundits in the offices of the *Independent*, *Telegraph* and *Mirror*. Picking up the stale sandwiches of bankers and hacks was better than being bombed by the Germans, but East Enders couldn't cope as they once had because the families which sustained them had evaporated. Fabian socialism with its founding suspicion of the ability of ordinary people to mind their own business had replaced matriarchs with middle-class professionals working for a state monopoly. 'Mum has lost ground steadily and comprehensively,' said Young's successors:

> An army of social workers now organises her children's and grandchildren's lives, often around principles and child-rearing practices with which she profoundly disagrees... The welfare state which was designed to help her has in the event taken her children and her role away from her.

The law of unintended consequences meant that the system assured the perpetuation of poverty. If you are a truly caring professional, you want to help those most in need. Top of the list were single mothers raising children without support. But giving them priority on council flat waiting lists provided a perverse incentive for single motherhood and its concomitant poverty. 'There are so many one-parent families around here nowadays,' said one East End woman:

> They are encouraged by social services. They claim and just get new equipment, several times over. They soon learn to play the system. There is no justice any more when you've always paid your way. Youngsters leave home and then claim on the state, they have babies to get a house. Older people are just not like that. East Enders are hard-working and proud. These people nowadays have no pride. The Government has taken away their self-respect.

The welfare state had a similar perverse effect on race relations. East Enders and the authors agreed that the sight of Bengali and Somali immigrants being given priority on council house waiting lists because they had more children, and therefore were in greater need, fuelled prejudice among those who had obeyed the rules and waited in line. The liberal professionals of the welfare state were aggravating the poverty and racism they said they opposed.

When the poor on whose behalf the Labour movement formed unions and a political party talked like this, and the intellectual heirs of the author of the 1945 Labour manifesto agreed with them, you knew that liberal-left certainties were vanishing.

Politicians take what ideas are in the air, and for the liberal-left middle class those ideas were increasingly conservative. Tony Blair and Gordon Brown were far more prepared to redistribute wealth and pump money into the public services than their critics from the Left were prepared to acknowledge. But Blair and Bill Clinton were as keen as Ronald Reagan and George W. Bush on breaking the state monopolies by getting private companies and charities to spend it. Similarly, New Labour and the Clinton Democrats declared themselves as tough on crime as their conservative opponents and as willing to debase themselves with hard-man posturing and backlash denunciations of do-gooding liberals. The American Christian right preached self-reliance, but the most fervent minister in Kansas would find it tough to match Gordon Brown's belief in the Protestant work ethic.

If the twentieth century in Britain was a leftish century with nominally conservative governments in charge, then standard liberal intellectuals at the millennium could begin to get the uncomfortable feeling that history was moving against them and the twenty-first would be a conservative century with nominally leftish governments in power. Many of their successes were guaranteed: women had been emancipated, the empires had gone and much else had been achieved. But the status of middle-class liberals was falling, and their decline in income, respect and influence could in large part be blamed on common men and women who didn't always vote as they should in elections, who didn't revolt as expected against the obscene inequalities of wealth and who took the welfare benefits that had been given with good intentions and failed to use them to lead admirable lives.

Such thoughts did not make the liberals disposed to like those who refused to stick to the script.

After the second Iraq war, the liberal middle classes hurled themselves at Tony Blair like a pack charging towards its prey. They seemed to think that the fury of their righteous outrage could dislodge him from power. He had lied, he had tricked them, he had exposed them to suicide bombers, he had fought an 'illegal war', he was the 'poodle' of the 'most right-wing US president ever'.

He had to go.

The Herbivores in the liberal media, the Liberal Democrats and rebellious Labour MPs kept saying they were speaking for progressive Britain, and only startled opinion pollsters noticed that they were doing no such thing. The leaders of the middle-class left had lost the ability to connect with working-class Labour voters and persuade them to support the causes that meant the most to them. One pollster wrote: 'Perhaps surprisingly', given the Conservative Party's leaders had supported the war in Iraq, 'Conservative voters are considerably less inclined to back the Blair Government's line on terrorism and the US relationship than are Labour supporters.' Perhaps he shouldn't have been surprised that working-class Labour voters were sticking with the Labour leadership. An international survey of anti-Americanism found the greatest support for the United States in Britain, and in many other developed countries, came from the working class and the upwardly mobile – people who associated the United States with economic progress and freedom from the prejudices of traditional societies, including the prejudices of the European left.

Shaken Labour MPs would return from Westminster to working-class constituencies, their ears filled with denunciations of the Prime Minister and predictions he would be gone within days. Their agents would tell them to calm down and remember their constituents were simple folk who lacked the education to know why it was 'illegal' to topple a fascist regime that was guilty of genocide. Don't worry, the agents told the MPs, your people take no notice of middle-class leftists.

Iraq blighted Blair's reputation, but it didn't destroy his administration. For all the liberal fury directed at him, he still won the 2005 general election.

There was a second reason why our pollster should not have been shocked about the gap between the working- and middle-class left. The previous thirty years had seen an estrangement between the classes. If the murderous fantasies of Shaw had vanished, the snobbery of Virginia Woolf was flourishing albeit in a more politically acceptable manner.

With the old factories gone, it became fashionable to talk as if the working class didn't exist, even though millions lived in humble circumstances with nothing to sell but their labour. A priceless leader in the left-wing *New Statesman*, which had once seen the working class as history's vanguard, announced in 2004:

> Socially and culturally, most Britons feel more European than ever, being more likely to spend a weekend in Perpignan than in Harrogate. Many could name the best restaurants in Barcelona and the best clubs in Rome [and] recommend truffle suppliers in rural France.

My colleagues on the *New Statesman* could indeed advise on where to stay in rural France, and I may be able to answer your questions about the truffle market if you let me make a few calls, but I'm not sure those who continued to work in menial jobs after the collapse of heavy industry would be as helpful.

Other commentators accepted that the working class lived on, but were obsessed by identity politics and patronized the living daylights out of those who didn't fit in. They failed to see that while it was commendable and essential to fight racism, sexism and homophobia, taking account of diverse identities could strengthen the pecking order if they forgot about class.

From the Seventies on, the public and to a lesser extent the private sector made strenuous efforts to give top jobs to women and people from the ethnic minorities, but because class played no part in their selection criteria the beneficiaries of the anti-discrimination measures were from the upper middle class as often as not. The women, blacks and Asians they employed had many differences, but usually they were of good family. In the name of diversity, everyone was the same. In the name of equality, privilege grew.

Supposedly egalitarian measures had the curious habit of favouring the comfortable. The huge expansion in university places that began in the Eighties resulted in the gap between the higher-education participation rates of the working and middle classes becoming wider than ever. For sound class reasons, Conservative politicians of the Sixties and Seventies were as keen as Labour politicians were on closing grammar schools because when you combined egalitarian comprehensives with a selective private system – as Britain and America did – you had the rich parents' dream. If their children were bright, they could go to a good private school. Competition for places was fierce, but generally limited by the parents' ability to pay. If their children were clots, parental wealth could still be decisive because rich parents could afford to pay the high prices of homes in the catchment areas of the best comprehensives. Either way, money talked, and in the name of helping others, the middle classes helped themselves. Poor but talented children who might challenge the children of the wealthy invariably went to second-rate comprehensives.

Researchers from the London School of Economics found that the promises to promote equality and diversity had turned out to be so much waffle. Contrary to all the self-regarding talk of old class differences not amounting to a hill of beans any more, Britain had become a sclerotic country at the beginning of the twenty-first century where social mobility was going backwards. In 1958, when Harold Macmillan was Prime Minister, he stuffed his administration with the dukes and lords he met on the grouse moors. None the less, a child born into aristocratic Britain in 1958 was far more likely to have broken away from his or her class and pursued a career that reflected his or her talents than a child born in 1970. Cherie Blair boasted in 2004 that 'whoever's calling the shots in this country, it isn't the people on the grouse moor'. Nevertheless Britain was a more class-ridden society in 2004 than 1958.

Michael Collins, a rare modern example of a working-class intellectual, kept a file of cuttings from the upmarket liberal press filled with ignorance about and disdain for the white working class. 'Gay pride has become a fun day out for south

London families,' said one columnist. 'No it hasn't,' said Collins, who had the advantage of coming from a south London family. 'A fun day out for my family and our neighbours is a visit to the theme park.' A Trotskyist columnist for the *Independent* applauded the black residents of an old people's home for having the kind of funky time white squares could never enjoy. 'Old Jamaicans wear splendid Rasta hats, while white 70 year olds wear cloth caps,' he wrote. 'Throughout the day the tape blasts out reggae...Can you imagine the uproar if someone stuck that on in a pensioners' centre full of white people?'

Needless to say, such ramblings dripped with condescension towards blacks and gays. Their role was to be exotics who brought homoerotic thrills or natural rhythm into the otherwise jaded lives of the pundits of Canary Wharf as they busily painted the white English working class that the Left had once meant to lead the march to socialism as the embodiment of nationalist reaction. Sir David Hare, a liberal playwright, some of whose fees from the subsidized theatre came from English taxpayers on modest means, said he found the idea of Englishness revolting.

'Most of us look with longing to the republican countries across the Channel,' he said. 'We associate "Englishness" with everything that is most backward in this country.'

You didn't need to ask who that 'us' was. The manner in which Sir David mistook his narrow circle of acquaintances for 60 million people was predictably Amisian. Still it was worth wondering about the seriousness of a serious playwright who hadn't grasped that the closest republic to England was France: a country cursed by mass unemployment, cronyism and racial hatred; the possessor of the largest white far-right party in the world and ghettos dominated by the brown far right in the shape of the Muslim Brotherhood.

Meanwhile the available evidence showed that the white working class was no less or more racist than the middle class and less racist than other ethnic groups. A 1997 study for the Institute for Public Policy Research found that 32 per cent of Muslims, Hindus and Sikhs and 29 per cent of Jews would have a problem if a member of their family married an Afro-Caribbean whereas only 13 per cent of white Britons said they would be repelled.

Such findings made no difference. As Julie Burchill said, 'the English working class is now the only group of people the chattering classes are happy to hear mocked and attacked'. Or as Collins put it, 'the vision of a multi-cultural Utopia needed its common enemy, and it was increasingly the tribe that played a major role in previous Utopian fantasies'.

At the end of his magisterial *Intellectual Life of the British Working Classes*, Jonathan Rose asked why 200 years of self-improvement through libraries, lectures, schools and news-papers organized by and for the working class had died. His conclusion was that the supposedly egalitarian and multi-cultural assault on the 'dead white men' of the classics increased middle-class advantage. When there was agreement on what the canon was, and everyone knew that, say, you couldn't be educated without knowing Shakespeare, it was relatively easy for the self-taught to catch up. But then Bohemia and the universities began to throw out cultural trends that had 'as brief a shelf-life as stock-exchange trends, and [which] depreciate rapidly if one fails to catch the latest wave in architecture or literary theory. The names that Bohemia adopted for itself – *avant-garde, advanced, progressive, le dernier cri, new wave, modernist, postmodernist* – reflect the Anxiety of Cool, the relentless struggle to get out in front and control the production of new cultural information.'

Spotting trends and selling them was turning into a big business in post-industrial societies. But each new wave carried high culture further away from the working class. Rose quoted the opinions of young working-class men of theatres and art house cinemas. 'Theatre goers? Someone well off,' said one. 'It's a class thing.' Then he searched the Modern Language Association of America's international database of academic books published between 1991 and 2000. He got 13,820 hits for 'women', 4,539 for 'gender', 1,826 for 'race', 710 for 'post-colonial' and a piddling 136 for 'working class'. He tried the list of periodicals and couldn't find one academic journal anywhere in the world devoted to proletarian literature and concluded:

> In Tony Blair's Britain as in many other Western nations, pro-fessionals in the creative industries have successfully reconciled bourgeois and Bohemian values. Affluent and ambitious, profit-motivated and style-conscious, they are sincerely committed to women's equality and genuinely interested in the literature, music, art and cuisines of non-Western peoples. But the bou-tique economy they have constructed involves a process of class formation where the accoutrements of the avant-garde are used to distance and distinguish cultural workers from more traditional manual workers.

From the theorists in the universities to the pundits in Canary Wharf, the intellectuals weren't interested in the work-ing class and the working class wasn't interested in the intellec-tuals.

You could not have found a more lethal way to kill left-wing politics if you had tried.

* * *

Shortly after George W. Bush became President of the United States, Thomas Frank returned to his native Kansas. Frank was like a figure from another age: generous, egalitarian and a stranger to the fashions of Bohemia. He was by a long measure the best left-wing writer in America. Yet he never achieved the global fame of Michael Moore and his imitators who told grateful foreigners how it was beyond them how their country had become the world's only superpower when 'stupid white men' led it.

It was not that Frank had any time for his nation's leaders, but he had the intellectual integrity to ask hard questions. Kansas posed dozens of them. It had once been the most radical state in the Union. The people of Kansas were so opposed to slavery that, while the rest of the country dithered, they started the American Civil War – all by themselves. In the 1890s, Kansas was at the centre of the populist movement that raged against the power of the bankers and railway owners, and terrified the American boss class of the day. Socialist newspapers sold in their hundreds of thousands. Plain-speaking Midwestern farmers denounced the devious East Coast elites as robbers and blackmailers as they threw the Republican state leadership from power.

One hundred years on and the American elite was more devious and more arrogant than in the Gilded Age. Agribusiness had driven small farmers to the wall. The little towns on the prairie, so beloved by American conservatives for their self-reliance and respectability, were dying: their shops closed by Wal-Mart; their young gone from the land in search of work. What's more, there were local imitations of the corruption of the Enron Corporation to outrage honest Midwesterners. Executives had looted millions from state utilities. Business leaders had held taxpayers to ransom by threatening to move their factories out of the state if their demands weren't met. Crony capitalists and Republican politicians had merged into a ruling class that was unable to distinguish between private gain and the public interest. Their programme for their fellow citizens was to deny them free health care, cut the taxes of the wealthy, privatize what few public assets remained and oppose any regulation of a rampant free market that was benefiting the few, rather than the many.

Their pride and pomp were revolting to behold.

And a revolt of the masses did sweep Kansas and many another American state. Unfortunately, it was not an uprising against rich conservatives in the American heartland but rich liberals in New York and Los Angeles. The insurgents claimed that the liberals formed the true elite that forced unchristian art on taxpayers, denigrated the family, legalized the murder of foetuses and corrupted the airwaves. These snotty aristocrats laughed at the aspirations of decent Americans while they sipped their lattes and drove their dinky European cars. Disgust at upper-middle-class liberalism had turned the once quasi-socialist Kansas into a state that was so far to the right George W. Bush didn't need to campaign in it.

Frank was a middle-class boy who had grown up in the wealthy Kansas City suburbs of Leawood and Mission Hills. He couldn't deny that he was witnessing a popular movement led by genuine working-class militants. The people had risen like lions from their slumber. But their cause, said Frank, and the interests of their class could not be further apart.

For decades Americans have experienced a populist uprising that only benefits the people it is supposed to be targeting. In Kansas we merely see an extreme example of this mysterious situation. The angry workers, mighty in their numbers, are marching irresistibly against the arrogant. They are shaking their fists at the sons of privilege. They are laughing at the dainty affectations of the Leawood toffs. They are massing at the gates of Mission Hills, hoisting the black flag, and while the millionaires tremble in their mansions, they are bellowing out their terrifying demands. 'We are here,' they scream, 'to cut your taxes.'

So far, so predictable: a conspiracy of rich men has fooled the humble into fighting for the mighty. But the reason why Frank never achieved the popularity of Noam Chomsky and Michael Moore was that he didn't just say that the working-class Republicans who helped bring Bush to power were the dumb victims of false consciousness. True, Frank left open the possibility that the vistas of endless prairie had driven many of them nuts, but he had to concede that there were faults on the Left. American liberals had stopped talking about class and to the working class, and the Democrats had become another pro-business party. (Bill Clinton's fundraisers were as willing to take Enron's loot as George W. Bush's.) The Democrats' abdication left the Republicans free to fight class-based culture wars and exploit some of humanity's deepest angers against elites.

Many on the American left would have agreed with that analysis, but Frank went further by showing how the liberals' faith in liberal democracy was fading. Foreign observers looking at the populist American right were dumbstruck by the success of anti-abortion campaigners in mobilizing support for the Republicans. Parliaments in every other democratic country had accepted abortion; surely, the backlash it inspired in the United States was proof that this was an alien land of religious extremists? It was, up to a point, but outsiders failed to notice that American liberals had not fought and won the argument for abortion in democratic elections, as they would have won it if they had gone in for the long haul.

Instead, they had persuaded the Supreme Court to legalize abortion with judge-made law in the 1973 case of *Roe v Wade*, and inadvertently given their conservative opponents a gold-mine of class resentment. As Frank noticed, *Roe v Wade*

> demonstrated in no uncertain manner the power of the legal profession to override everyone from the church to the state legislature. The decision superseded laws in nearly every state. It unilaterally squashed the then nascent debate over abortion, settling the issue by fiat and from the top down. And it cemented forever a stereotype of liberalism as a doctrine of a tiny clique of experts, an unholy combination of doctors and lawyers, of bureaucrats and professionals, securing their 'reforms' by judicial command rather than democratic consensus... Every aspect of the backlash nightmare seems to follow a similar path. Overweening professionals, disdainful of the un-washed and uneducated masses, force their expert (i.e., liberal) opinions on a world that is not permitted to respond.

Liberal Europe wasn't as different from the United States as it liked to think. If the peoples of Denmark, Ireland, France or Holland voted against the wishes of the European Union, Brussels would either order the recalcitrant country to vote again, in the cases of Denmark and Ireland, or ignore the results and carry on as before, in the cases of Holland and France. Mainstream liberals everywhere in Europe were far too keen on using the judges of the European Court of Human Rights to impose their views, while a list of their restrictions on free speech would fill the rest of this book. Highlights included:

Holocaust denial being made a criminal offence across the Continent; the Belgian courts banning a right-wing party for being right wing; Britain banning the incitement of religious hatred; the Danish newspaper *Jyllands-Posten* being investigated for publishing cartoons that murderously militant Muslims didn't like; and Michel Houellebecq, the only French novelist to find a foreign audience in a generation, being prosecuted for offending Islam. The point here is not to support right-wing Belgians or Holocaust denial, but to emphasize the indecent eagerness of the multi-cultural liberal states of Europe to restrict free speech and reach for their lawyers.

I've deliberately avoided mentioning the creaking gags about political correctness which so tickled the tummies of the British and American right in the period, but they did reflect the inclination of mainstream liberalism to avoid plain language and open debate. You couldn't help suspecting that the liberals doubted their ability to win open arguments and free elections and that their herd-like cohesion was now more defensive than confident. They were no longer the convinced force of the twentieth century but pinched and subliminally nervous people who lacked confidence in democracy.

We have travelled a long way from the student revolutionary Kanan Makiya realizing he would have to confront Saddam Hussein. We have seen a far left driven half-mad by the death of socialism produce apologetics for the totalitarian movements of the far right. We have seen the leading intellectual of the Arab world reflect mainstream Muslim opinion by refusing to confront crimes against humanity committed by Muslims against Muslims. We have seen the theorists in academe denigrate democratic values and produce a reactionary cultural relativism that was at best patronizing and at worst a form of racial determinism. We have seen the anti-globalization movement face up to injustices which were an affront to the conscience of the human race but fail to produce a universal political programme which could handle tyranny and genocide. We have seen the prosperity of modern society weaken the inclination to make selfless commitments whether in politics or daily life. We have looked at how the ideas of what was to become the twenty-first-century left were anticipated by John Major's Conservative government – and we were not surprised because many of the ideas of the new left were conservative. We have seen the European Union's shameful unwillingness to stop crimes against humanity on its borders, and the appeal of conspiracy theory to every fool with an Internet connection. Finally, we have seen that nice, decent liberals were nowhere near as nice or decent as they liked to think – or conspicuously liberal for that matter. Unsettling changes in society and their growing predilection for authoritarian measures had left them dogmatic and unsure about their commitment to the open traditions of liberal democracy.

Everywhere we have heard the refrain that the sicknesses of the world were the responsibility of the democratic countries, and we have seen the American electorate give support to that notion by choosing a government whose outlandish doctrines and conservative self-confidence appalled the majority of world opinion.

All in all, the liberal-left had not been in a worse state to confront fascism since the Thirties.

INTERMISSION

A Hereditary Disease

'IN OLD MOSCOW'
(Tune: Clementine)

In old Moscow, in the Kremlin,
In the fall of '39,
Sat a Russian and a Prussian
Writing out the party line.

Chorus:
Oh, my darling, oh, my darling,
Oh, my darling party line;
Oh, I never will desert you,
For I love this life of mine.

Leon Trotsky was a Nazi;
Oh we knew it for a fact.
Pravda said it; we all read it,
Before the Stalin–Hitler Pact.

Now the Nazis and the Fuehrer
Stand within the party line,
All the Russians love the Prussians,
Volga boatmen sail the Rhine.

Walter Gourlay, 1941

CHAPTER EIGHT

All the Russians Love the Prussians

*One of the easiest pastimes in the world is debunking de-
mocracy. In this country one is hardly obliged to bother any
longer with the merely reactionary arguments against popular rule, but during the last twenty years 'bourgeois' democracy has been much more subtly attacked by both fascists and
communists, and it is highly significant that these seeming
enemies have both attacked it on the same grounds.*

George Orwell, 1941

EVERYBODY KNOWS the story of the Thirties, or thinks they
do. Adolf Hitler's power grew and the leaders of the British
Conservative Party helped it grow further. Tory politicians
and a part of the wider right had a sneaking admiration for
Hitler and saw him as a bulwark against communism. Geoffrey
Dawson, the editor of *The Times*, and Lord and Lady Astor, the
political host and hostess of the day, made pandering to Nazis
respectable in the offices of Fleet Street and drawing rooms
of the aristocracy. Like Douglas Hurd, Neville Chamberlain
could on occasion look up and see clearly what was happening
around him. Three weeks before he sold out Czechoslovakia
at Munich in the autumn of 1938 he wrote: 'Is it not positively
horrible that the fate of hundreds of millions depends on one
man and he is half-mad?' But Chamberlain also thought that

America was 'a nation of cads' and that the French 'couldn't keep a secret for more than half an hour or a government for more than nine months'. On that basis, there was little to choose between one lot of bloody foreigners and another. Hitler may have been 'positively horrible' but a war to stop him destroying Czechoslovakia raised the even more 'horrible, fantastic, incredible' prospect that 'we should be digging trenches and trying on gas masks here because of a quarrel in a faraway country between people of whom we know nothing'. Chamberlain ignored the warnings of Winston Churchill and helped Adolf Hitler to become the master of Europe by agreeing to the dismemberment of Czechoslovakia at Munich in 1938.

By 1940 'Munich' and 'appeasement' were spat out and Chamberlain was the most despised Prime Minister in British history. Stalin had astonished the world by signing a pact with his sworn enemy Hitler, France had fallen to the German armies and Winston Churchill had taken over from Chamberlain. Britain stood alone in her finest hour.

And the Left? Well, it is a truth almost universally acknowledged that 1940 was also the Left's finest hour. Like Churchill, it spent the Thirties in the wilderness, issuing warnings that few heeded. It remained steadfast despite the discouragement, and helped force Chamberlain's resignation. History vindicated it by bringing victory in the war against fascism and victory in the 1945 general election that produced the nearest Britain has had to a socialist government. Our idea of what it means to be on the Left still invokes faded black and white images of the Wall Street Crash, the Great Depression, the Jarrow hunger marches, Mussolini's invasion of Abyssinia, the rise of Hitler, the Spanish Civil War, the persecution of the Jews and the betrayal of Munich. The radicalized middle classes of the day remain a model for educated people who want to make a political commitment.

It is a mistake to think that all the great novelists and poets of the Thirties were anti-fascist: W. B. Yeats, D. H. Lawrence and to a lesser extent T. S. Eliot were anything but. However, when the exceptions have been made it is the 'pink poets', the members of the Left Book Club and the readers of the *New Statesman* and *Manchester Guardian* who have defined the British intelligentsia's reaction to the lowest point of the twentieth century. Despite all the abuse that was thrown at them then and since, they don't come out of it badly because they got one big thing right. They knew the totalitarian right when they saw it, and realized it had to be fought.

W. H. Auden was the most attractive of them all. Although he had the privilege of attending private school and Oxford, he was a homosexual and had to manage with a society which treated his loves as crimes. He had gone to Weimar Germany largely because of its relaxed sexual mores. The Nazis stopped that. Auden returned to visit his friend and literary partner Christopher Isherwood in Berlin in 1934 and realized at once that 'a mixture of gangsters and the sort of school prefect who is good at Corps' was now in charge.

Back home, Churchill's decision to return the pound to the Gold Standard in 1925 – the monetarist madness of the day – guaranteed economic misery for the regions that depended on the traditional industries that had made Britain great. After the stock market crash of 1929, the established economic order appeared a fraud to Auden and many other thinking people: a malfunctioning machine which generated chaos and poverty. (That the socialist poets and novelists of the Thirties were almost without exception public-school boys who had done well out of the established order only made their embarrassed fury greater.) Meanwhile it was clear that the young men of the generation before who had died in the trenches of Flanders, and whose names were carved into school memorials and remembered in assemblies, had not sacrificed their lives for the 'war to end all wars'. By 1934, the First World War seemed a pointless act of butchery that had settled nothing and was leading to a greater and more terrible conflict. The combination of the capitalist slump and the fascist surge made all the bluff certainties of their fathers and teachers ridiculous.

Yet – and how to explain this? – good arguments about the need to confront the fascist menace did the Left no good. As far as the high politics of Britain was concerned the Left, the Labour Party and the pink poets might as well never have existed. The Thirties was like the Eighties, a decade of economic misery for many presided over by unchallengeable conservative politicians – 'safe, mediocre, hollow men'. When Auden went to Germany, the British Prime Minister was the gormless Ramsay MacDonald, the 'boneless wonder', as Lloyd George called him, who had split the Labour Party in 1931 so he could form a coalition with the Tories and engage in dalliances with duchesses. He once confessed to a colleague that 'often I am speaking and I have no idea how the sentence I am saying should finish'. John Major was a Pericles in comparison. The equally unimaginative Conservative leaders, Stanley Baldwin and Neville Chamberlain, succeeded MacDonald. Like their mediocre predecessor, they couldn't think of anything to do about Hitler other than appease him.

The hollow men kept winning elections none the less because the 'Hungry Thirties' weren't hungry for everyone. The Great Depression devastated parts of Scotland, Wales, Northern Ireland and the North, but the South and the Midlands were booming by the middle of the decade, and witnessing the birth of the consumer society. Home ownership exploded as skilled workers, foremen and clerks bought cars and the new £600 semis in south Birmingham and west London. Writers at the time and since who concentrated on the depressed areas missed the brute economic fact that average incomes rose in the Thirties. And as in the Eighties, the newly prosperous wanted American consumerism, American advertising and American entertainment, not socialist programmes to relieve mass unemployment.

The Thirties was the decade when refined leftists first cried 'No Logo!' Mars, Nescafé and Brylcreem proved to manufacturers that an active marketing department and strong brands were the essentials of commercial success. Sentimentalists believed the British masses were modern peasants who yearned for the designs of the Arts & Crafts movement and the personal service of the small shop. The managers of Woolworths – the Wal-Mart of the day – wisely ignored them and took the view 'that almost everything said about the character of the English people, their deep-rooted traditions, their snobbery and their unconquerable individualism, was – when you came down to the harsh facts of life – baloney'.

Many of the intellectuals of the time were as dismayed by suburbanization and consumerism as the modern enemies of McDonald's and Barratt homes. In 1937, John Betjeman asked for 'friendly bombs' to fall on Slough. While he waited for the Luftwaffe to oblige him, his friends applauded the sentiment and backed into a familiar dead-end for the twentieth-century left. On the one hand, they glamorized the working class and grew bitter when it failed to rebel. On the other, they despised the middle classes, who more often than not they distilled into the figures of their fathers.

The tension between idolizing and deploring the working

class runs through the left-wing poetry of the age. The poets see fascism with a clarity that 'realist' statesmen and respectable commentators could not match and warn of the coming disaster. Yet you can't help thinking a part of them wants disaster to hit not only the greedy, guilty middle classes, but the apathetic workers, who are more interested in Fred Astaire and Ginger Rogers than revolution. Disaster may encourage them to turn to socialism. At a minimum, it would allow the poets to say 'I told you so.'

The young C. Day Lewis spent the Thirties exhorting the masses to embrace socialism. When they refused to obey orders, he turned on them. In his 'Newsreel' of 1938, he lambasted the 'sleep-walking' audiences in cinema 'dream houses' who 'gape incurious' at the pictures on the screen of advancing fascist armies. Their apathy has made tyranny possible – 'what your active hours have willed'. With a touch too much relish he warned that they should:

> See the big guns, rising, groping, erected
> To plant death in your world's soft womb.
> Fire-bud, smoke blossom, ironseed projected –
> Are these exotics? They will grow nearer home:
>
> Grow nearer home – and out of the dream-house stumbling
> One night into a strangling air and the flung
> Rags of children and thunder of stone Niagaras tumbling,
> You will know you slept too long.

Then you'll be sorry, and wish you'd listened to me; just as the greedy consumers of petrol and Big Macs will be sorry and wish they'd listened to the Greens when the ice caps melt and the seawaters smash through the windows of their ghastly bungalows.

The belief that dark forces would destroy both the innocent and the privileged runs through W. H. Auden's great poems of the period. From 1932 when he wrote:

> Oh what is that sound which so thrills the ear
> Down in the valley drumming, drumming?
> Only the scarlet soldiers, dear,
> The soldiers coming.

Via his 'Letters from Iceland' which begins:

> It's farewell to the drawing room's civilised cry
> The professor's sensible whereto and why
> The frock-coated diplomat's social aplomb
> Now matters are settled with gas and with bomb.

To 'Spain (1937)' which says the 'flat ephemeral pamphlet and the boring meeting' are essential because:

> Time is short, and
> History to the defeated
> May say Alas but cannot help or pardon.

For all their contradictions, poets and socialist and trade unionist volunteers were prepared to fight against the fascist menace in the Spanish Civil War. The sight of intellectuals in battle is always a potentially ridiculous one, and Auden himself said that the global movement to stop Franco, Hitler and Mussolini overthrowing Spain's democratic government would fail because 'the intellectuals are supporting it'. There were conferences of artists in the Pyrenees, whose contribution to the war effort was doubtful, and writers who risked provoking a mutiny by blaring selections from their work through loud-speakers to the troops. More seriously, the intellectual left swallowed outright lies and refused to see that Stalin's Soviet Union was more interested in purging and murdering the liberal and left-wing opponents of communism than helping to defeat the fascist rebellion.

Their support for communism remains an indelible stain and is the main reason why respect for intellectuals – never a marked characteristic of the English, I admit – remains so low. By 1939, Auden was disgusted with himself for going along with the herd. He and Isherwood left Britain for America and, to the malicious delight of their many critics, ducked out of the war against fascism they had been warning about for years.

On the liner, Isherwood recorded in his diary that:

I turned to Auden and said: 'You know, I just don't believe in any of it any more – the United Front, the party line, the anti-fascist struggle. I suppose they're okay, but something's wrong with me. I simply can't swallow another mouthful.' And Auden answered: 'No, neither can I.' In a few sentences, with exquisite relief, we confessed our mutual disgust at the parts we had been playing and resolved to abandon them, then and there. We had forgotten our real vocation. We would be artists again, with our own values, our own integrity, and not amateur socialist agitators, parlour reds.

In the Fifties, Auden went further and renounced his best political poems like a father disinheriting delinquent children. He decided that when he said of the Spanish Civil War that 'History to the defeated/ May say Alas but cannot help or pardon' he was putting forward the 'wicked doctrine' that equated goodness with success. He refused to allow 'Spain

(1937)' to appear in his collected works, and produced a mercilessly accurate explanation of the persistent strain of racism in leftish thought that allows intellectuals to believe it is tolerable for others to suffer under depraved ideologies that they would never tolerate themselves.

> Our great error was not a false admiration for Russia but a snobbish feeling that nothing which happened in a semi-barbarous country which had experienced neither the Renaissance nor the Enlightenment could be of any importance: had any of the countries we knew personally, like France, Germany or Italy, the language of which we could speak and where we had personal friends, been one to have a successful communist revolution with the same phenomena of terror, purges, censorship etc., we would have screamed our heads off.

And yet and but and for all that, on the big question of fascism the 'parlour reds' were right. History did not help or pardon the defeated Spanish Republicans. The audiences who watched Fred Astaire and Ginger Rogers instead of reading the *New Statesman* did have to face 'Rags of children and thunder of stone Niagaras tumbling' outside the cinema doors in 1940. (As the owners of coastal bungalows may see the waves coming in.)

When the Battle of Britain began a trio of authors extolled the essential rightness of the Left. Working under the pseudonym of 'Cato' they wrote *Guilty Men*, the most rollicking assault on British Conservatism ever printed. Like millions of others, the young Michael Foot, then writing for the London *Evening Standard*, Peter Howard, a columnist on the *Sunday Express* and a former captain of the England rugby team, and Frank Owen, the *Standard*'s editor, were appalled and furious. They looked across to St Paul's from the roof of the old *Standard* building, and decided that if the Nazis were going to come they would nail their political dupes before the Wehrmacht reached London. They split up the work, and over a weekend in June 1940 produced one of the finest polemics in English literature – then went to a pub on the Gray's Inn Road to celebrate. It sold 50,000 copies in a week and 200,000 by the end of the year. No one who struggles to write for a living can view their success with anything other than undiluted envy.

Guilty Men was out in July, one month after the evacuation of Dunkirk and two weeks after the fall of France. It begins with the announcement that the ragged soldiers on Dunkirk's beaches were heroes in armies 'doomed before they took the field'. The cowardly and blinkered politicians of the Thirties had preordained the ruinous defeats that had left Hitler with Europe at his mercy. Appeasement and mass unemployment were two sides of the same coin. MacDonald, Baldwin and Chamberlain betrayed the unemployed at home and the national interest abroad. Hitler put Germany to work to prepare for war, while Britain still had 1 million unemployed in 1940.

The story has two heroes: Winston Churchill and the Labour Party, which had once 'been permeated with severe drenchings of pacifism' but had been ready to rearm and confront Hitler since 1935.

Each page rubbed a belief in the Left's moral superiority you can still find today. The Left was right; its flawlessness was beyond doubt. Clever, modest and misunderstood, it endured the wilderness years of the Thirties and returned to save its country in 1940. The standard exception to make at this point is for the apologists for Stalin, but they could say that their lapses were excusable because their main concern was to confront a psychotic cult of death from the far right.

Many did, not everything about the heroic left-wing narrative is wrong by any means. The liberal-left fought appeasement the hardest and put up anti-fascist candidates in by-elections to try to stop the Chamberlain Tories. The votes of Labour MPs forced Chamberlain out of 10 Downing Street after the British defeats of 1940, against the wishes of the majority of Conservative MPs who still wanted him to remain Prime Minister.

But the story isn't all cheery. Lessons for today's liberal-left can be found by looking at the minority who gathered around the Bloomsbury Group and the Communist Party. They didn't confront Nazism but were happy to go along with it.

Their motives were treason, reason and fear.

Of all people, the liberal intelligentsia seems best able by temperament and training to lead the search for the middle way. No phrase is dearer to our hearts than 'there is good and bad on both sides'. Our favourite colour is grey (or shades thereof). When presented with a choice between unacceptable alternatives – Hitler or carnage, Bush or Osama bin Laden, a capricious war or the perpetuation in power of Saddam Hussein – why shouldn't we be allowed to reject both without bullies accusing us of being Islamist or Baathist dupes?

I feel like a class traitor when I say it but the first lesson from the 'heroic' age of the Left in the Thirties is that it never works like that in a conflict in which your own society is involved. You can be a critical friend of one side or another, a very critical friend as often as not, but you have to choose which side you are on, and those who don't usually end up as the biggest villains of all.

For a while, the shifting alliances of the Thirties obscured the need for a decision. Anti-fascists on the Left who wanted a confrontation with Hitler didn't have to choose between opposing Nazi Germany and opposing Britain. The British government appeased Germany, so they were in the happy position of being able to condemn both. For the same reason, the pacifist left didn't have to choose between supporting the British war effort or trying to undermine it by urging peace with the Nazis. When the British Tories were doing everything they could to avoid war, pacifists too did not need to decide. Yet the knowledge that hard choices could arrive one day niggled away from the moment Hitler came to power in 1933.

Virginia Woolf, Clive Bell, an art critic and her brother-in-law, Bertrand Russell and others in the Bloomsbury Group were among the first on the liberal-left to think they could dodge them. As early as 1919, their friend J. M. Keynes had provided a 'root cause' to justify appeasement in his *Economic Consequences of the Peace*. The vindictive leaders of Britain and France had imposed a Carthaginian peace on Germany with the Treaty of Versailles, he said. Its punitive terms made a second conflict inevitable. The book's success guaranteed that Hitler's attempts to overturn the treaty's provisions would appear reasonable to a large section of liberal opinion, although, interestingly, Keynes himself did not go along with appeasement and had no hesitation in 1936 in condemning the fascist states as 'brigand powers who know no argument but force'.

His friends were not so certain, and the fear of another barbaric conflict pushed them towards neutrality, a slippery position which few people can stick to for long. The neutral has to believe that it doesn't matter who wins. Even if they managed to convince themselves that the 'root causes' of the rise of Hitler were all 'our' fault, even if there was every reason to be terrified about the prospect of a return to the slaughterhouses of the trenches, it clearly would have mattered if the Nazis had won. Woolf and her contemporaries had to find a way to block that thought out and avoid the moral and political obligation of opposing fascism. They did it by finding Nazis everywhere.

When a letter-writer to a newspaper asserted that the employment of women caused the unemployment of men, Woolf compared him to Hitler. 'Are they both not saying the same thing? Are they both not the voice of the dictator whether they speak English or German?' When the Church of England refused to allow the ordination of women vicars, she decided that the British establishment was as fascist as the fascist states of Europe. 'The whole iniquity of dictatorship, whether in Oxford or Cambridge, in Whitehall or Downing Street, against Jews or against women, in England or in Germany, in Italy or in Spain, is now apparent.' The universities were as bad. They should abolish academic gowns, medals, badges, she said, because 'the example of the fascist states' showed that uniforms could 'hypnotise the human mind'.

As the conservative critic Theodore Dalrymple commented, Woolf could not discriminate between 'a university degree convocation and a Nuremberg rally'. If she were alive today, she would be comparing America to Nazi Germany on Radio 4 and anti-terror laws to Sharia in her column in the *Independent*. Then as now, if you believe that everyone in power is a totalitarian, you needn't worry about actual totalitarians, and already your neutrality is tipping over into support for the other side.

The one authority figure Virginia Woolf confessed to loving was George Lansbury, and many others agreed that he was the most lovable man in the Labour Party of the Thirties. Although Lansbury was always identified with his East End constituency of Bow and Poplar, he was born into a poor Suffolk family. It fostered in him a love of his fellow creatures which beamed out from his ruddy cheeks. In *The Age of Illusion*, his portrait of the inter-war years, Ronald Blythe described him thus:

> He was gregarious. Humanity seethed, pullulated around him and he loved it. There were 12 children of his happy and candidly sensual marriage. There were workhouses, prisons, rallies, marches, congregations, emigrant ships, hospitals, parks, Parliament, palaces and they were all full of people. Reformers are always said to love people, though often what they love is tidiness. Lansbury never sacrificed human happiness to hatred of litter or to lawn-worship. Everywhere he went he broke down fences.

Supporters of all the radical causes of the early twentieth century trooped to his home at 39 Bow Road, and he welcomed them at the door. He allied with the suffragettes and the First World War's conscientious objectors without a thought for the short-term damage to his career. The butchery on the Western Front reinforced his Anglican pacifism and gave him a steadfast belief that all God's children must live in peace. He was a generous, honest and naïve man. In normal circumstances, he would have got nowhere in politics, but after Ramsay MacDonald and his supporters went off to join the Conservatives in 1931 there didn't seem to be anyone else to take over the rump of Labour MPs, and this saintly figure became the Leader of the Opposition.

Lansbury used his unexpected elevation to argue for pacifism. At the 1933 Labour Party Conference, he carried a motion against all war and called for a general strike if Britain entered another conflict. Like the Campaign for Nuclear Disarmament of the Fifties and Eighties, Lansbury believed that the shining moral example of a disarmed Britain would compel the dictators to mend their ways. 'The only path to peace is not to fight. Our people must give up the right to hold any other country, renounce imperialism and stand unarmed before the world. She will then be the strongest nation in the world, fully armed by justice and love.'

By 1935, other Labour leaders were beginning to wonder if love was all they needed. The rise of Hitler and Mussolini forced Clement Attlee and Ernie Bevin to ask if Britain shouldn't build some kind of national defence. They thought they had reached a deal with Lansbury to commit Labour to supporting collective security through the League of Nations, the forerunner of the United Nations.

At the 1935 Labour conference, the debate ranged back and forth until the adorable figure of Lansbury shambled on to the stage. The Labour Party is always partial to bouts of sentimentality and the sight of its old friend was too much for the delegates. There was prolonged applause and his comrades burst into a rendition of 'For He's a Jolly Good Fellow'. Lansbury explained that whatever his Parliamentary colleagues said he still believed that Britain should unilaterally disarm and hand over her empire to an international trusteeship. The spirit of the Lord was upon him. He intoned that war solved nothing and he didn't care if he went to the stake for saying so. 'It may be that I shall not meet you on this platform any more. (Cries of "No!") ... If mine were the only voice in this conference, I would say, in the name of the faith I hold, the belief that God intends us to live peacefully and quietly with one another. If some people do not allow us to do so, I am ready to stand as the early Christians did and say, this is our faith, this is where we stand, and, if necessary, this is where we will die.'

The readiness to declare yourself willing to be a martyr can make you very popular and nowhere more popular than at the Labour Party Conference. The hall erupted. Everyone loved Lansbury, except Ernie Bevin, the blunt trade unionist who was to have more influence on British history than any other working-class politician. As a leading figure in the party, he was furious that Lansbury had ignored party policy; as a trade unionist, he was angrier still that he had reneged on a deal.

He took to the stage and rasped: 'People have been on this platform talking about the destruction of capitalism. The middle classes are not doing too badly under capitalism and fascism. The only thing that is being wiped out is the Trade Union Movement. It is we who are being wiped out and who will be wiped out if fascism comes here.'

He turned to Lansbury and accused him of betraying Labour's National Executive Committee by refusing to stick to its agreed position. 'It is placing the Executive and the Movement in an impossible position to be hawking your conscience round from body to body asking to be told what to do with it.'

Uproar followed. Virginia Woolf burst into tears at the suggestion that her hero was no more than a common hawker and didn't calm down until she left the hall. Her husband, Leonard, said that Bevin 'had battered the poor man to political death'. So he had. The trade union block votes swung behind Bevin. Not a single leading Labour figure supported Lansbury. He had gone from being the star of the conference to its victim, and was deposed as leader shortly afterwards. Bevin relished his victory. 'Lansbury's been dressed in saint's clothes for years waiting for martyrdom. All I did was set fire to the faggots.'

Labour did gradually move towards a readiness to fight fascism, but its shift was nowhere near as fast as Michael Foot was to say in 1940. Not until 1937 was it clearly in support of rearming Britain to meet the Nazi threat, and it was Bevin and other Labour right-wingers who drove the change. Many on the Left opposed them and remained committed to disarmament and appeasement – along with a majority of public opinion. Appeasement was hugely popular, and the late twentieth-century fashion for casting Winston Churchill as a saint and Neville Chamberlain as a demon flatly contradicts the feeling of the time. On his return from agreeing the dismemberment of Czechoslovakia at Munich, Chamberlain found Downing Street stuffed with flowers. Shops sold Chamberlain dolls and companies bought space in newspapers to express their gratitude. The Archbishop of Canterbury called for a day of national celebration, and George VI and his wife, the late Queen Mother, dropped the pretence that the House of Windsor was above politics, and drooled over him. They sent the Lord Chancellor to bring Chamberlain on to the balcony of Buckingham Palace from where king, queen and statesman were applauded by adoring crowds.

Among Chamberlain's admirers were Bertrand Russell, Christopher Isherwood and the left-wingers of the Independent Labour Party. 'What do I care for the Czechs?' asked Isherwood. 'What does it matter if we are traitors? A war has been postponed – and a war postponed is a war which may never happen.'

Lansbury, meanwhile, launched a quixotic one-man campaign to do nothing less than bring peace on earth. Despite being nearly 80 and in mourning for his beloved wife, he dedicated the remainder of his life to a world tour to promote love and understanding. Inevitably, it took him to Hitler. It had to. The logic of pacifism was that there was nothing worse than war – not a bad logic, even if it was false – and pacifists had to convince themselves that the alternative to war was palatable.

The meeting of the two was almost comic. Paul Schmidt, Hitler's translator, described how his master fitted in Lansbury between two other English visitors: Sir Oswald Mosley, whom the Germans would probably have put in charge of a puppet government if they had invaded Britain; and the Duke of Windsor, the deposed Edward VIII, whom they certainly would have put on the throne. Schmidt said that Hitler greeted Lansbury with a tired and bored face. 'The Fuehrer was a man pale from sleeplessness, his complexion almost grey with somewhat puffy features, whose absent-minded expression clearly showed that he was brooding on other things. I almost felt sorry for the old gentleman from England. Again and again, he advanced his pacific plans with great enthusiasm and persistence. He seemed wholly unaware of Hitler's lack of interest, being obviously delighted with his replies, vague though they might be.'

James Griffiths, a miners' leader and Labour MP, remembered Lansbury telling him the only time the great leader was shaken from his boredom was when Lansbury got Schmidt to ask if Hitler had a message he could take to his Jewish constituents 'which will offer them some hope that the treatment of their people in Germany will be changed?'

When Schmidt came to the word 'Jew', Hitler jumped to his feet and, giving the Nazi salute, poured out a torrent of words.

'You need not trouble to translate,' Lansbury said to Schmidt. 'I know what the answer means.'

Even this performance couldn't shake Lansbury's conviction that the love of God and unilateral disarmament would appeal to Hitler's benevolent side. Lansbury emerged from the meeting still believing 'that Germany does not want war' and Hitler was a lost soul who might yet receive salvation in the Anglican Communion. 'I wished that I could have gone to Berchtesgaden and stayed with him a while,' he sighed on his return. 'I feel that Christianity in its purest sense might have had a chance with him.'

He was an extraordinarily silly man but many others on the liberal-left were sillier still. By early 1939, it was clear that the Munich Agreement had not brought peace but only encouraged Hitler to take the rest of Czechoslovakia and prepare to invade Poland. A reluctant and unprepared Britain declared itself ready to fight. The moment of choice had come, and Bloomsbury intellectuals chose to prefer a victory for fascism to the defence of their country and its democratic values.

Clive Bell talked of 'uniting the continent under German leadership' and demanded the 'censorship' of the 'warmongers' who criticized Hitler and Mussolini. *Peace News*, the journal of the Peace Pledge Union, whose members included such liberal grandees as Bertrand Russell and Aldous Huxley, responded to the Japanese attack on China by asserting: 'Clearly you cannot condemn Japan. It is war that is to be condemned.' Canon Stuart Morris, the union's Anglican organizer, joined the Link, a front for Hitler's admirers run by Admiral Sir Barry Domvile, a former director of naval intelligence. When Morris was attacked by the press for his support for neo-fascists, he replied that he thought the Link was a goodwill organization rather than a fascist party, but added that he was in favour of 'giving a great deal more away [to Hitler]. I don't think Mr Chamberlain has really started yet on any serious appeasement.'

The British People's Party, another fascist outfit, was more subtle than Oswald Mosley's Blackshirts. At its inaugural meeting the officers led by the Marquess of Tavistock announced that they had decided 'that far more could be achieved in the campaign by refraining from direct attacks on Jewry, [and] that the campaign against "usury" would bring about the same results and presented in this form would attract far more supporters to the ranks of the party'. (Their successors say 'Zionists' today.)

In July 1939, there was a by-election in Hythe. Domvile, the Marquess of Tavistock and the rest of the crew turned out to support the British People's Party candidate H. St John Philby, the Arabian explorer and father of Kim, who was also willing to betray his country. No surprise in that, but alongside them was Dr Maude Royden, a left-wing member of the council of the Peace Pledge Union. As Richard Griffiths, a historian of the upper-class far right said, Dr Royden could 'hardly have been unaware of the company she was keeping. The Conservative and Liberal candidates repeatedly pointed out Philby's fascist connections.'

As the German invasion of Poland on 3 September 1939 approached, you could see something strange happening to a part of the intellectual left, and it is happening again now. Woolf, Bell and the grandees who supported the Peace Pledge Union were clearly men and women of the liberal-left. They were not converts or turncoats who went from the Left to the Right. Virginia Woolf's support for women priests was fantastically advanced (the Church of England didn't accept that women could be ordained until 1992). Bertrand Russell championed free love and child-centred learning long before the Sixties. In the positions they and their friends adopted on domestic policy they gave no sign of moving towards the Conservative Party. Yet by July 1939, men and women like them with impeccable liberal credentials were campaigning for pro-Hitler candidates and arguing that he should be allowed to take over Europe.

A month later, the world got stranger still.

On 23 August 1939, Nazi Germany and the communist Soviet Union signed a non-aggression pact. This shocking fact was the greatest trauma socialists of my grandparents' generation had to confront. The communists had been the most ferocious enemies of fascism. They had formed popular fronts and organized volunteers to fight against Franco's fascists in the Spanish Civil War. Their record as Nazi Germany's most implacable enemy allowed anti-fascist leftists to ignore Stalin's crimes and excoriate Britain and France for failing to stand beside him in the struggle against Hitler.

When Britain and France finally inched towards doing what they wanted by telling Hitler that an invasion of Poland would mean war, Kremlinologists noticed that the Soviet Union was toning down its condemnations of Hitler. The diplomatic traffic between Berlin and Moscow increased through the summer of 1939, and diplomats started to reflect on an incredible thought: perhaps the communists and the fascists were preparing to form an alliance. The idea of the far left and the far right cooperating was unthinkable to the bulk of the Left in Britain and around the world. Whatever else they said about the communists, they were sure that they were the fascists' staunchest opponents and the doughtiest fighters in the struggle against Hitler and Mussolini. So the communists appeared, until on 23 August Stalin stood on his head and the Soviet Union and Nazi Germany agreed to leave each other in peace and carve up Poland, Finland and the Baltic states between them.

'All isms are wasms,' quipped a Foreign Office wag, which

wasn't true as fascism and communism had merged into a united totalitarian front against democracy. Nevertheless, for two years all the Russians did love the Prussians – on pain of death. The liner of the émigré Auden docked in New York and he described in 'September 1, 1939' how he sat in a bar, and saw 'the clever hopes expire/ of a low dishonest decade'. It felt that way to many on the Left. The Red–Brown alliance was one of those moments when everything people think they know turns out to be a lie. The time for a choice had come: did they support a war against fascism or go along with the communists and, by extension, Hitler?

For a few days, it looked as if even Harry Pollitt, the leader of the British Communist Party, would choose to oppose Hitler and Stalin. He was volcanic with rage. Despite everything, it is impossible to dislike him and his fury brought out his best side. Pollitt preferred plain, forceful English to the prefabricated slogans of most of his comrades. Rarer still, he had a self-deprecating sense of humour. (He told how once when he was in Wandsworth Prison a professional burglar said to him, 'serves you bloody well right, you've no respect for private property'.) He was a genuine working-class communist rather than a half-educated fanatic, who grew up in the slums of the North West. When Chamberlain flew to Munich, Pollitt asked his fellow citizens 'can we not see that our turn will come unless we make a stand now?' Hitler invaded Poland on 3 September 1939, and Britain made a stand by declaring war on Germany. At that instant, Moscow demanded that Pollitt oppose a war against 'the Fascist beast' he had been condemning for years.

It was too much, he told the Communist Party's Central Committee. 'I do not envy the comrades who can so lightly in the space of a week go from one political conviction to another...I am ashamed of the lack of feeling, the lack of response that this struggle of the Polish people has aroused in our leadership.'

If he'd been in Moscow, they would have shot him. As it was, he didn't have the strength of character to hold out for long against the herd and agreed to toe the party line. Walter Ulbricht, the worthless leader of the German Communist Party, explained what the new communist programme would be when he saved his skin by recanting on Radio Moscow a few days after the Hitler–Stalin pact. Nazi Germany, which had sent so many of his comrades to concentration camps, was no longer as bad as he had previously thought, he told the listeners. Britain was now 'the most reactionary force in the world'.

When the Second World War began, Britain faced a hot war against Nazi Germany and its supporters, and a cold war against the communist Soviet Union and its supporters. On Moscow's orders, British communists tried to rally as many people as possible from the wider left to the new cause of going along with Hitler. The story of how they did it is one of the murkiest and least remembered of the war years.

The Communist Party drew up 'the People's Convention' and organized a national movement against the wartime coalition government to go along with it. The convention was a typical communist front organization. It drew in naïve recruits with campaigns for higher living standards and better bomb shelters that no reasonable person could oppose. Once they signed up, only the politically astute would notice that the need to fight Nazi Germany was never mentioned. The communists instructed their fellow travellers that the 'real enemy' was Churchill and his Labour colleagues in the wartime coalition Cabinet. It was against them that the public meetings, propaganda, strikes and demonstrations were directed as the communists and their allies pushed their support for Stalin's alliance with Hitler as far as they dared.

As with the Cambodian genocide, it is worth looking at the backgrounds of those who blew the whistle and said that the Communist Party was trying to do Hitler's work for him. The loudest blast came from the publisher Victor Gollancz, a prim former schoolteacher who allowed the Left Book Club to become home for defenders of the Soviet terror in the Thirties. By 1940, he had had enough. Gollancz and Harold Laski, whom Margaret and Mohamed Makiya heard lecture at Liverpool University, went wild. Along with George Orwell they published a furious book, *Betrayal of the Left*, which demolished the communists and their sympathizers as effectively as *Guilty Men* demolished the appeasers.

'Can anyone,' asked Gollancz,

carry self-delusion to the point of being able to read through the file of the *Daily Worker* [the Communist Party newspaper] and still believe that the motive was any other than to weaken the will to resist? When, at the same time, you tell people that this is an unjust war, fought for no purpose but to increase the profits of the rich: when you jeer at any comment about the morale and heroism of the public and call it 'sunshine talk'; what possible purpose can you have but to stir up hatred of the government and hatred of the war, with the object of undermining the country's determination to stand up to Hitler?

Gollancz had an embarrassment of evidence to substantiate his attack. At the height of the Blitz on 7 September 1940, for example, a story in the *Daily Worker* read

CHEER BOYS CHEER

The blacker the news the more cheerful the Prime Minister
...Why worry boys? Only 1075 civilians have been killed and
only 800 out of our 13,000,000 houses have been destroyed
...The realities behind the Churchill blarney are the prospects
of more bombs and less [sic] sirens.

On 20 September the *Daily Worker* said, 'never has the
press been so degraded...every newspaper has discovered a
blessed word – endurance. Twenty-pound-a-week star writers
pay their tribute to the "courage and endurance" of the masses
...Strangely enough, they meet only big, strong, calm, quiet,
grim and patriotic members of the working class. What the
ordinary man is saying never reaches them.' On 18 October
1940, it claimed that 'Britain's Hitlers' were already 'over here'
and in the Cabinet. 'The working class knows it, and is not
going to be duped...into slackening the struggle of the people
against the enemies of the people.'

Strikes and protests followed. Eric Hobsbawm and Raymond
Williams, the two most respected left-wing intellectuals of my
youth, accepted the accommodation with Nazism and produced a pamphlet that defended the Soviet invasion of Finland
which the Hitler–Stalin pact had authorized. Hobsbawm and
Williams claimed that far from engaging in an imperial land
grab, Stalin was protecting Russia from an invasion by British
imperialists. I've read it twice to be sure, but nowhere do
Hobsbawm and Williams explain how a Britain which was on
her knees and couldn't defend her cities was in a position to
march on Moscow. Williams blithely admitted later that he and
Hobsbawm were just obeying the party's orders. 'We were given
the job as people who could write quickly, from historical
materials supplied for us. You were often in there writing about

topics you did not know very much about, as a professional with words.'

Many people on the Left who weren't convinced communists went along with the deception. Vicars, trade unionists and celebrities signed the People's Convention and prepared through public meetings and propaganda campaigns for a great rally at the Royal Hotel in Bloomsbury in January 1941, a time when Britain had no chance of winning the war and a fair chance of losing it.

Michael Redgrave, father of Corin and Vanessa Redgrave, and one of the few genuine stars the British film industry produced, was among them. He signed up because the convention seemed 'a good socialist document' written by people whose hearts were in the right place. He began to have doubts, but they were assuaged by the creepy figure of D. N. Pritt, KC, MP – a Wykehamist barrister who was on the wrong side of every great question of the mid-twentieth century. Despite everything, it is impossible to like him. Pritt was a type that is too common today: the two-faced civil liberties lawyer. In his time, he was Chairman of the Howard League for Penal Reform and the Bentham Committee for Poor Litigants: no one seemed more dedicated to holding the British state to the highest moral standards. But while fighting for justice at home, he excused and encouraged the worst injustice abroad. In 1937 he defended Stalin's show trials and concluded after one mockery of justice which might have pleased Saddam Hussein that the 'case was genuine and the trial fair'. If he and his fellow QC, Dudley Collard, had a criticism of the amazing admissions of guilt from former Bolsheviks accused of plotting with Adolf Hitler and Leon Trotsky to sabotage the Soviet Union, it was that their confessions were bogus. Not bogus because they had been tortured from them, but bogus because the real object of the devious defendants was to confess so that they could 'shield conspirators within the [Soviet] Union' who were still working for Hitler and Trotsky. Pritt recommended that Stalin must therefore redouble his efforts to find and exterminate the saboteurs who were still at large.

When Michael Redgrave's friends tried to warn him off, Pritt intervened. His chauffeur picked up Redgrave and drove him to Pritt's mansion near Reading. After dinner was served on Imperial porcelain from the tsarist era, they walked around the stream-bordered garden. Pritt comforted Redgrave by saying that Hewlett Johnson, the Dean of Canterbury, and other respectable men and women backed the convention. The poor actor knew nothing about politics. If he had he would have known that Johnson had told the readers of the Left Book Club that: 'The vast moral achievements of the Soviet Union are in no small measure due to the removal of fear...Nothing strikes the visitor more forcibly than the absence of fear.'

Reassured, Redgrave left Pritt and his collection of fine tsarist china 'in a sort of daydream' and returned to London to be the star attraction at the convention's dinner dance at the Royal Hotel.

It was quite an event. The rally attracted 2,234 delegates who allegedly represented 1.2 million trade unionists and political activists. Their number included serving soldiers as well as actors and deans, and the organizers claimed to have issued 632,000 pamphlets and 1,336,000 leaflets.

Harry Pollitt told the delegates that this was a 'gathering of those in deadly seriousness...who want to see the victory of the people of this country over its real enemies in the Churchill government and the policy it is pursuing at the present moment'. Everyone else agreed that Britain should sue for peace with Hitler because Churchill and the Labour Party were as bad as Nazi Germany. The Indian nationalist Krishna Menon, who went on to play a leading part in the struggle for independence, summed up the consensus when he said: 'There is no use in asking whether you would choose British imperialism or Nazism, it is like asking a fish if he wants to be fried in margarine or butter. He doesn't want to be fried at all!'

The Nazis were delighted, naturally, and their propaganda stations heaped praise on the convention. George Orwell looked on and wrote that 'the so-called People's Convention cannot conceivably win power in England, but it may spread enough defeatism to help Hitler very greatly at some critical moment'.

The newspapers agreed and savaged Michael Redgrave. For a while, it seemed as if every face he passed in the street was against him, as it does when the pack comes after you. The BBC banned him from the airwaves, along with twelve other celebrities who had signed the convention. Laurence Olivier and E. M. Forster rallied to their support. Forty Labour MPs circulated a letter against the ban, and Ralph Vaughan Williams withdrew permission for the BBC to broadcast his latest work.

The row blew over because the BBC's charge that Michael Redgrave was opposed to the war effort was ridiculous on a personal level – he tried to volunteer for the Navy and went on to make a string of patriotic war films from *The Way to the Stars* to *The Dam Busters*.

Precisely because he wasn't a supporter of Hitler or Stalin, Redgrave's motives and those of people like him remain interesting. It is platitudinous to say that communism and fascism were substitute religions whose adherents would adopt any tactic as long as their prophets assured them that it would bring the Promised Land closer to view, because it doesn't fully explain what made people communists in the first place, and why the likes of Michael Redgrave were their fellow travellers.

The 'heroic' years of the Left show that you should never underestimate the effect of parochialism on small minds that can't get beyond a hatred of injustice in their own countries. There was much more to hate in the Britain of 1940 with its poverty and imperial conquests than the Britain of today, and a good deal of what the supporters of the convention said was true. Many from the old gang of the Thirties were still in power in 1940 and 1941. In Churchill's mind the Second World War was as much a war to defend the British Empire as defeat Nazi Germany. Londoners didn't always show grim determination during the Blitz and they had no guarantee that they wouldn't face mass unemployment again when the war was over. What the vicars, trade unionists and celebrities couldn't understand was that the democratic system offered the chance of rectifying these evils. Then (and with far less justification now) political hatred moved from a rational complaint to an irresistible obsession that left the afflicted unable to fight against abuses in their own country while recognizing that there were greater abuses of power which they must defend the best of their country's democratic beliefs against. While the Battle of Britain raged and the cities burned, they found themselves on the far right simply by carrying on as they had done before.

A continental philosophical tradition that was very popular with the post-modern theorists held that violent prejudice flowed from irrational hatreds of the alien 'Other'. The Blitz contradicted it by showing that there was a leftish mentality that couldn't bring itself to hate 'the Other' when 'the Other's' bombs were exploding in the street.

The affair was quickly hushed up. Within six months, everyone involved in the demands of the People's Convention for strikes

245

against the war effort wanted to forget what had happened. Hitler invaded the Soviet Union on 22 June 1941 and British communists and their sympathizers instantly became passionate supporters of the Churchill government and the war effort. They airbrushed from their memories the time when they were on Hitler's side. The Churchill government had wanted to censor or arrest everyone associated with the People's Convention in January. By June, it was relying on the Soviet Union to take the full force of Hitler's armies. It was no longer politic to embarrass Stalin's British allies by raking up old muck, particularly as the Communist Party was now instructing the workers in Britain's factories to forget about strikes and work themselves to the bone.

George Orwell lacked their delicacy, and today the People's Convention is remembered only because of the controversies about his life and work. During the war, Orwell and his friends played a parlour game of guessing who would collaborate if Britain was invaded. (You can still play it today.) In March 1949, with the Second World War over and the Cold War beginning, he had a visit from Celia Kirwan, an old flame who was working for the Labour government Orwell supported. She was a member of the Information Research Bureau set up by Ernie Bevin, who by then was Labour's Foreign Secretary. Kirwan wanted to recruit democratic socialists, the only people who had consistently opposed communism throughout the Thirties and Forties. Orwell warned her she must be careful not to hire Stalin's sympathizers inadvertently and gave her names he had come up with in his party game. Most of the names on 'Orwell's list' were of thinkers who had said they supported Stalin, and one turned out to be a Soviet spy: Peter Smollett, an official in the Ministry of Information who had almost prevented the publication of *Animal Farm*. Other names Orwell either put a question mark against or dismissed as too undisciplined to be a truly committed communist. In the latter category was Michael Redgrave because of his support for the People's Convention which had served the interests of Hitler and Stalin. Orwell died in 1950 and therefore missed the commotion the discovery of his list would cause. Every time it resurfaces, the story is the same. Orwell is an informer. The revelation that he had grassed on potential communists was in the words of one recent book 'a body blow' from which 'his reputation as a left wing icon may never recover... As the *Daily Telegraph* noted: "To some it was as if Winston Smith had willingly co-operated with the Thought Police in *1984*".

In his study of Orwell, Christopher Hitchens gently argues that 'to be blacklisted is to be denied employment for political reasons unconnected with job-performance'. Stalin was laying waste to Eastern Europe in the late Forties, and the performance of Foreign Office employees charged with opposing him was likely to be affected if they were Stalin's supporters. It seems a straightforward point, yet nothing can stem the flow of accusations against Orwell. Over fifty years later in a letter to the *Guardian*, Corin Redgrave honourably defended his father's memory from the recurrent bad publicity Orwell's list brought, but then painted on a gloss. The People's Convention was not 'overtly a pacifist or even an anti-war document', he wrote. It merely 'addressed a very widespread suspicion of the government's intentions, and an even more widespread resentment at the lack of provision that had been made for the protection of people in the Blitz'.

That was not the whole truth, as the record of the speeches made at the convention shows, and the widespread belief that his list proved that Orwell was a nark reveals that a consoling myth from the Thirties lives on. The perennial daydream is that the Left is a happy family that includes the totalitarian left among its members. The totalitarian left may be a little wild on occasion, like an unruly teenager, but it is still family and its dirty laundry must never be washed in public. As with other passionate adolescents, the totalitarian left may at times appear preferable to the cautious and pragmatic old fuddy-duddies who win elections: more honest, more dedicated, more idealistic, more truly left. The survival of the myth of the family of the Left shows that a simple point is still being missed: the totalitarian left isn't a part of the family of the democratic left, but the enemy of the democratic left because it doesn't believe in democracy.

Orwell never asked to be a left-wing icon, or any other kind of icon for that matter. He had known there was no family of the Left ever since the communists attempted to murder him when he went to fight Franco in the Spanish Civil War. At the time Orwell passed his list to the Foreign Office, Stalin was slaughtering social democrats and Trotskyists across the newly conquered Eastern Europe. The killings didn't stop with distant relatives. Rather famously, Stalin and Mao devoted considerable energy to slaughtering communists. No one – not Hitler, Mussolini or the CIA – killed as many communists as communists did. If the Left of the Forties was a family, it was a family with Fred and Rose West in charge.

The communists and their allies dropped their support for Hitler only because he invaded the Soviet Union in 1941. Even after that, many intellectual pacifists refused to confront Nazism. John Middleton Murry, the distinguished critic and editor of *Peace News*, clung to the view that 'a Hitlerian Europe would not be quite so terrible as most people believe it would be'. Vera Brittain, whose *Testament of Youth* exposed the horrors of the First World War, lacked the moral imagination to confront the horrors of the Second. She dismissed the first reports of Hitler's gas chambers as 'fantastic'. When in 1945 she could deny them no longer, she complained that the British authorities were using them as a publicity stunt 'partly, at least to divert attention from the havoc produced in German cities by Allied obliteration bombing'.

It was for the best that the Nazis did not invade Britain and install a collaborationist government, and not only for the usual reasons. If they had, not every liberal-left reputation from the Thirties would have survived.

The French left wasn't so fortunate and many pacifist socialists made a terrible journey with the best of intentions. As he looked at the ruins of the Twin Towers in his native New York and then listened to the reaction to Islamist totalitarianism from the Left of the twenty-first century, the American socialist Paul Berman took what happened in the France of the Thirties as a parable for our times.

The leader of the French socialists was Leon Blum, and he knew that the Nazis had to be fought. But a large socialist faction supported by trade unionists and many left-wing intellectuals refused to follow him. The standard motives lay behind their pacifism: a justifiable horror at a conflict that would be worse than the First World War; and a well-founded suspicion of the military-industrial complex and the corporate media. But Berman spotted something more important in that time and in ours: the deadly consequences of the liberal belief in reason.

If they had looked the Nazis in the face, the French socialists would have realized that war was inevitable; you only had to read *Mein Kampf* to know that. Rather than see clearly, the socialists allowed a belief in reason to convince themselves that the German people could not have fallen for an insane cult. Why would they? Wasn't it almost racist to believe that they were not as rational and decent as the French? Take Hitler's attempt to expand the German Reich, perhaps when you saw through the spin it wasn't as threatening as the warmongers maintained. Was it not the case that the Treaty of Versailles had imposed punitive conditions on Germany at the end of the First World War? Wasn't this the 'root cause' of the dispute, and was it not reasonable for Hitler to ask that Germans should be freed from control by the Poles and the Czechs and returned to their mother country? Hitler may have been from the extreme right and they may have been from the democratic left, but an argument wasn't wrong just because Hitler made it.

As in Britain, many French socialists were enthusiastic supporters of the Munich Agreement. They believed, said Berman, in the 'simple-minded optimism' of nineteenth-century liberalism – a 'liberalism of denial'. Human beings were essentially rational. Politicians and journalists who said otherwise were the tools of the arms corporations and media empires that were leading France into a pre-emptive war.

'The anti-war socialists,' writes Berman,

gazed across the Rhine and simply refused to believe that millions of upstanding Germans had enlisted in a political movement whose animating principles were paranoid conspiracy theories, blood-curdling hatreds, mediaeval superstitions and the lure of murder. At Auschwitz the SS said 'Here there is no why.' The anti-war socialists in France believed no such thing. In their eyes, there was always a why.

There was a price to pay even before the fall of France. Clearly, the French socialists couldn't begin to show solidarity with the German socialists who were being persecuted by Hitler. How could they protest at their treatment or organize parliamentary debates calling attention to their plight when they were making excuses for the Hitler who was doing the persecuting? Then there were the Nazis' Jewish victims. The anti-war socialists couldn't tolerate racism. Yet they were determined not to let their sympathies get out of hand. Weren't the Jews always showing their wounds and trying to make others feel guilty for their past suffering? Hitler might be going a bit far, but wasn't it true that a disproportionate number of industrialists and financiers were Jewish? And wasn't it also the case that their leader, Leon Blum, who was urging France to enter a bloody and worthless confrontation with Germany, was, as it happens, Jewish, too?

In 1940, Hitler gave irrefutable proof of his intentions when he invaded France. The French extreme right under the leadership of Marshal Pétain proposed a collaborationist government. Blum and some socialists chose to fight on and ended up dead or in concentration camps, but among their former comrades were socialists who made their accommodation with the new order and

began to see a virtue in Pétain's programme for a new France and a new Europe: a programme of strength and virility, a Europe ruled by a single-party state instead of by the corrupt cliques of bourgeois democracy, a Europe cleansed of the impurities of Judaism and of the Jews themselves, a Europe of the anti-liberal imagination. And in that very remarkable fashion, a number of the anti-war socialists of France came full circle. They had begun as defenders of liberal values and human rights, and they evolved into the defenders of bigotry, tyranny, superstition and mass murder. They were democratic leftists who, through the miraculous workings of the slippery slope and a naïve rationalism, of all things, ended as fascists.

Long ago, you say? Not so long ago.

Indeed not. If people assume that everyone on the Left is good, if they can't tear their eyes from abuses close to home to see the darker world beyond, if they pretend that they are not taking sides when they opt for neutrality and then compound the fault by believing that the irrational has rational causes, then disgrace inevitably follows.

PART TWO

Raging Fevers

Only one faction in American politics has found itself able to make excuses for the kind of religious fanaticism that immediately menaces us in the here and now. And that faction, I am sorry and furious to say, is the Left. From the first day of the immolation of the World Trade Center, right down to the present moment, a gallery of pseudo-intellectuals has been willing to represent the worst face of Islam as the voice of the oppressed. How can these people bear to reread their own propaganda? Suicide murderers in Palestine – disowned and denounced by the new leader of the PLO – described as the victims of 'despair'. The forces of al-Qaeda and the Taliban represented as misguided spokespeople for anti-globalization. The blood-maddened thugs in Iraq, who would rather bring down the roof on a suffering people than allow them to vote, pictured prettily as 'insurgent' or even, by Michael Moore, as the moral equivalent of our Founding Fathers.

Christopher Hitchens, 2004

CHAPTER NINE

'Kill Us, We Deserve It'

Nobody move. Everything will be OK. If you try to make any moves, you'll endanger yourself and the airplane. Just stay quiet.
Mohamed Atta to the passengers and crew of American
Airlines Flight 11 from Boston to Los Angeles,
11 September 2001

ALTHOUGH Mohamed Atta could demonstrate his hatreds in a brutal fashion, he was hopeless at explaining them. In his last will and testament, the 33-year-old Egyptian showed little more than a loathing of women. 'I don't want a pregnant woman or a person who is not clean to come and say good-bye to me because I don't approve it,' he instructed. 'I don't want any women to go to my grave at all during my funeral or on any occasion thereafter.' These were strange demands from a man who was to spend his last nights in American strip clubs, but an attraction to and fear of emancipated women fuels Islamism and all our other religious reactions. To be fair, Atta also had difficulties with the boys, for he continued, 'the person who will wash my body near my genitals must wear gloves on his hands so he won't touch my genitals'.

He wrote the will in 1996. The FBI found final instructions to his fellow hijackers in his luggage, instructions which he must have written a few hours before he went out to murder.

Somewhat ungratefully in the light of the strenuous apologetics that were to be made on his behalf, he didn't mention Palestine, Kashmir, Chechnya or any other Muslim grievance of the day, let alone castigate the World Trade Center's brokers for being a part of an unequal economic system. Apocalyptic religion filled his mind, not politics. 'You will be entering the happiest life, everlasting life,' he promised the hijackers. 'Be cheerful, for you have only moments between you and your eternity, after which a happy and satisfying life begins.' To get themselves in shape to meet Allah and all his virgins, the hijackers must 'shave the extra hair from the body. Pray. Purify your head. Cleanse it from dross.' They were to 'put on tight clothes' because 'this is the custom of the good predecessors. Allah blessed them, for they tightened their clothes before battle.' His men were to carry on praying all the way to the airport, and when they boarded their planes they were to say, 'Oh God open all the doors for me.'

Atta didn't have a word of compassion for those he was about to kill, and I suppose it would have been surprising if he had. More unusually, he barely acknowledged their existence. Terrorists usually employ some kind of humbug about the innocent dead not being as innocent as their grieving families would have you believe. They picked the wrong moment to walk by a military base, for example, or drank in a pub used by soldiers. Atta said nothing about why thousands had to die.

Perhaps he thought his choice of targets would make the 'root cause' of death self-evident. Attacking the Pentagon spoke for itself, but while the World Trade Center was a symbol of modern business, crashing planes loaded with crew, passengers and aviation fuel into the middle of New York risked killing the poor along with the rich, the brown and black along with the white, the Muslim along with the Christian, Jew, Hindu and atheist. All they would have in common is that they would all be civilians. Atta did not think it worth his while to blame the victims. If the papers he left were a true guide, he barely thought about them. Their class, colour and creed didn't matter. Who died and how many died depended on the will of a pitiless god.

Three weeks after 9/11, Tony Blair asked the 2001 Labour Party Conference: 'If they could have murdered not 7,000 but 70,000 does anyone doubt they would have done so and rejoiced in it?'

If Blair had gone on to 700,000, no reasonable person could have doubted him. The bombing of London on 7 July 2005, which produced a small number of fatalities by Islamist standards, made his case better than larger massacres. Two of the four British-raised murderers exploded their rucksacks on London Underground's Circle Line: one in the tunnel by Aldgate station and one in the tunnel on the approach to Edgware Road. Aldgate is on the edge of George Lansbury's East End, just on the wrong side of the dividing line between the glass towers of the City and the narrow streets of the slums. Most people knew that the East End was the home of Britain's largest Bengali community, and British Muslims knew it better than most. Similarly, Edgware Road station is in Bayswater, and the Lebanese restaurants and Egyptian cafés of London's Arab quarter fill the streets around it.

Shezad Tanweer, the Aldgate bomber, was a nice boy who worked in his father's fish and chip shop until he returned from a holiday in Pakistan boasting of his new godliness and his admiration for Osama bin Laden. If he had thought about whom among his fellow countrymen and women he wanted to kill and why, he might have got out at the next stop and exploded his bomb in the heart of the City.

Before he embraced Islamism, Mohammad Sidique Khan was a respectable young man. He worked in a school and his mother-in-law had been to a Buckingham Palace garden party. He might have changed trains at Edgware Road and in two stops been in Maida Vale, one of London's richest suburbs. In the event, neither Tanweer nor Khan worried that bombs in Aldgate and Edgware might kill many Muslims whose interests they professed to champion. It didn't matter who they killed or how many they killed, as long as they killed.

Like ordinary terrorists, ordinary murderers offer a reason for selecting their victims: she died because she said she didn't love me; he died because he was muscling in on my corner of the heroin market. A blank absence of discrimination marked out the Islamist targeting of civilians. If victim and bomber were to come back to life, the latter would be unable to tell the former why he had died rather than the next man or woman.

The murders of 202 people in the Bali bar bombings of October 2002 offered further embarrassment to those trying to find a respectable 'root cause' to explain away atrocity, and not only because thirty-eight Indonesians died along with the Australian, British and other tourists. Osama bin Laden did give a reason, but it wasn't the right one. He said Australians died because Australia was an *anti-imperialist* rather than an imperialist power, whose troops had reversed the annexation of (largely Catholic) East Timor by (largely Muslim) Indonesia, which had so angered Noam Chomsky twenty-five years before. Australia had taken back conquered Islamic land therefore Australians must die. In Madrid in 2004, the 'root cause' of the atrocity was Spanish support for the war in Iraq. Yet the Islamic Combatant Group did not attempt to attack government or military targets, it just blew up commuter trains carrying supporters and opponents of the Spanish presence in Iraq alike. The second Intifada was as big a disaster for the Palestinian cause as the first was a success because Hamas was in charge of most of the violence, and Hamas killed any Jew it could – Jews on buses, Jews in pizza restaurants, Jews in bars – and freed Israel to unilaterally draw new borders and protect them with a wall.

There was a grotesque vignette when Chechen Islamists seized a school at Beslan in southern Russia in 2004 that captured the almost whimsical nature of the violence. Early on, the terrorists made what looked like a humane gesture and allowed twenty-six mothers with young children to leave the school. There was a catch: each mother could take only one child. Zalina Dzandarova had two children at the school: a toddler, Alan, and a 6-year-old daughter Alana.

She made an instant decision to save her son. She tried to pass her daughter to her sister-in-law, but the Islamists caught her and pulled the child away.

> Alana was clinging to me and holding my hand firmly. But they separated us, and said: 'You go with the boy.' I cried. I begged them. Alana cried. The women around us wept. One of the Chechens said: 'If you don't go now, you don't go at all. You stay here with your children...and we will shoot all of you.' I didn't have time to think what I was doing. I pressed Alan even stronger to myself, and I went out, and I heard all the time how my daughter was crying and calling for me behind my back. I thought my heart would break into pieces there and then.

The 'root cause' of the school siege was Russia's cruel war in Chechnya and the colonization of the Chechen cause by Islamists, but it can't explain why they freed one child, but not another and eventually precipitated the deaths of 344 civilians, 186 of them children.

Atta set the pattern of blanket enmity. His instructions to his fellow hijackers go on at tedious length about the pious thoughts that must be in their heads and the need for tight trousers. He acknowledges that murder is the business of the day only in passing when he says that 'if God grants one of you a slaughter, you should perform it as an offering on behalf of your father and your mother, for they are owed by you.' The *New York Review of Books* asked Kanan Makiya and an Arab colleague, Hassan Mneimneh, to explain his thinking. They spotted that Atta had used *dhabaha* – 'slaughter' – rather than the more natural and normal Arabic, *qatala* – 'kill'. Atta was explicitly invoking the memory of that model totalitarian citizen, Abraham, whose creepy willingness to sacrifice his son on God's orders was celebrated by Judaism, Christianity and, in Islam, with the ritual slaughter of sheep on the 'feast of the sacrifice'. Makiya and Mneimneh said that in Atta's mind the victim was a gift from God, a substitute for the sheep a gracious Lord put in the place of Abraham's son. Atta's martyrdom and the thousands of death it brought was a 'private act of worship'. The rich world was learning about 'a terrifying new form of nihilism'.

Nihilist it was. Violence was the only point of the violence because the Islamist dream of a Caliphate – a sexist, homophobic, racist, imperialist theocracy that would oppress about a billion Muslims – was impossible, as well as being undesirable from the traditional liberal perspective. But whether Islamism was as new an ideology as Makiya thought was open to question. Without doubt, the alliance between al-Qaeda and the Taliban theocracy foretold a new terror from which we are unlikely to escape. Those who said the twenty-first century began on 11 September 2001 meant that the prospect of a tyrannical state or arms dealers handing weapons of mass destruction to Islamists or another sect whose name we don't know yet would never be unthinkable again. It would nag in the background from then on, like a jarring low hum.

As an ideology, however, Islamism wasn't all new. Osama bin Laden proved it when he celebrated his dead minions' successes in New York and Washington and – at last! – gave the 'root cause' of the attacks. Interviewed by Al-Jazeera in October 2001, he had the presence of mind to mention the wars in Palestine, Kashmir, the Philippines, Somalia, the Sudan and all the other countries where Islamists were rubbing up against other cultures. This clearly wasn't just throat clearing, he was engaged, but his surge of energy came when he let out the elated cry: 'The values of this Western civilization under the leadership of America have been destroyed. Those awesome symbolic towers that speak of liberty, human rights and humanity have been destroyed. They have gone up in smoke.'

He didn't say that the towers were a symbol of capitalism – as a poor little rich boy from Saudi Arabia's second wealthiest family bin Laden made an unconvincing anti-capitalist – but of 'liberty, human rights and humanity'. On the other side of the divide and the other side of the coin, the Christian fanatic Jerry Falwell showed a similar disgust for the freedoms of modern society. Like bin Laden, he believed that the atrocities were an act of God. The Lord was punishing the United States for 'the gays and the lesbians who are actively trying to make that an alternative lifestyle, the ACLU, People for the American Way, all of them who have tried to secularize America. I point the finger in their face and say "you helped this happen". '

It was the best of the West Islamism was against not the

worst, and its detestation of Enlightenment values was nothing new. Since the beginnings of modern democracy in the American colonies of the eighteenth century, plenty on the Right had dreamed of liberty and human rights going up in smoke. By 'the Right', I don't mean the American Republicans or the British Conservatives or the French Gaullists, but the deep right of the counter-revolution that raged against the American and French Revolutions and the slow evolution of Britain into a democratic society. In the eighteenth and nine-teenth centuries, it took the form of aristocratic reaction and ethnic nationalism. In the twentieth, 'scientific' racism and fascism. The themes and arguments of the vile tradition appeared with remarkable consistency in Saddam Hussein's Iraq, Iran, the Sudan, as well as the ideologies of the Islamist terror groups.

As early as 1770, one Cornelius de Pauw, a Dutch naturalist, sounded like half the novelists and playwrights in Britain today (and all the novelists and playwrights in France) when he poured scorn on everything American. You could tell it was a blighted continent by its animals, he said. They were 'for the most part inelegantly shaped and badly deformed'. Many lacked tails; others suffered from a disproportion between the number of digits on their front and back feet. America was a land 'inundated by lizards, snakes and by reptiles and insects monstrous in their size and in the strength of their poison'.

Their sickness was contagious. When well-bred European animals crossed the Atlantic with pedigrees guaranteed by the *Ancien Régime* and fingers and toes in perfect proportion, 'their size diminished' and they lost 'a part of their instinct and capacity'. Dogs stopped barking and women became infertile.

It was here that de Pauw got to the nub of his argument. His real subject was European women (and men) who went to live in the experiment in democracy, not his alleged specialism of natural history. Today's anti-American Europeans scream about McDonald's and Wal-Mart and can't bring themselves to acknowledge the valuable as well as the trashy in American high and popular culture. De Pauw anticipated them and upheld the virtues of aristocratic Europe by saying that America's evil climate passed on the deformities of its animals to its human population. The inherent inferiority of the new democracy was evident because 'in all of America, from Cape Horn to the Hudson Bay, there has never appeared a philosopher, a scholar, an artist, or a thinker whose name merits being included in the history of science or who has served humanity'. (This in 1770 when Paine, Franklin, Jefferson, Hamilton and Washington were alive and getting ready to kick.)

Or as the English novelist Margaret Drabble said in 2003

My anti-Americanism has become almost uncontrollable. It has possessed me, like a disease. It rises up in my throat like acid reflux, that fashionable American sickness. I now loathe the United States and what it has done to Iraq and the rest of the helpless world . . . There, I have said it. I have tried to control my anti-Americanism, remembering the many Americans that I know and respect, but I can't keep it down any longer. I detest Disneyfication, I detest Coca-Cola, I detest burgers, I detest sentimental and violent Hollywood movies that tell lies about history.

De Pauw is a joke today, although his contemporaries treated him with respect, and Margaret Drabble's display of the persistence of class hatred of American vulgarity is more daft than serious. No one should find Friedrich Nietzsche, a proto-Nazi philosopher, or Martin Heidegger, an actual Nazi philosopher, funny and both, naturally, were against American democracy. Nietzsche feared it couldn't be confined. 'The faith of the Americans today is more and more becoming the faith of Europeans,' he wailed. Heidegger believed that Hitler's Germany must offer a virtuous alternative to America, 'the site of the catastrophe'.

A dread infected the philosophers of the counter-revolution as it disturbs their heirs among the pseudo-leftist theorists of today. They feared the masses would abandon their prince-lings, priests and thinkers and embrace a democratic culture that would push their former rulers and sages to the margins. 'Images of America have always haunted the European psyche,' wrote Richard Wolin, a historian of irrational ideas:

> Among Europeans America has often assumed the form of a nightmare vision, a degenerate image of Europe's own future. Such judgments, however, reveal more about the state of the European mind than they do about America per se. They betray the anxieties and obsessions of European scholars and intellectuals confronted with modernity, 'progress' and the discomforting specter of democratization...This dystopian view of America is hardly a thing of the past. [It] informs a certain anti-intellectual spirit that pervades contemporary cultural life – a spirit best expressed by the fashionable view that Reason and the Enlightenment, instead of setting us free, are a curse.

You find similar fears and obsessions in Islamism. Sayyid Qutb of the Muslim Brotherhood and the chief ideologue of Islamist terror, was shocked into a famous demonstration of repressed sexuality when he visited a dance at a church hall in that fleshpot of the Rockies, Greeley, Colorado, in 1949. 'The hall swarmed with legs…Arms circled arms, lips met lips, chests met chests, and the atmosphere was full of love.' There is disgust in these words, but an attraction too. The swarming legs of Greeley were for Qutb a manifestation of the *jahiliyya* – the paganism Muhammad had fought in Arabia. For Qutb, paganism had returned to dominate not only sex-obsessed Americans but also the Muslim states. Qutb had no doubt that only violence could cleanse the pagan world and return it to the truths of early Islam. The Prophet Muhammad waged war against paganism and so must today's revolutionary vanguard of true believers 'using whatever resources are practically available'. Yet even as Qutb demanded the annihilation of paganism, he acknowledged the seductive appeal of prosperity and democracy. They brought 'marvellous material comforts and high-level ambitions', he said with a mixture of admiration and fear.

But democracy and prosperity could not be for the Islamic Caliphate he wished to restore, any more than the thinkers of the counter-Enlightenment believed that they could be for Europe. Islamism differs from conventional Muslim belief in that it is a political movement, which sees the answer to every moral and social problem in the dictatorial implementation of Islamic teaching. Its founders were explicit about which modern political tradition they were drawing on. Hassan al-Banna, the Egyptian who created the Muslim Brotherhood in 1928, responded to the inability of the Muslim world to compete with Western colonial powers by arguing that only a restored and pure Islamic Caliphate could end the humiliation of the Arabs, and only violence could bring that restoration. He followed the example of other opponents of Western democracy by organizing his followers in 'falanges' modelled on General Franco's, and admiring Hitler's brown shirts.

Abul Ala Mawdudi, who founded Jamaat-i-Islaami, the south Asian sister organization of the Muslim Brotherhood in 1945 in British India, described how his Islamist Utopia would be totalitarian.

> A state of this sort cannot evidently restrict the scope of its activities. Its approach is universal and all-embracing. Its sphere of activity is coextensive with the whole of human life. It seeks to mould every aspect of life and activity in consonance with its moral norm and programmes of social reform. In such a state, no one can regard any field of his affairs as personal and private. Considered from this perspective the Islamic state bears a kind of resemblance to the fascist or communist states.

Democracy was unacceptable to the thinkers of the ultra-right because it weakened and corrupted the chosen people be they Muslims or Germans. Notions of purity run through reactionary thought and – though its sympathizers hated the comparison – through communism. It may be the God-given purity, which gave the absolute monarchs of Europe a divine right to govern. It may be the purity of the tribe with its organic connection to blood and soil. It may be the pure faith that came from submission to the teachings of the popes, rabbis or the Koran. Or it may be the purity of the classless society that freed workers from alienation. Whatever purity's origin, modernity fouled the clear pool. Hitler admired the British racist theorist Houston Stewart Chamberlain because Chamberlain believed that people could belong only to the organic *Volk* with roots deep in *Blud und Boden*. Democracy revolted Chamberlain because a foreigner could become British by the legal process of acquiring the right to be a resident, rather than the biological process of being born into the tribe's bloodline. He said British citizenship was debased because it could be had 'by every Batuso nigger' for two shillings and six-pence. When Hitler talked of America and Britain being Jew-ridden, he meant that the citizenship laws of the democracies had corrupted racial purity.

Islamists substituted religion for race but the thought was the same. For Qutb the infectious spread of *jahiliyya* had so stained Muslim purity that 'true Islamic values could never enter our hearts'. The whole environment of modern Muslim states, 'people's beliefs and ideas, habit and art, rules and laws is *jahiliyya*'. The ubiquity of the corruption made challenges to its hegemonic power appear futile. But bin Laden none the less declared war on America in the Nineties. His *casus belli* had nothing to do with the concerns of the Left. It was the sacrile-gious presence of American troops in the holy land of Saudi Arabia which infuriated him. They were there to protect the kingdom from invasion by Saddam Hussein, who hadn't been overthrown in 1991 when the world had the chance – a deci-sion that you could make the 'root cause' of the 9/11 attacks, if you wanted to play consequences. (And why not? It made as much sense as any of the other root causes offered at the time.)

Bin Laden was convinced that American power was puny because its pampered soldiers weren't willing to die for their cause. He bragged to the Clinton administration that his followers 'love death as you love life. They inherit dignity, pride, courage, generosity, truthfulness and sacrifice from father to father... These youths are different from your soldiers. Your problem will be how to convince your troops to fight, while our problem will be how to restrain our youths to wait for their turn in fighting.' Their suicidal sacrifice had a strategic purpose. In bin Laden's mind the sight of young men destroying themselves would shock the Muslims out of the corruptions of paganism and turn them into warriors in the army of God.

In *Occidentalism*, their account of prejudices about Western democracy, Ian Buruma and Avishai Margalit show that a relentless theme of the enemies of democracy from the romantic nationalists in the nineteenth century to fascist Germany and Japan in the twentieth is that it produces flabby and effeminate societies, run by money-grubbing traders and equivocating politicians. Each wave of ultra-rightists asserted that the armies of the democracies will be no match for warriors ready to kill and be killed on the orders of a charismatic leader. Nationalist, fascist and Islamist alike believed that a 'rootless, arrogant, greedy, decadent, frivolous cosmopolitanism' drove the trading cities of the democracies. They all condemned Western thought for upholding the cold and specialized reasoning of the scientific method rather than the holistic mysteries of tribe and church. They all believed that the citizens of the democracies were bourgeois cowards; too selfishly fearful for their personal safety to risk a confrontation.

The messianic worship of pure blood and the idolization of blood sacrifices are at the root of fascism, and it is an enormous mistake to ennoble the fascist critique of 'corrupt' and 'hypocritical' democracies by pretending it is just an extension of the ordinary arguments and confrontations of democratic debate. If you oppose genuinely disastrous American policies, you most emphatically are not aiding and abetting totalitarianism, although far too many on the American right are now prepared to say that you are. Nor do critiques of blind faith in the market or progress lead you into the camp of anti-Enlightenment mystics. You are not echoing fascist themes because fascism along with its predecessors in the counter-Enlightenment and successors in Islamism was not a rational critique of this or that failure of a democratic government, but an assault on democracy and human rights as malign in themselves. At times of crisis in the last two centuries, the counter-revolutionary argument has proved very popular: for who has not felt the lure of the tribe and a yearning for the heroic? Who has not thought democratic freedoms were no antidote to frustrated ambitions and daily miseries, or not been revolted by unregulated markets allowing sharks in suits to make fortunes in the City and Wall Street and worthless exhibitionists to become celebrities?

Fascism's case against democracy ended with the assertion that, in any case, democracy was a façade that hid the real rulers of the world – the Freemasons, the conniving foreigners or the Jews. Their schemes could be undone if those who knew the best interests of the chosen people shook them from their lethargy by seizing power or taking the battle to the citadel of their enemies.

The US commission on the 9/11 attacks found that Atta had bought the whole package. He was a man lost in a conspiratorial wilderness where nothing was what it seemed. The commission sent its researchers to talk to students who knew him when he studied in Germany and found he had 'virulently anti-Semitic and anti-American opinions, ranging from condemnations of what he described as a global Jewish movement centered in New York City that supposedly controlled the financial world and the media, to polemics against governments of the Arab world'. Even Saddam Hussein was an 'American stooge' in Atta's mind, whom Washington left in power 'to give it an excuse to intervene in the Middle East'. Atta's father was an Egyptian lawyer from the same mould. He dismissed the evidence against his son and said he had been framed by a sinister conspiracy of Jews.

With commendable frankness, the Islamists described

how they were against every aspect of post-Enlightenment modernity. Yussuf al-Ayyeri, one of Osama bin Laden's closest associates, who went under the *nom de guerre* Abu Muhammad, explained that all history was a 'perpetual war between belief and unbelief'. By 'belief', he meant his version of Islam, which 'annuls all other religions and creeds' and must destroy them or be destroyed. The past century had seen repeated assaults on the faithful, he explained. The first form of unbelief to attack was 'modernism', which led to the emergence in the lands of Islam of states based on ethnic identities and territorial dimensions rather than religious faith. The second was nationalism, which, imported from Europe, divided Muslims into Arabs, Persians, Turks and others. The third form of unbelief was socialism.

None of the above is to deny that Islamism has Islamic roots. Many careful scholars have written about its links to and departures from mainstream Muslim traditions. But this book is about the rich world's liberal-left and how it can come to pander to its enemies and betray its friends. Looking at how Islamism continued the fascist traditions of the counter-Enlightenment shows why it should have been easy to oppose. Many in 2001 found opposition easy, but a part of the Left wiggled and waffled as it made excuses for the extreme right.

Not since the Sixties had leftish magazines known the popularity they enjoyed in the months after 9/11. The then new journalistic phenomenon of the blogosphere bounced articles around the Net from radical journals that the readers of the blogs had never heard of or given up on years before.

Abuse followed by the electronic equivalent of the sack-load. Leftist reporters on the receiving end felt that American conservatives might have invented the Internet so they could denounce traitors on their websites and invite their readers to direct their anger to the culprits' inboxes. However loud the furious cries became, guffaws drowned them out. There was almost a carnival atmosphere in cyberspace as bloggers took their knives to the latest moral idiocy, gobbled it up and waited with broad smiles for the next course.

After 'blog' the next neologism the bloggers created was 'fisking'. Novices surfing the Net would see perplexing links headlined 'click to see *The Nation* given a thorough fisking' or 'Michael Moore fisked to within an inch of his life here'. Old hands would announce 'I'm going to fisk this' and beam with pride when friends congratulated them with cries of 'well fisked' and 'you're a natural, born fisker'.

The entry in *The Jargon File* dictionary of technical slang reads,

> **fisking:** n. [blogosphere; very common] A point-by-point refutation of a blog entry or (especially) news story. A really stylish fisking is witty, logical, sarcastic and ruthlessly factual; flaming or hand waving is considered poor form. Named after Robert Fisk, a British journalist who was a frequent (and deserving) early target of such treatment.

The unfortunate Fisk was a Chomskyan foreign correspondent for the London *Independent* who could see the good in every system of government but his own. He was on the Afghan border in December 2001 as the American-led forces fought the Taliban and al-Qaeda, and filed an account of his treatment at the hands of Afghan refugees. Andrew Sullivan, a British journalist based in the States who became the first blogger to reach a mass audience, performed the first fisking when he took it apart.

Like so many of his kind, Fisk didn't do light and shade. But he began with an unintentionally comic introduction which Evelyn Waugh could not have improved on.

'They started by shaking hands. We said, "*Salaam aleikum*" – peace be upon you – then the first pebbles flew past my face. A small boy tried to grab my bag. Then another. Then someone punched me in the back. Then young men broke my glasses, began smashing stones into my face and head. I couldn't see for the blood pouring down my forehead and swamping my eyes.'

If *Independent* readers thought their correspondent was the victim of an unprovoked assault, he swiftly put them right. Even when Fisk was on the floor, battered and bleeding and at his assailants' mercy, guilt rather than fear overwhelmed him. 'I understood. I couldn't blame them for what they were doing. In fact, if I were the Afghan refugees of Kila Abdullah, close to the Afghan-Pakistan border, I would have done just the same to Robert Fisk. Or any other Westerner I could find.'

Sullivan said this example of the victim blaming himself was a 'classic piece of leftist pathology'. Fisk was saying that 'some-one – anyone – is either innocent or guilty purely by racial or cultural association. An average Westerner is to be taken as an emblem of an entire culture and treated as such. Any random Westerner will do. Individual notions of responsibility or morality are banished, as one group is labelled blameless and another irredeemably malign.' Fisk reinforced Sullivan's point by saying that the men who nearly killed him 'should never have done so but [their] brutality was *entirely the product of others*'. He was forced to punch an attacker in the mouth, but he didn't blame him for provoking the violence. The Afghan was 'innocent of any crime *except that of being the victim of the world*'.

Such masochism – 'I would have done just the same to

Robert Fisk' – was hard to match, but my then editor at the *New Statesman* came close when he wrote its most notorious leader since the whitewashing of Stalin in the Thirties. Mohamed Atta didn't bother to blame the workers in the World Trade Center for their own deaths, but the *Statesman* like many other journals of the Left was prepared to find incriminating evidence on his behalf.

> American bond traders, you may say, are as innocent and as undeserving of terror as Vietnamese or Iraqi peasants . . . Well, yes and no, because Americans, unlike Iraqis and many others in poor countries, at least have the privileges of democracy and freedom that allow them to vote and speak in favour of a different order. If America seems a greedy and overweening power, that is partly because its people have willed it. They preferred George Bush to both Al Gore and Ralph Nader. These are harsh judgments but we live in harsh times.

A harsh judge of my former editor would have noted that al-Qaeda declared war on the United States when Bill Clinton was its President and Al Gore its Vice-President, and that Islamism was the sworn enemy of the human rights that robust campaigner for the underdog, Ralph Nader, had spent his life defending. Michael Moore deserved credit for realizing that the dead of New York included people who did vote for Al Gore and Ralph Nader, but then he went and spoilt it all by bellowing: 'If someone did this to get back at Bush, they did so by killing thousands of people who DID NOT vote for him! Boston, New York, DC and the planes' destination of California – these were places that voted AGAINST BUSH.'

The stupid white man seemed to think it was wrong for al-Qaeda to direct its fire against Woody Allen's Manhattan but reasonable to crash planes into Thomas Frank's Kansas City.

The *London Review of Books* in Bloomsbury invited its regular contributors to share their thoughts with its academic readership. The former friends of the Iraqi opposition were unable to bring themselves to think about the nature of an extreme right they had once castigated. Writing from Columbia University in New York, Edward Said mentioned Muslim Americans' fear of a backlash, which was real but largely groundless, mercifully, and criticized the crudity of George W. Bush for saying that he wanted the people who had attacked his country taken 'dead or alive'. He said it was a 'horrible deed' but couldn't bring himself to discuss or criticize the Islamist ideology. To understand is not to pardon, but to ignore is, and what was shocking about Said and so many of his fellow intellectuals was their determined unwillingness to see al-Qaeda for what it was. Mary Beard, a Cambridge classics don, cleared her throat by saying 'the horror of the tragedy was enormously intensified by the ringside seats we were offered through telephone answering machines and text-messages', and then got down to business. 'But' – there was always a but –

> when the shock had faded more hard-headed reaction set in. This wasn't just the feeling that, however tactfully you dress it up, the United States had it coming. [Not very tactfully in her case, the families of the dead could be forgiven for thinking.] But there is also the feeling that all the 'civilised world' (a phrase which Western leaders seem able to use without a trace of irony) is paying the price for its glib definitions of 'terrorism' and its refusal to listen to what the 'terrorists' have to say.

The rub was that like many other members of the leftish intelligentsia, she did not listen to what the 'terrorists' had to say. Writer after writer was incapable of grasping that people with brown skins were as capable as people with white skins were of forming a fascistic movement and murdering and oppressing others. Whether the apparently uniform ignorance was a true reflection of all the views of the *LRB*'s learned contributors is an open question. There was a minor intellectual scandal when Professor David Marquand, a distinguished writer on British politics, revealed that the editor had refused to publish a piece he had written praising Tony Blair for his handling of the crisis. She told him she couldn't 'square it with my conscience to praise so wholeheartedly Blair's conduct since September 11. I feel quite strongly that the US response, and *ipso facto* ours, has been at the very least questionable.' (Even liberal literary editors censor, but they usually dress it up more tactfully than that.)

Leftish intellectuals said the attacks were really about Palestine, although none of the hijackers was Palestinian, or an inchoate protest against global capitalism, even though al-Qaeda received the petro-dollars of Saudi plutocrats. All shared an instant reaction to the 9/11 atrocities that they must have been the fault of the United States or the West.

Sexist judges used to say that women who went out in miniskirts were 'asking for it'. Their provocative dress was the 'root cause' of their rape. So it was with the intellectual left after 9/11. We 'had it coming'; we were the root cause of our own murder. In mitigation, you could say that if women wore veils or never went out then the incidence of rape would fall. Equally if Western powers had left East Timor under Indonesian rule, promised not to oppose Islamists if they attempted to take over Saudi Arabia or any other state, ended their efforts to promote democracy and women's rights and imposed Sharia law on their Muslim minorities, they would have been on the receiving end of fewer assaults. The old sexist judge and the modern literary intellectual are not entirely wrong. The fault with their victim-blaming reasoning is that the victimizers disappear behind the wall of excuses. Just as judges once removed responsibility from rapists and didn't want to know why some men raped and others did not, so intellectual leftists made mass murder appear a natural response to external provocation and didn't ask themselves if any free society could remain free if it didn't provoke Islamists.

The Left's critics attacked it at the time for wanting to appease al-Qaeda, but the charge was too kind. Giving Hitler territory in Czechoslovakia appeared a rational solution to German grievances. Even if it proved to be a disaster, you can understand why the appeasers thought their policy of accepting Hitler's demands would avert war. The difference in 2001 was that the Islamists couldn't have what they wanted because the Caliphate they wanted was impossible. Rather than listening to what bin Laden was saying, leftish intellectuals adopted a stance for which I can find no precedent: they urged the appeasement of demands that hadn't been made. They used bin Laden as an ally to promote their own wish list and called for a limit to globalization, the withdrawal of Israeli troops from the West Bank or a rerun of the disputed 2000 American Presidential election. The contrast with the Thirties isn't flattering. Say what you like about the appeasers of Munich, but they studied Hitler, even if they got him wrong. Their successors didn't know what the Islamists wanted and didn't want to find out.

I was no different. My instant reaction to the 9/11 attacks was that they were a nuisance that got in the way of more pressing concerns. Throughout the Nineties, I had been writing about the overweening power of big business and how it could corrupt democratic governments. I had lambasted New Labour for its love of Conservative crime policies and attacks on civil liberties for years. Attacking Tony Blair was what I liked doing – what got me out of bed in the morning. Accepting that fascism is worse than Western democracy, even Western democracies governed by George W. Bush and Tony Blair, sounds easy in theory, but it is very difficult to do in practice when you are a habitual enemy of the status quo in your own country. Seeing fascism for what it is means shaking yourself out of old habits and looking at the world afresh. In my case as a journalist, it involved going to the trouble of finding new contacts and thinking through new arguments, as well as the unpleasantness that comes with disagreeing with people you took to be friends and finding yourself on the same side as people you took to be enemies. The easy option, for me at any rate, was to carry on as if nothing had happened. I berated Bush for failing to predict and prevent the atrocities, as if a child could have seen them coming at bedtime on 10 September 2001. I followed up with articles calling for the Americans to suspend the invasion of Afghanistan because Oxfam and Christian Aid said the bombing campaign would stop aid reaching starving villagers and millions would die in a famine. (In the event, they did not die. Instead, 3.5 million refugees returned home once the Taliban was gone.)

My pieces weren't written in good faith. I wanted anything associated with Tony Blair to fail because that would allow me to return to the easy life of attacking him. If propagating scare stories from Oxfam and Christian Aid allowed me to undermine him, then I was more than prepared to do it. Like the fellow travellers with the Hitler–Stalin pact, I couldn't walk and chew gum at the same time: criticize the faults of democratic governments while supporting democracy against its enemies. The Taliban and al-Qaeda were the embodiment of everything I was against – superstition, mass murder, racism, misogyny, ignorance, tyranny – but as I said before, people oppose what they know.

Not that anything I or anyone else in the leftish press said mattered. After 9/11, intelligent liberals, as well as conservatives, denounced and mocked the views of self-deluding leftists in equal measure. In *How Mumbo-Jumbo Conquered the World*, his dissection of modern delusions, Francis Wheen said that the claims of a portion of the Left to possess a sceptical intelligence had been destroyed by its inability to look squarely at a cult of death. 'Like generals who fight the last war instead of the present one, socialists and squishy progressives were so accustomed to regarding American imperialism as the only source of evil in the world that they couldn't imagine any other enemy.'

The conservative historian Geoffrey Wheatcroft said that Marxism had died long before the Berlin Wall came down. Democratic socialists had given up as well and embraced market economics to varying degrees. The 9/11 atrocities marked the death of something vaguer: a leftist mentality or style that flourished without practical left-wing politics. It wasn't just that 'clever and famous people' had made fools of themselves – they had done that many times before – but that 200 years after the French Revolution 'a large part of the progressive tradition' had made a final declaration of bankruptcy.

There was, and is, a distinction between the practical and intellectual left. In the 1930s, the 'practical' left on either side of the Atlantic weren't much interested in communism, but got on with making the New Deal, or preparing the Labour Party to win a decisive election. It was the intellectual left, or part of it, which lost its heart to Stalin. But if those Stalinoids were nasty enough when they explained away the Moscow trials, they weren't silly, and they could plausibly believe that history was on their side. To re-read that catalogue of nonsense [written after 9/11] is to realize that their descendants simply aren't serious any longer. If the old Leninist left was buried politically in the rubble of the Berlin wall, the literary-academic intelligentsia disappeared morally in the ashes of ground zero.

We last met Wheatcroft when he was in a tizzy about 'those chatterers' winning the argument against Margaret Thatcher in the Eighties. Now – after two decades of waiting – he could at last say that they had discredited themselves beyond rehabilitation.

He couldn't have been more wrong. When New York and Washington were bombed in 2001, you were a bankrupt crank if you said America had it coming. When they came for London in 2005, conventionally minded BBC presenters would gasp if an interviewee suggested that there was more to Islamist violence than a dislike of British foreign policy.

Up to a point, the eruption of liberal bad faith was the fault of George W. Bush and Tony Blair, but only up to a point. Longer-term trends in both the liberal mainstream and the nihilist left had created the ideal circumstances for millions of people who considered themselves thoughtful and honourable to make a nonsense of their beliefs.

CHAPTER TEN

The Disgrace of the
Anti-War Movement

*Though in neither case was the nature of the regime the
reason for conflict, it was decisive for me in the judgement as
to the balance of risk for action or inaction. Both countries –
Afghanistan and Iraq – now face an uncertain struggle for the
future. But both at least now have a future. The one country
in which you will find an overwhelming majority in favour
of the removal of Saddam is Iraq. I am proud – was proud
and remain proud – of this country and the part it played,
especially our magnificent armed forces, in removing two vile
dictatorships and giving people oppressed, almost enslaved,
the prospect of democracy and liberty.*

Tony Blair, 2004

ON 15 FEBRUARY 2003, about a million liberal-minded people
marched through London to oppose the overthrow of a fascist
regime. It was the biggest protest in British history, but it was
dwarfed by the march to oppose the overthrow of a fascist
regime in Mussolini's old capital of Rome where about 3
million Italians joined what the *Guinness Book of Records* said
was the largest anti-war rally ever. In Madrid, about 650,000
marched to oppose the overthrow of a fascist regime in the
biggest demonstration in Spain since the death of General
Francisco Franco in 1975. In Berlin, the call to oppose the

overthrow of a fascist regime brought demonstrators from 300 German towns and cities, some of them old enough to remember when Adolf Hitler ruled from the Reich Chancellery. In Greece, where the previous generation had overthrown a military junta, the police had to fire tear gas at leftists who were so angry at the prospect of a fascist regime being overthrown, they armed themselves with petrol bombs. The French protests against the overthrow of a fascist regime went off without trouble. Between 100,000 and 200,000 French demonstrators stayed peaceful as they rallied in the Place de la Bastille, where in 1789 Parisian revolutionaries had stormed the dungeons of Louis XVI in the name of the universal rights of man. In Ireland, Sinn Fein was in charge of the protests and produced the most remarkable spectacle of a remarkable day: a peace movement led by the IRA. Only in the newly liberated countries of the Soviet bloc were the demonstrations small and anti-war sentiment muted.

The protests against the overthrow of a fascist regime weren't just a Western European phenomenon. From Calgary to Buenos Aires, the Left of the Americas marched. In Cape Town and Durban, politicians from the African National Congress, who had once appealed for international solidarity against South Africa's apartheid regime, led the opposition to the overthrow of a fascist regime. On a memorable day, American scientists at the McMurdo Station in Antarctica produced another entry for the record books. Historians will tell how the continent's first political demonstration was a protest against the overthrow of a fascist regime.

Saddam Hussein was delighted and ordered Iraqi television to show the global day of action to its captive audience. The slogan the British marchers carried, 'No War – Freedom for Palestine', might have been written by his foreign ministry. He instructed the citizens of Baghdad to march and demand that he remain in power. Several thousand went through the streets carrying Kalashnikovs and posters of the Great Leader.

No one knows how many people demonstrated. The BBC estimated between 6 and 10 million, and anti-war activists tripled that, but equally no one doubted that these were history's largest coordinated demonstrations and that millions, maybe tens of millions, had marched to keep a fascist regime in power.

Afterwards, nothing drove the protesters wilder than sceptics telling them that if they had got what they wanted, they would, in fact, have kept a fascist regime in power. They were good people on the whole, who hadn't thought about the Baath Party. Euan Ferguson, of the *Observer*, watched the London demonstrators and saw a side of Britain march by that wasn't all bad.

There were, of course, the usual suspects – the Campaign for Nuclear Disarmament, the Socialist Workers' Party, the anarchists. But even they looked shocked at the number of their fellow marchers: it is safe to say they had never experienced such a mass of humanity.

There were nuns. Toddlers. Women barristers. The Eton George Orwell Society. Archaeologists Against War. Walthamstow Catholic Church, the Swaffham Women's Choir and 'Notts County Supporters Say Make Love Not War (And a Home Win against Bristol would be Nice)'. One group of SWP stalwarts were joined, for the first march in any of their histories, by their mothers. There were country folk and lecturers, dentists and poulterers, a hairdresser from Cardiff and a poet from Cheltenham. I called a friend at two o'clock, who was still making her ponderous way along the Embankment – 'It's not a march yet, more of a record shuffle' – and she expressed delight at her first protest. 'You wouldn't believe it; there are girls here with good nails and really nice bags.'

Alongside the girls with good nails were thoughtful marchers who had supported the interventions in Bosnia, Kosovo and Afghanistan but were aghast at the recklessness of the Iraq adventure. A few recognized that they were making a hideous choice. The South American playwright Ariel Dorfman, who had experienced state terror in General Pinochet's Chile, published a letter to an 'unknown Iraqi' and asked, 'What right does anyone have to deny you and your fellow Iraqis that liberation from tyranny? What right do we have to oppose the war the United States is preparing to wage on your country, if it could indeed result in the ouster of Saddam Hussein?'

His reply summed up the fears of tens of millions. War would destabilize the Middle East and recruit more fanatics to terrorist groups. It would lead to more despots 'preemptively arming themselves with all manner of apocalyptic weapons and, perhaps, to Armageddon'. Dorfman also worried about the casualties – which, I guess, were far higher than he imagined – and convinced himself that the right course was to demand that Bush and Blair pull back. Nevertheless, he retained the breadth of mind and generosity of spirit to sign off with 'heaven help me, I am saying that I care more about the future of this sad world than about the future of your unprotected children'.

I don't think any open-minded observer who wasn't caught up in the anger could say that Dorfman was typical. Hose Ramos Horta, the leader of the struggle for the freedom of East Timor, noticed that at none of the demonstrations in hundreds of cities did you see banners or hear speeches denouncing

Saddam Hussein. If this was 'the Left' on the march, it was the new left of the twenty-first century, which had abandoned old notions of camaraderie and internationalism in favour of opposition to the capricious American hegemon.

They didn't support fascism, but they didn't oppose it either and their silence boded ill for the future.

In *Saturday*, his novel set on the day of the march, Ian McEwan caught the almost frivolous mood: 'All this happiness on display is suspect. Everyone is thrilled to be together out on the streets – people are hugging themselves, it seems, as well as each other. If they think – and they could be right – that continued torture and summary executions, ethnic cleansing and occasional genocide are preferable to an invasion, they should be sombre in their view.'

Most people, me included, are not like Ariel Dorfman. In moments of political passion, we are single-mindedly and simple-mindedly sure of our righteousness. From the day of the marches on, liberal-leftish politicians and intellectuals kept up a vehement and slightly panicky insistence that they were right and their goodness was beyond question. In fairness to all of those who didn't want to think about the 'occasional genocide' or ask Heaven's forgiveness for recommending that the Baath Party be left in power, they were right in several respects.

The protesters were right to feel that Bush and Blair were manipulating them into war. They weren't necessarily lying in the lawyerly sense that they were deliberately making up the case for war – nothing that came out in the years afterwards showed that they knew Saddam Hussein had no weapons of mass destruction and thought 'what the hell, we'll pretend he does'. But they were manipulating the evidence. The post-mortem inquiries in America convicted the US administration of 'Collective Group Think': a self-reinforcing delusion in the White House that shut out contrary information and awkward voices. Lord Butler's inquiry in Britain showed that Tony Blair turned statements that the Joint Intelligence Committee had hedged with caveats into definite warnings of an imminent threat. Before the Labour politician Robin Cook resigned in protest against the war, he pointed out to Tony Blair that several details in his case that Saddam had chemical weapons couldn't possibly be true. Cook told his special adviser David Mathieson after the meeting that Blair did not know about the detail and didn't seem to want to know either.

'A half truth is a whole lie,' runs the Yiddish proverb, and if democratic leaders are going to take their countries to war, they must be able to level with themselves as well as their electorates. If Blair had levelled with the British people he would have said that he couldn't be sure if Saddam was armed, and even if he was there was no imminent danger, but here was a chance to remove a disgusting regime and combat the growth in terror by building democracy, and he was going to take it. Instead, he spun and talked about chemical weapons ready to be fired in forty-five minutes. If the Labour Party had forced Blair to resign, there would have been a rough justice in his political execution.

The war was over soon enough, but the aftermath was a disaster. Generals, diplomats and politicians covered their own backs and stabbed the backs of their colleagues as they piled blame on each other, but for the rest of the world pictures released in 2004 of American guards with pornographic smirks on their faces standing beside the tortured and sexually abused bodies of Iraqis at the Abu Ghraib prison encapsulated their disgust. To those who knew that the Baathists had had tens of thousands tortured and murdered at Abu Ghraib, the pictures were evidence of sacrilege. It was as if American guards had decided to gas a Jew in Auschwitz while their superiors turned a blind eye.

Just as dozens of generals, politicians and diplomats shifted the blame, so journalists and academics produced dozens of books on the troubles of the occupation of Iraq. One point demanded far more attention than it got. Fear of an upsurge in terrorism was as strong a force as anti-Americanism in motivating opponents of the war who knew next to nothing about Iraq. Yet hard-headed and principled Iraqis, who knew all about the ghastly history of their country, failed to understand the appeal of fascism. The exiled Kanan Makiya and others worried about coping with the consequences of totalitarianism when the Baath Party was overthrown. They talked about how many people you could reasonably put on trial in a country where the regime had made hundreds of thousands complicit in its crimes against humanity, and wondered about truth and reconciliation commissions and amnesties. They expected the invaders to be met with 'sweets and flowers' and assumed Baathism was dead as a dynamic force. They didn't count on its continuing appeal to the Sunni minority all too aware democracy would strip them of their status as Iraq's 'whites'. They didn't wonder what else the servants of the Baath could do if they didn't take up arms. Wait around for war crimes trials or revenge from the kin of their victims? Nor did they expect to see Islamist suicide bombers pour into Iraq. Despite vocal assurances from virtually every expert who went on the BBC that such a pact was impossible, Baathists and Islamists formed an alliance against the common enemy of democracy.

Abu Musab Zarqawi, the leader of al-Qaeda in Iraq, wasn't against elections because he was worried they would be rigged or because he couldn't tolerate American involvement in the political process, he was against democracy in all circumstances. It was 'an evil principle' he said as he declared a 'fierce war' against all those 'apostates' and 'infidels' who wanted to vote in free elections and the 'demi-idols' who wanted to be elected. Democracy was a 'heresy itself' because it allowed men and women to challenge the laws of God with laws made by parliaments. It was based on 'freedom of religion and belief' and 'freedom of speech' and on 'separation of religion and politics'. He did not mean it as a compliment.

His strategy was to terrorize Iraq's Shia majority. To Sunni Islamists they were heretics, or as Zarqawi put it in his characteristic language 'the insurmountable obstacle, the lurking snake, the crafty and malicious scorpion, the spying enemy, and the penetrating venom'. Suicide bombers were to murder them until they turned on the Sunni minority. He explained, 'I mean that targeting and hitting them in [their] religious, political, and military depth will provoke them to show the Sunnis their rabies and bare the teeth of the hidden rancour working in their breasts. If we succeed in dragging them into the arena of sectarian war, it will become possible to awaken the inattentive Sunnis as they feel imminent danger and annihilating death.'

Journalists wondered whether the Americans were puffing up Zarqawi's role in the violence – as a foreigner he was a convenient enemy – but they couldn't deny the ferocity of the terror. Like Stalin, Pol Pot and Slobodan Milosevic, they went for the professors and technicians who could make a democratic Iraq work. They murdered Sergio Vieira de Mello, one of the United Nations' bravest officials, and his colleagues, Red Cross workers, politicians, journalists and thousands upon thousands of Iraqis who happened to be in the wrong Christian church or Shia mosque.

How hard was it for opponents of the war to be against that?

Unbelievably hard, it turned out. The anti-war movement disgraced itself not because it was against the war in Iraq, but because it could not oppose the counter-revolution once the war was over. A principled left that still had life in it and a liberalism that meant what it said might have remained ferociously critical of the American and British governments while offering support to Iraqis who wanted the freedoms they enjoyed. It is a generalization to say that everyone refused to commit. The best of the old left in the trade unions and Parliamentary Labour Party supported an anti-fascist struggle regardless of whether they were for or against the war, and American Democrats went to fight in Iraq and returned to fight the Republicans.

But again, no one who looked at the liberal-left from the outside could pretend that such principled stands were commonplace. The British Liberal Democrats, the continental social democratic parties, the African National Congress and virtually every leftish newspaper and journal on the planet were unable to accept that the struggle of Arabs and Kurds had anything to do with them. Mainstream Muslim organizations were as indifferent to the murder of Muslims by other Muslims in Iraq as in Darfur. For the majority of world opinion, Tony Blair's hopes of 'giving people oppressed, almost enslaved, the prospect of democracy and liberty' counted for nothing. The worst of the lot were the organizers of the British anti-war demonstrations who turned out to be not so much against war but on the wrong side.

The producers of the 2006 series of the reality TV show *Celebrity Big Brother* told the contestants they must play a game in which they pretended to be animals. Among the housemates was a former star of *Baywatch*, a 46-year-old transvestite, a TV presenter whose career appeared to be over when the body of a young man bobbed to the surface of his swimming pool, an ageing actress, who had not had a hit for years, and the leader of the Stop the War coalition.

'Would you like me to be the cat?' the leader of the Stop the War coalition asked the ageing actress in a slow, numb voice.

'Yes please!' said the ageing actress.

The leader of the Stop the War coalition got down on all fours and began to purr.

'Here pussy, pussy, pussy... Yessss,' said the ageing actress. 'More tickles, it's OK... Oooh, little pussy cat... there, there pussycat.'

The leader of the Stop the War coalition slowly licked his lips.

'You stay there, I'll get you some milk, you like that don't you?' said the ageing actress.

She cupped her hands and offered make-believe milk to the leader of the Stop the War coalition. 'Yes, good pussy cat,' said the ageing actress.

The leader of the Stop the War coalition stuck in his tongue and began to slobber.

'That's right, delicious!' said the ageing actress. 'Good girl, good girl.'

The leader of the Stop the War coalition pulled back his head and licked his moustache.

'You've got cream all over your whiskers,' said the ageing actress, sympathetically. She stroked the leader of the Stop the War coalition's cheek and bushed his moustache back into place.

'Who's a good puddycat. *Yeessss*, good puddycat.'

Bored with licking her cupped hands, the leader of the Stop

the War coalition moved his head towards the ageing actress's lap and purred. She didn't mind and stroked his back.

'Oooh yes,' she said. 'Has it been a trying day with all those people coming into the house, has it? You just like being alone with your mummy, don't you?'

The leader of the Stop the War coalition crawled an inch further forward and shoved his head towards her crotch.

George Galloway, the leader of the Stop the War coalition, the first candidate for an allegedly far-left party to win a seat in Parliament since 1951 and a man who modestly told his rivals on *Celebrity Big Brother* that '1.5 billion Muslims know who I am', was always a good crawler.

Galloway was a bombastic Scottish Labour MP who combined blood-curdling rhetoric with a whining sentimentality, like many a political thug before him. In the Nineties, his political career appeared to be dead. Contrary to popular prejudice, successful politicians don't always love the sound of their own voices. The ones who get on learn to hold their tongues and speak for a purpose. Galloway was too fond of grandstanding to make it in the best of times for the Left. When New Labour took charge, many Scottish bruisers from the old left found preferment under Tony Blair, who, like all prime ministers, needed his enforcers. But Galloway missed the boat, and perhaps never wanted to board it. He seemed an irrelevant backbencher who could hope only for the occasional appearance on talk radio, but he proved that a minor politician from democratic Britain could build an alternative career in the Arab dictatorships.

Their state-controlled media quoted approved foreigners at length and gave Galloway the attention he could not get at home. The bleak and apparently unending tyranny of totalitarian Iraq and the ephemeral glitz of *Celebrity Big Brother* seem as far apart as it is possible to be. But the anti-war movement should not have been surprised that Galloway ended up as an exhibit on a TV freak show. The celebrity and the totalitarian share a desire to have their faces in every newspaper and on every television screen. Both are what the British playwright Heathcote Williams called 'psychic imperialists', who want to colonize the minds of millions.

In 1994, twelve years before he crawled round the Big Brother house, Galloway made his first steps towards stardom when Iraqi television showed him bending the knee before Saddam Hussein. He gave the most emphatic demonstration of the switch on the Left from opposing to supporting Baathism when he flew to Baghdad in the aftermath of the first war against Saddam and declared: 'I thought the President would appreciate to know that even today, three years after the war, I still meet families who are calling their newborn sons Saddam... Sir, I salute your courage, your strength and your indefatigability. And I want you to know that we are with you until victory, until victory until Jerusalem.'

As the realization sank in that their friends and families had joined marches led by a saluter of a genocidal tyrant, a few British broadcasters found the social courage to break with their class and quote Galloway's words back at him. Indignantly, he replied that he wasn't praising Saddam but praising the Iraqi people – a defence that couldn't stand up to thirty seconds' fisking. If you are in front of President Saddam Hussein and call him 'Sir', he could reasonably suppose that you were addressing him rather than the Iraqi people. If you continue, 'I salute *your* courage, *your* strength and *your* indefatigability', you would say nothing to change his mind, particularly if you also say, 'I thought the President would appreciate to know that even today, three years after the war, I still meet families who are calling their newborn sons Saddam.'

Many people lose their bearings when confronted with a mighty potentate and gabble whatever comes into their heads – Unity Mitford said that sitting next to Adolf Hitler was 'like sitting beside the sun' – but Galloway's servility wasn't an aberration. He became friends with Tariq Aziz, Saddam's foreign minister. The British human rights organization Indict had testimony from witnesses who saw Aziz shoot Iraqi prisoners at close range, and credible reports that he had advance knowledge of the gassing of Halabja. Galloway preferred to dwell on the funky side of the alleged war criminal and remembered with fondness the night he danced with Aziz on 'the crowded dance floor of a North African nightclub'. Uday Hussein was a greater sadist than his father. He ordered the torture of Iraqi footballers who didn't play well for his team and raped any woman who attracted him. Galloway greeted the torturer and rapist with, 'Your Excellency, very, very nice to see you again.' In his autobiography, published in 2005, eleven years after he had first sucked up to the dictator, Galloway proved that his was not a transient infatuation when he said that Saddam's slaughter of the Kurds and Shia in 1991 was understandable because it took place during 'a civil war with massive violence on both sides'.

After the 2003 war, the *Telegraph* accused him of being in Saddam's pay. He sued and the *Telegraph* lost. The US Congress cross-examined him about what had happened to money he had raised for a charity for starving Iraqi children, and, by the universal agreement of the deferential media, Galloway wiped the floor with them. His accusers didn't realize that they were letting him off the hook. They thought that the worst charge they could level at him was that he was corrupt, when corruption is a common and readily understandable vice. To flatter a tyrannous regime because it has bribed you is deplorable, of course, but to do so unbribed because you admire it of your own free will is more chilling and more common, as the histories of every totalitarian movement from Bolshevism to Islamism proved. With Galloway, you could no more explain away his subservience by citing the 'root cause' of corruption than you could diminish Islamist atrocities with the 'root cause' of globalization.

If you listened to what Galloway said, you once again noticed a difference with what had gone before. With the brief exception of the two years of the Hitler–Stalin pact, twentieth-century fellow travellers had to choose between communism and fascism, but, as the theorists had shown, in the twenty-first century you could refuse to be 'judgemental' about any system as long as it was anti-democratic.

Galloway saluted the fascistic perpetrator of racial extermi-nation campaigns, but he was just as keen on communism. When he praised Saddam for building up the Iraqi economy, he compared him favourably to Stalin and, implicitly, Mao – 'just as Stalin industrialised the Soviet Union, so on a different scale Saddam plotted Iraq's own Great Leap Forward' – rather than Hitler – for the autobahns – or Mussolini – for making the trains run on time. Meanwhile he lamented 'the disappearance of the Soviet Union', and said it was 'the biggest catastrophe of my life', and when asked about his admiration for Fidel Castro the dictator of Cuba, he said, 'I don't believe that Fidel Castro is a dictator.' When Saddam was gone, Galloway went to Baathist Syria, even though it was the sworn enemy of Baathist Iraq, and applauded it as 'the last castle of the Arab dignity and the Arab rights'. Saddam had launched an unprovoked war against Iran, but when Hezbollah, Iran's terrorist proxies in the Lebanon, began a war with Israel a finger-jabbing Galloway bellowed to a rally in London that 'Hezbollah has never been a terrorist organization. I am here, I AM HERE, to glorify the Lebanese resistance, Hezbollah, and I AM HERE to glorify the resistance leader, Hassan Nasrallah.'

Stalinism, Castroism, Islamism, Baathism...the old distinctions no longer held. Any ism would do as an alternative to democracy, which he explained in an unguarded moment, wasn't meant for poor, brown people. 'In poor third world countries like Pakistan, politics is too important to be left to petty squabbling politicians. Pakistan is always on the brink of breaking apart into its widely disparate components. Only the armed forces can really be counted on to hold such a country together.'

Such was the leader of the Stop the War coalition, a man offered columns by the *Guardian*, the parish magazine of the 'liberal' English middle class, and buttered-up with oily profiles in the *New York Times*, the parish magazine of the 'liberal' American middle class. A respectable movement of the Right or the Left would have refused to have anything to do with him, but the fever George W. Bush provoked and the waning power of liberal principles meant that not one heckler raised a voice in protest when he addressed the London marchers who were so eager to chant 'not in my name'.

A theme of this book is that ideas on the fringe are worth examining. Not only do the thoughts of apparently inconsequential figures – Michel Aflaq, Karl Marx, Friedrich Hayek, Sayyid Qutb – take off, but the extreme parties magnify trends in wider society. In Britain's case, the British National Party magnified the racial hatred of immigrants and the UK Independence Party magnified the British suspicion of foreign interference. The Greens expressed the longing for a pre-industrial pastoral life, and the media junkies of the

Revolutionary Communist Party exaggerated the trite contrarianism of mainstream journalism. The Socialist Workers' Party, Galloway's backers and the real force behind the Stop the War coalition, distinguished itself by taking the opportunism and control-freakery of conventional politics and pushing it further than any democratic party would dare.

Everyone with a conscience on the Left knew how immoral the SWP could be, but the delusion that the Left was a family meant that public denunciations were rare. Just after the 2003 war, Mike Marqusee, the best and to my knowledge only American Marxist cricket writer, broke the silence and allowed years of expatriate frustration at the state of the British left to let rip. Every time he joined a campaign, he found that the SWP was trying to take it over. Almost ninety years on from 1917, its leaders behaved as if they were preparing the Bolshevik Party for a *coup d'état*. Marqusee explained that they 'consider themselves *the* vanguard and despite the lip-service to pluralism retain the conviction that they *alone* offer the movement proper leadership...Doubt and agnosticism have no place – indeed they are regarded as weaknesses. Truth is reified in the form of a jargon. Instead of sober assessment of our success and failures, strengths and weaknesses, we're offered empty boosterism.'

No one outside the cult could dispute that. The staged meetings and the mechanized speakers who churned out slogans like concrete mixers disgorging cement drove away potential recruits. The politburo issued the line and the members toed it, whatever it was. 'What has disturbed me most in working with the SWP has been their flagrant ethical relativism,' continued Marqusee. 'This is an ancient foible of the Left – a conviction that the class struggle, or the building of the revolutionary party, or the sheer evil of the forces we find ourselves up against justifies any behaviour, no matter how dishonest, duplicitous, or destructive to others. In their competition with the rest of the Left, in their drive to maintain control (including control of their own members) anything goes.'

Only the Jehovah's Witnesses seemed as remote from modern life as the few thousand Leninists still trying to work out why the proletariat hadn't put them in power. But in apathetic times when politics is at the margins of most people's lives, a regimented sect can take charge. The SWP disciplined members filled the empty chairs on campaign steering committees, and ensured that movements that had little to do with Bolshevik revolution followed their agenda. Only later when the apathetic had allowed the SWP to run a show did innocents learn that anything did indeed go on the modern left.

Take the fascist conspiracy theory. Globalise Resistance, an anti-capitalist organization dominated by the SWP, first proposed a worldwide day of protest against the second Iraq war at the 'Cairo Conference' of anti-war activists. The delegates sounded as if tsarist Russia and Nazi Germany had inspired them rather than well-meaning peace campaigns when they declared that the 2003 war against Iraq was the result of a 'Zionist plan, which targets the establishment of the greater State of Israel from the Nile to the Euphrates'.

Beyond the convergence of far-left and far-right ideas lies a second reason for taking a good look at the organizers of the anti-war marches. Because they said they were on the Left, they had to face an argument which was soon to confront men and women with real power in the centre-left governments of Europe, South America and South Africa. All right, it ran, you say the war against Iraq was illegal, and you wish it had never happened, you're appalled by the casualties and sickened by Bush. That's fine and good and you have a point, but now that far-right psychopaths are ravaging the country, are you going to stand up for your social democratic principles and support their victims, or does anything go for you too?

The October 2004 Labour conference was a rare phenomenon: a party political conference that might have changed the government of the country. Tony Blair may not have alienated his working-class voters, but his middle-class supporters were furious. The failure to find weapons of mass destruction Saddam could launch in forty-five minutes, or forty-five years for that matter, had destroyed his reputation in the media. The hacks were out to get him, the herd of independent minds was preparing to stampede and Gordon Brown was getting ready to take power. If Labour Party members and the trade unions had revolted and called for the immediate withdrawal of British troops from Iraq, the vote of no confidence from his own party conference would have finished him.

'Nobody ever got rich betting against Tony Blair,' sighed the unlucky gambler Mike Smithson who ran a tip sheet on the Net for political punters. Blair survived to face the next crisis, thanks to the most unlikely ally to come to his rescue in his charmed career: the socialists of the Iraqi trade union movement.

It had once been the strongest in the Middle East. On May Day in 1959, it got half a million people on to the streets of Baghdad – an impressive turnout in a country that then had a population of 7 million. No totalitarian leader can tolerate free unions, and Saddam followed the examples of Stalin and Hitler and crushed independent activity while setting up 'yellow unions' – state-controlled front organizations, one of which was led by Chemical Ali, the poisoner of the Kurds. The few trade union activists who survived went underground.

Exposure meant torture and imprisonment, followed by exile or execution. By the time of Saddam's overthrow, the Baathists had reduced the movement to a few hundred clandestine socialists and communists. With remarkable speed, the underground came out of hiding and the exiles returned to build a trade union movement of about a million in the most frightening conditions. Naturally when confronted with independent organizations signing up workers without regard to ethnicity or creed, the Baathists and the Islamists did what any other fascistic movement would have done and killed them.

At every Labour event I went to at the time, I would meet Abdullah Muhsin, a middle-aged Iraqi with thick curly hair and a winning smile. The international representative of the Iraqi Federation of Trade Unions had no money and no office. He often had no home to go to, and had to sleep on friends' floors. All he had going for him was a moral argument, which tugged at the roots of the old left. He collared trade union leaders and said words to the effect of, 'Look, we opposed the war too, but now it is over we are fighting the forces of reaction which represent everything you are against. If you go along with the demands of Blair's enemies to end the occupation immediately, you will be condemning your comrades to death. It's all right, you can still oppose Bush, American troops have raided our offices and we would more than welcome it if you condemned that and all their other catastrophic mistakes. But now the war is over, you must make a stand against fascism.'

His arguments produced a touching display of internationalism I never expected to see in that seedy time. The British trade union movement is the oldest in the world, and what successes it had achieved came from its members sticking together. Even though they woke up every morning wondering if they hated Tony Blair more than they hated George W. Bush, most of its leaders recognized the universal duty to show solidarity with the victims of oppression and swung their votes behind Blair as their predecessors had swung them behind Ernie Bevin in 1935.

The star of the conference was a figure as unlike the portly docker as it is possible to imagine. Shanaz Rashid, an Iraqi exile and member of the socialist Patriotic Union of Kurdistan, stunned delegates with the rawness of her emotion. The liberation of Iraq, she said, was a dream she had had all her life. When, after Saddam had been defeated, she landed at Baghdad airport, she had kissed the ground, and 'wept for my freedom! Freedom that you take for granted!'

She described how her relatives had been tortured and murdered by Saddam, and how the West had ignored their plight. 'Surely there is no dishonour in helping me to get my freedom?' she said. 'You may feel you can attack your leader, but it is Mr Blair who has stood up to Saddam and has freed my people!' Simon Hoggart of the *Guardian* wrote that:

> by this time her face, viewed on the two giant screens, had crumpled with a mixture of rage, frustration and relief. 'Yes, there have been difficulties, yes there have been mistakes, perhaps many mistakes. No, you didn't find weapons of mass destruction. But for the great majority of Iraqis, WMD were never an issue. We never understood the argument about them. All we wanted was to be free! Free! *FREE*!' she cried, her voice peaking dangerously as TV sound engineers ripped off their earphones and stuffed tissues up their bleeding noses. 'Please, please, do not desert us in our hour of need!'

To a conference that was in the middle of a convoluted discussion about whether British troops should leave when the Iraqi government asked them, or go somewhat earlier, this was an alarming dose of first-hand feeling. Nobody knew how to cope. As Ms Rashid fled from the stage, all passion spent, she was followed by a Marian Grimes from Edinburgh, whose voice was as low and mumbly as Ms Rashid's was high-pitched and furious.

'I'm finding it very difficult to follow that,' she said, but she soon found a way: she simply ignored it, and didn't address a single point that Ms Rashid had made. Nor did any of the troops-out-now people. They simply pretended she hadn't been there.

What Shanaz Rashid said was both true and false. It was true that America and Britain had freed Iraq, and that big truth got the Labour Party behind Tony Blair, but it wasn't the case that all Iraqis were shouting 'All we wanted was to be free! Free! FREE!' If they had been, British and American troops wouldn't have died in a long war. That there was a long war ate into Tony Blair's credibility as much as the failure to find chemical weapons, but it also ate into the credibility of those among his opponents who watched the march of al-Qaeda and the Baath Party with indifference or enthusiasm. As the liberal-left of the Thirties found, you have to decide which side you're on. No amount of saying the Prime Minister was a liar and a poodle could stop it evading the choice, however hard it pretended otherwise.

The leaders of the anti-war demonstrations made theirs. As the fighting began, a writer for *Socialist Worker* said that 'the best response to war would be protests across the globe which make it impossible for Bush and Blair to continue. But while war lasts by far the lesser evil would be reverses, or defeat, for the US and British forces.' Once the conventional fighting was over, George Galloway got the mixture of viciousness and sentimentality just right when he backed the beheaders and the suicide bombers by purring: 'These poor Iraqis – ragged people, with their sandals, with their Kalashnikovs, with the lightest and most basic of weapons – are writing the names of their cities and towns in the stars, with 145 military operations every day, which has made the country ungovernable.'

By their own lights, the organizers of the anti-war protests were being logical. If there had been an easy victory in Iraq, America might have been able to put more pressure on Syria and Iran or invaded Syria and Iran or, worse still, encouraged the Syrians and Iranians to rise up. They might have faced a Middle East running short of dictators to salute.

Making friends with your enemy's enemy is a familiar tactic, but it is not as uncomplicated as it seems. More often than not, you have to betray your old friends when you conclude your pact. Like Gerry Healy before them, the organizers of the anti-war demonstrations and their friends treated Iraqi left-wingers like criminals because they refused to take up arms against the Americans as the script of the rich world's left said they must. Instead of supporting the far right, the uppity natives said they wanted to escape from al-Qaeda and the Baath and participate in free elections.

Iraqi trade unionists in particular were met with the most implacable hatred. After George Monbiot addressed the European Social Forum in Paris in 2003, the anti-globalization movement moved to Alexandra Palace in north London for its 2004 conference. Speaker after speaker supported the 'resistance'. No one booed when one said that those who questioned the motives of the suicide bombers who were daily murdering (mainly Muslim) civilians were guilty of 'anti-Islamic racism'. John O'Farrell from *The Blanket*, a radical Belfast paper, noted the frantic evasiveness of the anti-globalizers about the true nature of their new comrades in Iraq. 'All speakers were coy about the specifics of the "resistance". There was no specific mention of the Shi'ite cleric Al-Sadr and his Madhi Army, nor Zarqawi and his fellow kidnappers and decapitators, nor even of Al-Qaeda, and its own take on the rights of women and the existence of gays.'

After covering up for the far right, the campaigners for global justice screamed down the Iraqi left. 'Subhi al Mashadani, the leader of the Iraqi Federation of Trade Unions never got to speak,' said O'Farrell. 'For an hour, he was barracked by a handful of English and Turkish Trots, who surged towards the stage when he attempted to address the 2,000 strong audience. After being attacked on his arrival at Alexandra Palace earlier that day, the ESF's security took no chances and dragged a furious Mashadani from the stage for his own protection.'

George Galloway matched his sycophancy towards Saddam Hussein with his hatred of Abdullah Muhsin whom he described as an 'Iraqi Quisling'. (A peculiar insult as Vidkun Quisling was a Norwegian who collaborated with fascism rather than opposed it.) Meanwhile the leaders of the Stop the War coalition issued a draft statement that recognized that the Iraqis had a right to resist 'by whatever means they find necessary'. They withdrew it after protests, but no one who was paying attention could doubt the growing affection between the modern equivalents of the Russians and Prussians. Mick Rix of the train drivers' union said he couldn't 'be associated with remarks that attack decent trade unionists' and resigned from the Stop the War coalition.

He got out just in time because the brave resistance that Western leftists thought it Islamophobic to criticize was showing what it thought of Iraqi leftists in the most graphic manner.

In the twentieth century, Hadi Saleh would have been recognized as a socialist hero for dedicating and risking his life for the welfare of humanity. Saleh was a printer and trade union organizer whom the Baathists arrested as soon as they came to power in 1968. He sat on death row for five years. They let him go, and he fled to Sweden with his wife. Like many in the Iraqi Communist Party he lost his faith in Moscow after it cut deals with Saddam and started a long journey towards constitutional politics. In the Seventies and Eighties when Iraq was a closed society with its secrets protected by Moynihan's Law, Saleh and his comrades worked to educate the then Left on the nature of Saddam's regime. Tiny victories – getting this international conference to pass a resolution condemning the treatment of an Iraqi dissident, or that social democratic party to recognize the free trade union movement – were momentous events because they proved that some people in the West understood what Saddam's regime represented and were prepared to speak out. As you might expect, he had to live with the constant fear of assassination.

Saleh opposed the war of 2003, but returned home after it was over. From next to nothing he and his comrades built a mass movement in the face of the indifference or hostility of the Americans, who were so lost in conservative dogma they didn't grasp that free societies and free trade unions go together. He knew his life was in danger. 'Yes, it's a risk for civil society organisations, including trade unions. Extremists who targeted those trade unionists, both teachers and engineers, killed them under the notion that they are collaborating with a state created by the Americans, so by definition those are collaborators and legitimate targets. We call on our brothers and sisters in the international community to support us to make sure that our rights in organising formal unions freely and openly are guaranteed and ensured.'

They came for him, of course. The professional nature of the torture wounds on his body suggested that 'they' were Baathist secret policemen rather than bin Ladenists. When he was dead, they took his union records to give them the names of more people to kill.

I've never felt as ashamed of my trade of liberal journalism as I did at the time of his murder. The comment pages of the *Guardian* were a platform for every variety of apologist for Islamist terrorism and the Baathist 'resistance', although my colleagues couldn't be intellectually consistent and provide the same service to white queer bashers, European neo-Nazis and Christian fundamentalists. The *Independent*, which had been launched in 1986 as a sober alternative to its narrow-minded rivals, gave up on serious journalism and its dividing lines between news and opinion, and turned its front pages over to agit-prop which wouldn't have made it into a student newspaper.

The British press is meant to be biased. The BBC boasts that it questions without fear or favour. But when you hire upper-middle-class arts graduates, pay them well and allow them to work, eat and sleep together in west London, there's bound to be a 'Collective Group Think'. In Iraq's case, it did not come out in the hard questions they asked the other side, but the soft questions they asked their own side. For years, the BBC's attack-dog presenters couldn't manage to give one opponent of the war a tough interview. Not even George Galloway.

My colleagues were rich men and women by British standards, let alone world standards. They kept silent so they could maintain the illusion that the family of the 'Left' was flawless. No one would have tortured them if they had spoken out. No one would have beaten their genitals, broken their bones, strangled them with an electric flex and then stolen their address books so they could do the same to their friends. The worst they would have got was Naomi Wolf's punishment of being 'looked at with contempt at dinner parties', which was a badge of honour at the time.

When I asked my colleagues why an anti-war movement being led by apologists for Saddam Hussein was not a story, when a Countryside Alliance led by neo-Nazis would have been, they said, 'Well, the people who went on their demonstrations didn't agree with Galloway and the SWP. They followed Robin Cook, Jacques Chirac, Gerhard Schroeder and the Liberal Democrats.' This was true up to a point. 'And anyway,' they continued, 'it didn't matter' – an answer which showed how little they understood their country.

Christians, Jews, Hindus and Buddhists demonstrated against the 2003 war, but the only religious group the Stop the War coalition promoted was an outfit called the Muslim Association of Britain. Its speakers and propaganda appeared at anti-war meetings and its officers co-organized the anti-war marches. Most British Muslims knew little about it because it was an Arab organization and most British Muslims' families were from the Indian subcontinent or East Africa. It turned out to be the closest Britain had to a branch of the Muslim Brotherhood and was, by twentieth-century standards, a movement of the extreme right. Its favourite cleric – a preacher its spokesman described as a 'shining example of moderation' – was the Qatari-based Yusuf al-Qaradawi, who issued fatwas that would have once offended leftist sensibilities. On the right to freedom of conscience, he ruled that a grown-up Muslim who decided to convert to another religion or become an atheist 'is a traitor to his religion and his people and thus deserves killing'. Female genital mutilation on the other hand was fine by him – 'whoever finds it serving the interest of his daughters should do it, and I personally support this under the current circumstances in the modern world'. He was also prepared to excuse a little light wife beating – 'if the husband senses that feelings of disobedience and rebelliousness are rising against him in his wife, he should try his best to rectify her attitude by kind words, gentle persuasion, and reasoning with her...If this approach fails, it is permissible for him to admonish her lightly with his hands, avoiding her face and other sensitive areas.' When a moderate Egyptian cleric, Mohammad Sayed Tantawi, condemned the murders of Israeli children by suicide bombers, Qaradawi asked, 'has fighting colonizers become a criminal and terrorist act for some sheikhs?' Gays had to die too, apparently. 'Muslim jurists hold different opinions concerning the punishment for this abominable practice. Should it be the same as the punishment for fornication, or should both the active and passive participants be put to death? While such punishments may seem cruel, they have been suggested to maintain the purity of the Islamic society and to keep it clean of perverted elements.'

Neither he nor the Muslim Association of Britain supported al-Qaeda, but all but the most committed marchers were shocked out of their hatred of Bush and Blair for a moment when they read the Muslim Association of Britain's leaflets on the rights and wrongs of executing apostates.

Shocked the naïve may have been but candid revolutionary socialists had to look to the future. They couldn't deny that the calls for the murder of free thinkers, Jews and homosexuals came from the real radical anger that threatened the status quo: the anger of the Islamist right. When they looked around without illusion, they couldn't help but notice that there were hardly any communist revolutionaries left. Beyond a few Maoists in Nepal, no one was taking up arms and overthrowing governments in communism's name. Marxism was no longer an ideology which could move men and women to kill and be killed. It was as irrelevant to the human race as the Arian heresy, as Kanan Makiya's former friends had wailed.

However, the outlook wasn't all bleak. Revolutionary socialists could be cheered by the sight of millions of people who hated the United States and 'capitalist' democracy, as they did; who hated globalization, Hollywood and consumerism, as they did. More to the point, among the millions were tens of thousands who – when you got down to the basics – wanted to kill Americans. All the revolutionary socialists had to do was forget about the belief of these millions in the literal truth of an early medieval holy book, their elevation of their god over free men and women, their hatred of intellectual freedom, their homophobia, their antisemitism, their supernatural conspiracy theories, their misogyny, their use of state oppression in Taliban Afghanistan, the Sudan and Iran, and their condemnations of godless communism . . . and they might even be comrades.

There was certainly no hope left elsewhere. The leaders of the anti-war movement learned that hard lesson in the months after the great anti-war march. Try to imagine their exultation on that day. All their lives they had been waiting for a revolution that never came. The working class, whose vanguard they had appointed themselves to be, failed to notice their existence. Their voices had gone hoarse screaming slogans in half-empty halls, and the revolt of 1968 was half a lifetime away. They were getting old. They were looking tired. Outside the secure walls of their sects, the few strangers who spared them a glance treated them as living fossils – one of history's dead ends.

Then on a bright cold day in February, the clocks struck thirteen and the leaders of the Socialist Workers' Party found that they were in charge of a 1-million strong demonstration. Think of that: 1 million people. The biggest demonstration

Britain had seen. Think of how long it takes 1 million people to file through the streets of London. Imagine standing on a stage in Hyde Park and for the first time in your revolutionary career addressing not hundreds, but hundreds of thousands, and seeing hundreds of thousands more beyond the park gates pressing towards you, like the St Petersburg proletariat in November 1917.

The masses were with the revolutionary vanguard. They had come to them, chanted their slogans and carried their banners. The anti-war march must have seemed the revolutionary moment of their dreams. They'd waited all their lives for this, and it turned their heads, of course it did. The leaders of far left talked of direct action, of a general strike on the day war began, of the overthrow of an elected Prime Minister...anything seemed possible in the weeks after 15 February 2003, until the masses turned out in May 2003 for the local elections and the far-left parties in the Socialist Alliance did...as dreadfully as ever.

It didn't occur to them that the masses had looked at the leaders of the far left when they took to the stage at Hyde Park and wondered who the bloody hell they were. Anti-war votes went to the Liberal Democrats and the far left won just one seat in Preston, a Lancashire town not previously noted as a hotbed of revolutionary socialism. It must have been a lot to take. To go from 1 million marchers waving your placards to one council seat in Preston (Town Centre Ward) was a precipitous fall. They were used to yet another 'inevitable crisis of capitalism' failing to arrive, but this was too much. Any political movement would have to reconsider its strategy after such a disaster. Did they look around and reflect that perhaps they should not be too downhearted? Did they think that the apparently unimportant victory in Preston (Town Centre Ward) was worth dwelling on? For something rather wondrous had happened. A white atheist communist won because the priests in Preston's mosques were so disgusted by the war they instructed the faithful to abandon Labour and vote for him.

The far left had no future – that had been clear for decades. But if it could downplay its Marxism and appeal to Muslim grievance, maybe it could make it as a communalist party exploiting support for political Islam. Their theorists had been saying since the early Nineties that if they got into bed with Islam they could 'try to win some of the young people who support it to a very different, independent, revolutionary socialist perspective'. Perhaps that daydream consoled them. Perhaps it allowed them to pretend to themselves that they were covertly building up the radical left rather than riding the Islamist tiger. Maybe they no longer believed in their hearts in 'independent revolutionary socialist perspectives' – no one else did – and just wanted to ally with the real threat to the established order.

For whatever reason, the game was on. Ken Livingstone, the Mayor of London, whom we last saw mourning at Gerry Healy's funeral, invited Qaradawi to London and defended him against furious gays, Hindus, Jews, humanists, socialists, feminists and liberals who wondered what had happened to the tolerant politician they thought they had elected. Meanwhile the Socialist Alliance was effectively wound up and the SWP and Galloway formed Respect, a party with the specific aim of appealing to alienated Muslims.

I can't find a time before 2003 when a part of the Left consciously adopted a communalist strategy. The old left told immigrants that what mattered was that they were workers united in a common struggle with their British brothers and sisters against the boss class. It was often a myth – not always, but often – but it was a benign myth that played down racial and religious differences. The left of the Sixties fought racism with the decent belief that differences in skin colour or religious faith counted for little when set against the universal claims of common humanity. (No cliché was more pleasing to the liberal of the time than the assertion that racism was wrong because we were all the same under the skin.) By 2003, we had a part of the Left which was playing identity politics by trying to build support on the back of Muslim grievance, and nowhere more so than in George Lansbury's old constituency of Bethnal Green and Bow.

Galloway's alliance of white far left and brown religious right took much of the Muslim vote and returned him to Parliament in the 2005 general election as the first Respect MP. For the East End's Bengalis and Somalis – by now referred to by everyone as *the* Muslims – the outlook was grim. The great wave of Islamic revivalism had already pushed many Muslim immigrants away from British culture and the jobs and social mobility integration brought with it. Now they had a new political party which emphasized their separateness. When British Muslims already had the highest unemployment rate in the country, it was not helping them to pile bricks on the ghetto walls.

The British National Party understood what was going on in the slums far better than middle-class commentators, and saluted the arrival of a fellow communalist party. 'The victory of George Galloway and his Soviet/Islamic Front Group Respect, which is run by an Islamic/Socialist Workers Party alliance, is a welcome victory,' the BNP said. It 'demonstrates very clearly to the [white] British voters that the Muslim community, when it forms an ethnic bloc in an area, chooses to vote only for those political parties that explicitly promote the interests of the Muslim community itself'.

The language was as ugly as the party, but the BNP was seeing Britain clearly. It predicted that whites would be provoked into adopting their own version of identity politics and vote for its candidates in ever-greater numbers, which they did.

Would it have made a difference if the liberal mainstream had been as principled as the old left and opposed the war in Iraq but then supported Iraq's largely Muslim population as they tried to build a new country? Couldn't it have asked itself why it didn't take sides when Baathists and Islamists murdered Iraqis and drove them towards sectarian warfare? Maybe a liberal stand wouldn't have convinced Muslim voters that the anti-war movement wasn't defending the best interests of Muslim Iraqis. But the point was that the extreme was magnifying trends in the mainstream once again and the liberals didn't even try to stand by their principles. They stayed silent as a part of British Islam went off into the wilds, and they are going to have to live with the consequences.

CHAPTER ELEVEN

The Liberals Go Berserk

The bitter old New York socialists had learned that deep streaks of naiveté run through the liberal heart. Let a few thunderbolts of social rage and political distress fall across the country, and the naïve liberals would make their fatal leftward lurch and the disaster would occur. They would look at the achievements of America's socialists and trade unions and reformers and civil rights leaders, and the naïfs would curl their lips in scorn at the paltriness of democratic progress. The naïve liberals would out-Stalin the Stalinists while all the time imagining themselves to be sweetly untainted by any ideology. They would go on binges of posturing and ultra-radicalism until every last achievement the social democrats had built over the years lay in shambles.

Paul Berman, 1996

IN THE RUN-UP to the overthrow of Saddam Hussein, the rich world's liberals were in danger of becoming ridiculous. At no point before in history had their ideals seemed so dominant. About two-thirds of the world's nations were democracies at the end of the twentieth century, not always very good democracies, but making a start none the less. Meanwhile the language of human rights was becoming the way the world talked about the relationship between citizens and states. The non-governmental organizations the liberals most admired – Amnesty International, Human Rights Watch, Médecins Sans

Frontières – had successfully raged against oppression and mass suffering, and become 'players' in global politics. Governments consulted them and feared their criticisms. The organizers of international summits invited them to attend their meetings and share their thoughts with the powerful. In *Bridget Jones's Diary*, her retelling of *Pride and Prejudice*, Helen Fielding summed up the kudos of liberal interventionists when she made her modern version of Mr Darcy, not a landed aristocrat, but a 'top-notch human rights barrister' and 'total sex god': there was no more worthy or desirable occupation for the modern hero. The human rights conventions and inter-national criminal courts with which liberals sought to bind states offered unprecedented protection against crimes great and small. As democracy spread to South America and Asia, it seemed reasonable to believe that high standards of justice, which would have been impossible while the European empires and totalitarian systems of communism and fascism were alive, would become global norms. A twentieth century dominated by massacre would be succeeded by a twenty-first century dominated by liberal law.

When asked why they were going along with George Galloway and his kind, the liberal anti-war marchers protested that they didn't support totalitarianism and wanted nothing more than to uphold these exacting standards. And I can see how they managed to convince themselves that their virtue remained intact. They followed sober and responsible politi-cians such as Robin Cook and Gerhard Schroeder: leaders who were committed to multilateralism and conciliation, which were good principles to have. They opposed George W. Bush and Tony Blair because they didn't believe that Saddam Hussein posed an imminent threat and they feared an upsurge in al-Qaeda violence when the fighting began – and these were undeniably good grounds for opposing war. They worried about how lopsided and dangerous a world with only one superpower would become when that superpower resorted to force without the support of a clear majority of the democratic nations, and this, too, was a reasonable worry for all who weren't American – and for many Americans as well.

Hundreds of millions of liberal-minded people felt the same – not just in Europe, but in South and Central America, Canada, the Middle East, South Africa, India, Australia and Asia. Yet for all their reasonableness, and all their good and intelligent arguments, they were in danger of becoming vicious, self-defeating and fraudulent. Ridiculous, in short.

Saddam Hussein was against everything represented by Amnesty International and all the other admirable non-governmental organizations. No anti-liberal, anti-democratic tyrant could be further from the professed principles of the British Liberal Democrats, the European Social and Christian Democrats and the African National Congress. He was an embodiment of the mass terror and racism of the twentieth century which they said they wanted to escape.

When a war to overthrow him came, the liberals had two choices. The first was to oppose the war, remain hypercritical of aspects of the Bush administration's policy, but support Iraqis as they struggled to establish a democracy.

The policy of not leaving Iraqis stranded was so clearly the only moral option, it never occurred to me that there could be another choice. I did have an eminent liberal specialist on foreign policy tell me that 'we're just going to have to forget about Saddam's victims', but I thought he was shooting his mouth off in the heat of the moment. From the point of view of the liberals, the only ground they would have had to concede if they had stuck by their principles in Iraq would have been an acknowledgement that the war had a degree of legitimacy. They would still have been able to say it was catastrophically mismanaged, a provocation to al-Qaeda and all the rest of it. They would still have been able to condemn atrocities by American troops, Guantánamo Bay, and Bush's pushing of the boundaries on torture. They might usefully have linked up with like-minded Iraqis, who wanted international support to fight against the American insistence on privatization of industries, for instance. All they would have had to accept was that the attempt to build a better Iraq was worthwhile and one to which they could and should make a positive commitment.

A small price to pay; a price all their liberal principles insisted they had a duty to pay. Or so it seemed.

The second choice for the liberals was to do the wrong thing for the right reasons. To look at the Iraqi civilians and the British and American troops who were dying in a war whose central premise had proved to be false, and to go berserk; to allow justifiable anger to propel them into 'binges of posturing and ultra-radicalism' as the Sixties liberals had done when they went off the rails. As one critic characterized the position, they would have to pretend that 'the United States was THE problem and Iraq was *its* problem'. They would have to maintain that the war was not an attempt to break the power of tyranny in a benighted region, but the bloody result of a 'financially driven mania to control Middle Eastern oil, and the faith-driven crusade to batter the crescent with the cross'.

They chose to go berserk.

In 2003, while his friends in Washington were enjoying their brief moment of triumph, the neo-conservative thinker Robert Kagan tried to warn Republicans that the apparently feeble liberals of Europe had a latent power. On the face of it, Europe

– and by extension the countries and organizations that favoured the multilateralism associated with the ideals of Europe – was a joke. It talked loudly and carried a small stick. For all the high-sounding speeches from the inhabitants of 'Paradise' about 'never again' and human rights, they relied on the Americans to stop the atrocities in Bosnia and Kosovo and condemned them when they didn't intervene in Rwanda. Militarily, the United States could have won the war in Iraq without the support of a single ally, including Britain. Economically, it could afford to rebuild Iraq, even if the task took decades, as it did in Western Europe and Japan after the Second World War. But Kagan warned that *politically* a split in the democratic world would be calamitous. The European opponents of the war in Paris and Berlin, and all the organizations and liberal-minded people there and elsewhere who said they supported human rights, had the power to deny America moral legitimacy by saying the war was 'illegal'. Logically, they should then have followed through and demanded that the Americans release Saddam Hussein from prison and restore him to the presidency that the invading forces had 'illegally' stolen from him. But, as the theorists of the Eighties and Nineties had anticipated, there wasn't much call for logic in a post-modern world that welcomed self-righteous fury without positive commitments.

A paradoxical consequence of the emphasis on human rights law was that it reinforced this post-modern tendency to angry indifference. Judges in the courts of liberal democracies treated all abuses of human rights equally – and rightly so. A crime by a tyrant and an identical crime by those who sought to overthrow the tyrant were equal in the eyes of the law, and, again, that was as it should be. The legalistic approach, however, allowed no distinctions. Unless revolutions are peaceful, and, unfortunately, they rarely are, a judge must be passionate about the crimes but indifferent about whether the tyrant stays in power or not. Good judges aren't a guide to how the politically motivated should behave because, by definition, good judges can't commit to a cause because commitment would compromise their impartiality.

If the liberals decided that they hated Bush enough to play at judges and lawyers, the long-term effect on American public opinion would be to reinforce isolationism and the demands for the United States to bring its legions home – and not just from Iraq. In defiance of the stereotype, Americans have always cared what the rest of the world thinks about them, said Kagan. Their Declaration of Independence said they must have 'a decent respect for the opinion of mankind'. Paine, Jefferson and Franklin said from the start that American democratic values should be universal. 'Because Americans do care,' argued Kagan, 'the steady denial of international legitimacy by fellow democracies over time will become debilitating and perhaps even paralyzing.'

He didn't think of a further consequence – maybe because it was too scandalous to imagine. What would be the effect of pretending that it was illegal to overthrow a genocidal regime on Iraqis who were struggling to build a better country? The answer came soon after the invasion when the liberals gave aid and comfort to the Islamists and the Baathists. The 'insurgents' were able to use the liberals' slogans – 'It's all about oil!' 'It's illegal!' – and to taunt their opponents with the indisputable fact that even their supposed liberal allies in New York, London, Berlin and Paris didn't support them.

The push for a democratic Iraq had American military and financial power behind it, but liberals the world over denied it moral support and legitimacy, which matter more. In the eyes of liberal opinion, the millions of Iraqis who voted for a new government were little better than the receivers of stolen goods.

Richard Dawkins was a typical case. A polemical scientist who had pulverized religious fundamentalism in Britain and the United States, he couldn't see beyond Bush to an Iraq that was being pulverized by Islamists. In a letter to the press just after the war he summed up the liberals' raging indifference when he gloated, 'Now Bush is begging the United Nations to help clean up the mess he created in Iraq, there is a temptation to tell him to get lost. It is a temptation to which I hope the United Nations will succumb. US armed forces are "overstretched", and that is exactly how they should be.'

It wasn't just the far left who treated Iraqis who wanted a democracy as irritants or 'Quislings', and those who pretended it was when they came out of their berserkers were deceiving themselves. Stephen Sackur, a BBC foreign correspondent in Brussels, described the contrast between the reaction of his Iraqi wife's family and that of his European friends to the news that American troops had found Saddam Hussein hiding in a hole.

> Suddenly Saddam's haggard face is before us. This man has been a constant presence in my wife's imagination, to a lesser extent in mine too. He is our personification of evil and yet, perversely, without him we would never have met. A US medic is examining the tyrant's wild hair for lice and ticks; his mouth is open for a cursory inspection. He's like a horse being prodded by a vet – the whole scene so improbable that we simply stare, gobsmacked. In the Baghdad auditorium, local journalists are on their feet screaming Arabic curses at the big screen, others are clapping, laughing, crying. One, my wife tells me, repeatedly hollers 'Play it again! Play the tape again!' Our phone

starts ringing. Zina's mother is beside herself, giddy with joy. Saddam ruined her life, but at least she lived long enough to see him humiliated. And now he's locked up in a cage while politicians, lawyers and the world's wise men discuss his fate. And that surely is a cause for celebration at the end of this sour, violent, divisive year. But then again, maybe not. Even this week one acquaintance here in Brussels expressed his disgust at the sickening behaviour of what he called 'Iraqi Uncle Toms' who expressed delight at Saddam's capture simply to please their American masters. He means my wife, I suppose, or the millions of other Iraqis both in and out of their Saddam-free homeland who are coming to terms with a novel emotion this new year: hope of something better.

Cardinal Renato Martino agreed with Sackur's acquaintance in Brussels. He upheld the worst traditions of the Catholic Church when he said that far from being exultant at the arrest of Saddam he felt pity for 'this man destroyed, [the military] looking at his teeth as if he were a beast'. Meanwhile the idea that it was morally worthwhile for Sackur's Iraqi mother-in-law to see the tyrant who had ruined her life and infested her nightmares brought low was anathema to an eminent liberal QC in Cherie Blair's Matrix chambers who said that pictures of Saddam Hussein in his underpants were a breach of his human rights. If Saddam wanted to sue, he had a 'cast-iron case'.

I could go on. In fact, I could go on and on with examples of bad faith, and turn this into an encyclopaedia of liberal hypocrisy. The short point is that the ideology of the new far left or new far right, or however you wish to characterize the nihilist mentality we saw developing in the universities and the anti-globalization movement, was now mainstream. There was the same commitment-phobia: the leaders of the anti-war marches in Britain who saluted Saddam or mused about executing apostates were the exception – most who marched behind them just grew impatient if you asked which Iraqis they were supporting and what type of Iraq they wanted to see. The idea that liberalism imposed the obligation to support others who shared liberal values was as beyond most liberals as it was beyond most of those who called themselves socialists.

There was also an ominous echo of the theorists' debasement of language, as liberals spoke of Iraq in the passive voice and stripped sentences of human agency. Al-Qaeda and the Baathists vanished from the liberal press so that their crimes could become the responsibility of the Americans. Typical of thousands of reports was this from the *Independent* on the murder of Marla Ruzicka, a brave American Green Party activist and aid worker, by an Islamist suicide bomber in Baghdad on 16 April 2005. The piece was headlined, 'The senseless death of the woman who fought George Bush', which read as if her murder wasn't a premeditated act by a religious fanatic from the ultra-right but George Bush's fault. Her legacy 'should put many politicians in America, and in our own country, to shame', the *Independent* continued, while carefully – and shamefully – avoiding criticism of her killer. Euphemisms replaced proper nouns. You could read accounts of the violence in Iraq for months without learning whether Baathists and Islamists were planting the bombs or whether American occupiers had driven reasonable Iraqis to take up arms. Spelling out who was doing what to whom – the first responsibility of journalism – might have had the uncomfortable consequence of making readers wonder whether they ought to oppose anti-liberal forces. Better to keep it murky and cover Baathists and Islamists under the coy label of 'the insurgents'.

For the rich world's liberals, America was 'the hegemon' of both the theorists' and anti-globalizers' imagination, and, as with the theorists and anti-globalizers, no movement which fought the hegemonic could be unequivocally condemned. The theorists' reliance on attacks on their opponents' hypocrisy went mainstream too. The protests against George W. Bush felt like a great leftish mobilization, but it did not produce a new generation of left leaders. The only global figure to emerge was Michael Moore, and his film *Fahrenheit 9/11*, the most profitable documentary of all time, was the defining cultural moment of the protests. It was an embarrassingly shabby piece of propaganda, which worked on the correct assumption that its audience would be so angry it wouldn't care if what intelligence it had was insulted by honking factual errors and clunking internal contradictions. The high point was a countdown to the beginning of the war in Iraq in March 2003. As a voice intoned '*ten, nine, eight, seven...*' the screen was filled with images of Baathist Baghdad. Moore brushed aside the millions forced into exile and the mass graves and torture chambers and decided instead to present life in one of the worst tyrannies of the late twentieth century as sweet. Happy Iraqis enjoyed simple pleasures (*six...five*). Merry children flew kites (*four...three*). Blushing lovers got married (*two...one*). And just as a lovely little girl reached the bottom of a slide, the countdown reached zero and explosions filled the screen. The camera cut to a man holding a dead baby, standing by a pickup truck full of corpses.

Presented with propaganda which might have come from the studios of the dictators of the Thirties, the jury at the Cannes Film Festival and audiences in art house cinemas on every continent did not protest at the whitewash of totalitarianism, but rose to their feet and cheered themselves hoarse.

These weren't marginal Trotskyists heading from the far left to the religious right, but mainstream liberal consumers unable and unwilling to find a way to oppose George W. Bush while retaining (or discovering) the smallest concern for the victims of fascism.

The refusal to think about a middle course sent the liberal organizations with the most to lose from a collapse of faith in universal human rights spinning off into the wasteland of moral relativism. Five years ago, if you could have asked journalists, diplomats, academics and the victims of oppression themselves who they would have trusted above all others to stay sober in a crisis my guess is that they would have nominated Amnesty International. Peter Benenson, one of the great Englishmen of the twentieth century, set it up as a rigorously, almost ascetically, impartial body. At first, Amnesty dealt only with prisoners of conscience who espoused non-violence. It didn't matter which side they were on in the Cold War, or any other war, because Amnesty didn't concern itself with politics. Such was Amnesty's fastidiousness that when it expanded its remit to cover opposition to the death penalty, there were tormented debates among Amnesty members about whether a campaign that would be as concerned with saving common criminals as political dissidents would dilute the purity of the movement's purpose. I can't think of another political institution which through its moral exactness had earned the right to have its word accepted without challenge. When others spoke, the media scrutinized them and rounded up opponents to put a contrary view. When Amnesty spoke, what it said was incontestable.

Its reputation couldn't survive the aftermath of 9/11. The first sign that it was losing its compass came when Tony Blair cited Amnesty International's reports on Iraq in a dossier on his reasons for going to war. In September 2002, he urged MPs to

> read about the routine butchering of political opponents; the prison 'cleansing' regimes in which thousands die; the torture chambers and hideous penalties supervised by him and his family and detailed by Amnesty International. Read it all again and again. I defy anyone to say that this cruel and sadistic dictator should be allowed any possibility of getting his hands on more chemical, biological or even nuclear weapons.

Faced with the prospect of Tony Blair removing the regime it had denounced for thirty-four of its forty-one years, Amnesty cracked. Blair's description of the terror in Iraq was 'opportunistic and selective', it snapped. Strictly speaking, Amnesty should have kept its mouth shut. All that should have mattered to its leaders was whether Blair was quoting their reports accurately – which he was: Blair was 'selective' only in that he underplayed the scale of the terror. Amnesty couldn't admit that because the crisis was pushing it away from the necessary impartiality of any human rights worker or judge into a sly political posturing with echoes of the Thirties. If it took sides in the war, Amnesty's history would have forced it to come out for a democratic Iraq. But support for Bush, however limited, would have appalled its members. Equally, it couldn't support the Saddamists and Islamists. So in true Virginia Woolf style, Amnesty, along with a large segment of liberal opinion, pretended that both sides were equally bad and America and Britain were moral equivalents of totalitarian movements and states. Bizarre proclamations came out of Amnesty press conferences, and none was wackier than the claim that the American prison camp at Guantánamo Bay 'has become the Gulag of our times, entrenching the notion that people can be detained without any recourse to the law'. A brief pause to look at its own files would have shown Amnesty that in Solzhenitsyn's Gulag the secret police executed several million and drove countless millions more to early deaths from starvation, disease or exhaustion. The denial of constitutional rights at Guantánamo Bay was both a scandal and a recruiting tool for al-Qaeda. There were credible accounts of torture; however, those who made them were serious men and women who did not go on to allege that the American guards had executed a single prisoner or encouraged one inmate to die of starvation, disease or exhaustion. It is not a competition, as I said, but this wasn't even a comparison.

There's always a hangover after a liberal binge, and Amnesty's hands trembled so violently after its bender, they dropped the ball. Human rights are universal or they are nothing. Relativists have to diminish their importance and say they apply only to favoured groups, races or classes. In the nineteenth century European imperialists said that the colonials didn't need freedom of speech and other rights the British took for granted back home because they were 'lesser breeds without the law'. The twentieth-century communists and parts of the socialist left dismissed 'bourgeois freedoms' as irrelevant to people with nothing to eat. Irene Khan, Amnesty's Secretary General, showed that a twenty-first-century cultural relativism could be as condescending when she told the *Financial Times* that 'if you look globally today and want to talk about human rights, for the vast majority of the world's population they don't mean very much. To talk about freedom of expression to a man who can't read the newspaper, to talk about the right to work to someone who has no job; human rights means nothing to them unless it brings some change on these particular issues.'

You can blame Bush and Blair for creating a mental climate where even Amnesty International thought that human rights 'don't mean very much' if you wish, but it is as valid to blame the leaders of the rich world liberals. I don't know what went through the minds of Amnesty's officers but I could see around me how liberal journalists and politicians were contorting themselves. Because Bush was as good as his word and didn't impose a pliant dictator on Iraq – as I expected him to – people who once believed in human rights and free elections had to disassociate themselves from their old principles for fear of being accused of 'neo-conservatism' at dinner parties.

Human Rights Watch, which had made its name as a rival to Amnesty with its investigations into Saddam's Iraq, tied its tongue in knots as it tried to find a way to oppose the war to overthrow him. Kenneth Roth, its director, came up with a canting formula that there was no humanitarian purpose to the war because, although there had been mass slaughter, ethnic cleansing and environmental destruction over thirty-five years, 'no such slaughter was then ongoing or imminent' at the precise moment in 2003 when the war began. His lawyerly point was that although the Baathists were still killing, they were killing at a *slower* rate than in the past; the numbers of rapes and the intensity of the persecution of ethnic minorities were not up to their previous speed and nothing could be done until Saddam pulled his socks up and improved the strike rate. The British political philosopher, Norman Geras, explained Human Rights Watch's new take on human rights thus: 'The criteria for humanitarian intervention by Kenneth Roth (among others) would allow a regime that had just massacred, let us say, two million of its own people, but had finished massacring them, to stand with its sovereignty and international legitimacy intact.'

Médecins Sans Frontières was the only one of the major human rights organizations to hold on to the principles that had seemed to embody the highest hopes for the new century on 10 September 2001. Its founder, Bernard Kouchner, a former French socialist minister, was an evangelist for saving humanity. He made his motto 'mankind's suffering belongs to all men', as he laid out the duty of the rich world to intervene to save the poor world from crimes against humanity. Kouchner had worked in Biafra, Cambodia, Thailand, El Salvador, the former Yugoslavia, Rwanda and Afghanistan. He knew Sergio Vieira de Mello, Nadia Younes, Jean-Sélim Kanaan, Fiona Watson and many of the other brave men and women from the United Nations that al-Qaeda murdered in Baghdad in 2003. There was a touch of the Old Testament prophet about him and after accepting that the Bush administration had made catastrophic errors, he turned to liberals from the rich world who thought they could sit out the Iraq calamity, and thundered: 'As for us, as so often draped in our certitudes, let us not imagine ourselves protected from barbarism. Europeans' lukewarm interest in maintaining their American and British alliances won't protect them. Those who think so commit a fearsome mistake of analysis. Soon, the Americans won't be the only target of the fanatics, but all democrats, all moderate believers, and first of all, women.'

Kouchner's denunciations of complacency didn't get his fellow Europeans quite right. They were frightened. The Middle East was just across the Mediterranean and the EU had a large Muslim minority with a strong Muslim Brotherhood presence. But they weren't willing to fight fanaticism not only because of the passivity their post-modern Paradise encouraged, but for a practical reason that the US conservatives who roared about the terrorist threat never grasped. I don't mean to diminish the suffering caused by the bombings in Madrid and London when I say that Islamist violence in Europe after 9/11 was tolerable. Europe could live with a few dozen or few hundred casualties once every couple of years. The fear of a catastrophic conflict in the future nagged away, but it didn't feel like a war.

By the time you read this, maybe the body count will have risen and forced Europeans to think a little less glibly, but in the five years after 9/11, the combination of fear and a relatively small number of casualties brought the ideal conditions for appeasement. In the liberal and social democratic movements of Europe, fear led to denial, as it did in the Thirties, and every upsurge of Islamism was blamed on the root cause of Western provocation. Like the British liberal-left outside the Labour Party, the French left just gave up on principled thought and chanted the slogans of Trotskyists. In Spain, the Madrid bombings brought to power the Spanish socialists on whose behalf my mother had boycotted General Franco's oranges a generation before. Their conservative rivals had seemed certain to win the election until they were caught spinning that the atrocities were the work of Basques rather than Islamists and the Spanish electorate punished them for playing politics with murder.

In a videotape found near the scene, a Moroccan Islamist set out the bombers' demands.

We declare our responsibility for what happened in Madrid exactly two and a half years after the attacks on New York and Washington. It is a response to your collaboration with the criminal Bush and his allies. This is a response to the crimes that you have caused in the world, and specifically in Iraq and Afghanistan, and there will be more, if God wills it. You love life and we love death, which gives an example of what the Prophet Muhammad said. If you don't stop your injustices, more and more blood will flow and these attacks will seem very small compared to what can occur in what you call terrorism.

The brave Spanish socialists, whose grandparents had fought fascist armies that marched with the slogan 'Long Live Death!' on their lips, collapsed before Islamists who declared 'We Love Death' and ordered the immediate withdrawal of Spanish troops from Iraq. Fascism wasn't ancient history in Spain. It had survived until 1975, and many socialist politicians were old enough to remember reading in Franco's school textbooks about how a conspiracy of Freemasons and Jews threatened Spanish purity. They showed no fellow feeling with Iraqis who were enduring what their grandparents had endured. A few weeks before the bombs, the Socialist International met in Madrid. Barham Salih, a leader of the Kurdish left, told the leaders of the mainstream European left that:

Good Social Democrats should be making the moral argument that the war of liberation in Iraq came too late for so many innocent victims of Saddam's fascist tyranny. And the lesson for the international community is that it must be prepared to act in time and pre-empt terrible tragedies to happen again anywhere else in the world. I call upon your help to Iraqi democrats in this critical juncture of the history of the Middle East. To help us transform our country from the land of mass graves and aggression, to the land of peace, justice and democ- racy. I can see an Iraq that is democratic, that is an anchor for peace in this troubled part of the world and a partner to civilized nations in pursuit of the universal values of human rights and justice.

No good did his stirring words do him. As far as the Europeans were concerned, the unnecessary war had brought death into the Paradise of Fortress Europe, and that was the end of it. Like children in a playground, the leaders of the Spanish socialists screamed that Bush was a 'liar' and Blair was a 'dickhead' and fled – leaving their comrades in the lurch.

For Germans, the second Iraq war marked the moment when they finally shrugged off their wartime guilt. They had built an admirable liberal democracy in the west and taken over the Soviet satellite in the east, and had nothing to feel guilty about. However, the German liberal-left didn't stride forward with confidence but wiggled away from the past, with a deviousness which could be seen all over the liberal world. The propaganda of the German Social Democrats and Greens implied Bush was now closer to Hitler than the Germans were as it concentrated on denouncing America's 'war of aggression'. The phrase had Nazi parallels, but, as a German commentator noted, to get away with the analogy, the German left had to ignore 'the countless real victims of Saddam's regime' and the 'uncomfortably familiar echoes of Nazi slogans in the anti-Semitic ideology and thrust of the Baath regime'.

Like John Major's Tories during the Bosnian war, the mainstream European left didn't want to participate in a war to overthrow Saddam themselves, as was their right, but they also wanted to deny the legitimacy of others who were prepared to fight.

* * *

Kanan Makiya returned to Baghdad in 2003 and found he was a bit of a star. Members of the Baghdad intelligentsia had passed around samizdat copies of *Republic of Fear* for years, and many doors opened for him. Kanan used his clout with his new friends and the American occupiers to get back the family home, which his parents had fled thirty years earlier when the Baathists accused them of being members of an international conspiracy of Freemasons. His main concern was whether his fellow Iraqis would be able to cope with the aftershocks of tyranny. How could a nation which had suffered so much come to terms with its past? he asked himself. How could torturer and victim live in the same country? Makiya and his colleagues answered their questions by creating the Iraq Memory Foundation in the Makiyas' old home. They followed the example set in Germany, Cambodia and South Africa, and amassed millions of files. Nothing was to be missed so that if they ever had the chance of peace, Iraqis would be able to confront their own history and reach a truce with their past.

The foundation collected 2.4 million pages from files captured by Kurdish guerrillas, which described the preparations for the Anfal extermination campaign; 800,000 pages describing in revolting detail what Saddam's armies did to the people of Kuwait; and an estimated 3 million pages on how the Baathists initiated members, indoctrinated schoolchildren and persecuted Iraqis for the capital crime of failing to respect Saddam Hussein. Makiya wanted more. He wanted to build a gigantic archive which would counter the decades of silence and fear with a true map of the totalitarian state.

'My instinct was to put everything I had out on the web,' he told me, 'to let it all come out.'

But full disclosure is not a straightforward policy. Although South Africans cite the virtues of 'truth and reconciliation', the two don't always go together. How much truth can the survivors of a totalitarian society take? If people learn the identities of torturers and informants, they can take revenge. In Iraq, as in Nazi Germany and the Soviet Union, the secret police had forced the closest friends of its targets to turn into narks to save their skins. Did their victims need to know that?

Yet secrecy was no answer either. The experience of Eastern Europe after the fall of communism had shown that ruthless politicians were capable of leaking partial extracts from the reports of the old secret police to discredit rivals. Because their smeared targets didn't have access to the files they had no means to rebut the false accusations.

Makiya turned to Germany, the country that knew more about confronting totalitarianism in its fascist and communist guises than any other. Marianne Birthler, the official in charge of the archive of old Stasi files, welcomed him and his colleagues to her Berlin office – which, in a nice touch, was housed in the old headquarters of the East German secret police – and explained how to balance the demands of confidentiality and openness.

The Germans and the Iraqis got on famously, and Makiya was bowled over by Germany's dedication to preserving the historical record. At a joint news conference, the ever-exuberant Makiya declared that applying the lessons of Berlin back in Baghdad 'will change the way Iraqis think of themselves in an infinitely better way'.

He wanted German archivists to come to Iraq to teach Arabs and Kurds what they knew about preserving the past for the historians, novelists and poets of the future, as well as the victims of torture and the families of the dead. There was a snag. The German government refused to allow its officials to cooperate with Iraq as a protest against the 'illegal' war. Its

Foreign Minister was Joschka Fischer, a member of the 1968 generation of radicals who had hung around the fringes of the terrorist wing of the German far left in his youth before calming down and going on to lead the pacifist Green Party into government. Like George Lansbury before him, he had hawked 'his conscience round from body to body asking to be told what to do with it', before finally deciding to drop his pacifism and allow German troops to intervene to stop crimes against humanity in the Balkans. Iraq, though, was beyond the pale, and the German Foreign Office refused to give German officials permission to travel to Baghdad to share their expertise.

'Just come, anyway,' cried Makiya. His Germans friends said they would love to but couldn't.

This little act of spite can stand for the parochialism and selfishness of the mainstream liberal-left. Just as the European Union limited poor world imports into its Paradise, so it refused to export the best of its values. Foolishly as well as selfishly, it pretended that there was no longer a need to confront the demons of the past.

CHAPTER TWELVE

The Jews, *the* Muslims and – er – *the* Freemasons

To take only the subject of the Jews: it would be difficult to find a form of bad reasoning about them which has not been heard in conversation or been admitted to the dignity of print.

George Eliot, 1879

ON THE SATURDAY of the 2003 demonstration against the war in Iraq, I watched as about 1 million people marched through London, then sat down to write for the *Observer*. I pointed out that the march's organizers represented a merger of far left and far right. Be careful, I said. Saddam Hussein's Iraq has spewed out predatory armies and corpses for decades. If you are going to advocate a policy that would keep him in power, you should talk to his victims, whose number included socialists and liberals – good people, like you. The next day I looked at my emails. There were a lot of them. The first was a fan letter from Ann Leslie, the *Daily Mail*'s chief foreign correspondent, who had seen the barbarism of Baathism close up. Her cheery note ended with a warning, 'you are not going to believe the antisemitism that is about to hit you'.

'Don't be silly, Ann,' I replied. 'There's no racism on the Left.'

I worked my way through the rest of the emails. I couldn't believe the antisemitism that hit me.

I learned it was one thing being called 'Cohen' if you went along with liberal orthodoxy, quite another when you pointed out liberal betrayals. Your argument could not be debated on its merits. There had to be a malign motive. You had to be in the pay of 'international' tycoons or 'neo-conservatives'. You had to have bad blood. You had to be a Jew.

Try it for yourself if you don't believe me. Go on to a leftish website and put your email address at the bottom of a piece expressing doubt about a part of current liberal-left thinking – praise an aspect of American policy or condemn al-Qaeda. You can call yourself Cathleen ni Houlihan for all the difference it will make, the odds are you will be accused of 'Zionism'.

I directed my leftish correspondents to the Patriotic Union of Kurdistan, a member of the Socialist International that had decided after being on the receiving end of one too many extermination campaigns that foreign invasion was the only way. No good. I tried sending them to the Iraqi Communist Party, which opposed the invasion but understood the possibilities for liberation that were beyond many of the fine minds of the Western intelligentsia. No good, either. As the months passed, and Iraqis were caught between a criminally incompetent occupation and an 'insurgency' so far to the right it was off the graph, I had it all. A leading figure on the British left asked me to put him in touch with members of the Iraqi opposition. 'I knew it! I knew it!' he cried when we next met. 'They want to recognize Israel.' I experienced directly what many blacks and Asians had told me: you never can tell with racism. Where people stand on the political spectrum says nothing about their visceral beliefs. I found the far left wasn't confined to the chilling Socialist Workers' Party but contained many scrupulous people it was a pleasure to meet and an education to debate. Meanwhile, the centre was nowhere near as moderate as it liked to think. One minute I would be chatting to a BBC presenter who seemed a civilized man; the next, he would be screaming about how the Jews were using the Holocaust to extort money from gullible Germans. One minute I would be thinking that a liberal academic had an almost pedantic regard for correct form; the next he would be raving that only supporters of Israel wanted Saddam Hussein overthrown.

All around me, liberal London descended into the radical chic of the ultra-right. A writer for *Index on Censorship*, which W. H. Auden's friends had founded in 1972 to defend freedom of speech, gloated about the ultimate censorship of Theo van Gogh, the Dutch film-maker, who was murdered by a knife-wielding Islamist for opposing the subjugation of Muslim women. The real villain according to *Index* was not the murderer but van Gogh, a 'free-speech fundamentalist' who had incited his own murder when he went on a 'martyrdom operation' and 'roared his Muslim critics into silence with obscenities'. The *Independent* and *New Statesman* produced neo-Nazi iconography, while an article reprinted by the *London Review of Books* won the praise of a former leader of the Ku Klux Klan for explaining that a Jewish 'Lobby' controlled American foreign policy. The Church of England's General Synod, university lecturers and architects called for boycotts of Israel and none of them felt the need to explain why they didn't demand boycotts of states which had committed far greater crimes against humanity, up to and including genocide. When you asked them why they were singling out Jews for special treatment, they cried that the Jews always said that criticism of Israel was 'antisemitic', even though no serious scholar, journalist, Jewish organization or Israeli politician did anything of the sort.

I can see now that going along with fascistic ideas to some degree was a way of subliminally coping with the Islamist threat, or of letting Bertrand Russell's fallacy of the superior virtue of the oppressed turn anger at the treatment of the Palestinians into sympathy for the Devil. The desire to appease terrorists by agreeing with their prejudices and outrage at oppression in the West Bank and Gaza shepherded the herd of independent minds to the extreme right, and you can't deny that many enjoyed the trip.

Imagine the thrill. To intellectuals of a certain age, the assassin of a film-maker could seem like a doomed existential hero striking a blow against the system – even if it was the system of free speech and rights for women they nominally believed in. The flirtations with antisemitic imagery and argument, and the treatment of Israel as a special case to which double standards applied, were also a merciful release of pressure.

'For anyone who inhabits Western culture,' wrote the American writer Christopher Caldwell,

> the Holocaust made that culture a much more painful place to inhabit – and for any reasonably moral person, greatly narrowed the range of acceptable political behavior. To be human is to wish it had never happened. (Those who deny that it did may be those who can't bear to admit that it happened.) But it did. If there's a will-to-antisemitism in Western culture – as there probably is – then the Arab style of Judeophobia, which is an antisemitism without the West's complexes, offers a real redemptive project to those Westerners who are willing to embrace it. It can liberate guilty, decadent Europeans from a horrible moral albatross. What an antidepressant! Saying there was no such thing as the gas chambers is, of course, not

respectable. But the same purpose can be served using what Leo Strauss called the *reductio ad Hitlerum* to cast the Jews as having committed crimes identical to the Nazis'. They must be identical, of course, so the work of self-delusion can be accomplished. We did one, the Jews did one. Now we're even-steven.

Beyond the release from the burden of the past, lay the relief of letting out repressed emotion. Outsiders don't understand the enfeebling self-consciousness of political debate on the middle-class liberal-left: they can't imagine the thoughts strangled and tongues bitten to avoid giving the smallest offence to audiences overanxious to find it. The director of a prison reform charity once told me that he struck all metaphors and similes from his speeches. Even if it was a bland cliché of 'the government is like a rabbit caught in the headlights' type, he wouldn't use it because he knew half his listeners would stop listening to him for thirty seconds as they double-checked that he had not unintentionally insulted a disadvantaged or ill-favoured group.

Once, however, a figure or group became an approved object of hatred, pent-up feeling burst over it. You can't understand the sexist abuse heaped on the 'bitch' Margaret Thatcher and the homophobic abuse levelled at Peter Mandelson for his 'closeness' to Tony Blair without grasping the joy of release. The admiration of pacifists for suicide bombers and the relish with which formerly prim Labour ministers enjoyed the perquisites of office after 1997 are further examples of the riots which follow when leftish puritanism breaks down.

I didn't understand that at the time and was merely baffled. The moment when my bewilderment settled into a steady scorn came when the *Guardian*'s online talkboards carried a discussion about me and another supporter of the war from the Left with a Jewish name, which was entitled: 'David Aaronovitch and Nick Cohen Are Enough to Make a Good Man Anti-Semitic'. The political incorrectness was too much for one contributor. Rightly, she protested that naked bigotry infused the debate. The *Guardian* readers should have head-lined it 'David Aaronovitch and Nick Cohen Are Enough to Make a Good Man, *or Woman*, Anti-Semitic'.

I resolved then to complete two tasks: to apologize to Ms Leslie, which took me a matter of minutes, and to learn more about antisemitism, which took a little longer. Like Margaret Makiya forty years earlier, I ran into – er – the Freemasons.

Critics of this book could make a tough-minded case that anti-semitism doesn't matter although I doubt many will have the courage to argue it. Those Jews who survived the twentieth century are generally secure, they could say. Enemies who make no distinction between soldiers and civilians attack Israel and the Islamist Iranian regime threatens 'to wipe it off the map', but it remains the strongest military power in the region and can look after itself. As for the echo of the old antisemitic laws in the demands from Anglicans, architects and academics for sanctions on Israel but not, for instance, on the Sudan – get real: universal values are for the birds. Leftists had a respectable record of exposing the dark corners of the far right in South Africa, the American Deep South, Pinochet's Chile, Franco's Spain and the Colonels' Greece. Only the bravest had much to say about the Soviet Union, China or Cuba. Overall, the democratic right opposed those monstrosities. But it's not a competition, as you keep saying. Looking back, good came out of the activism of both sides. Equally, good will come from our obsession with Israel. If Moynihan's Law makes it easier to attack Israel because it is a democracy with a free press and independent judiciary, so what? That doesn't make what Israel does right. The Palestinians need help in a fight against racism and collective punishment. Just give it, and don't ask too many questions about the helpers' double standards. You've kept saying that the modern obsession with hypocrisy is disproportionate and conceals a cowardly unwillingness to tackle greater vices. Well then, mean what you say. Who cares if the motives of Israel's opponents aren't as high-minded as they pretend? The loss of Palestinian land, the barrier of partition sneaking across the West Bank, the humiliations endured at the hands of Israeli forces and the poverty of the overwhelming majority of the Palestinian population are evils which are worth fighting.

I willingly concede that this argument makes a great deal of sense until you ask a question I've delayed asking for too long: what is antisemitism?

George Orwell wrote that 'there are two journalistic activities that always bring you a comeback. One is to attack the Catholics and the other is to defend the Jews'. I will start with Catholics by pointing out that the first modern antisemitic conspiracy theory of politics had no Jews in it. Racist laws had confined Jews to ghettos when the modern world began with the industrial revolution and the Enlightenment. Even the maddest thinkers in Europe could not bring themselves to maintain that persecuted Jews were the secret rulers of the world. The supporters of the far right needed a conspiracy theory none the less to explain away the revolutions of the eighteenth century. When American revolutionaries scandalized them by drafting bills of rights, separating church and state and rejecting the rule of George III, when the French revolutionaries overthrew the king who loved them and the

Holy Mother Church that succoured them, the counter-revolutionaries could not accept that millions of American and French men and women had revolted of their own free will. Diabolic conspirators must have duped the masses into rejecting sacred authority.

In 1797, eight years after the start of the French Revolution, L'Abbé Augustin Barruel, a French Jesuit priest in exile in Britain, exposed the conspirators. He launched the tradition that led to modern fascism with a *Da Vinci Code* for the counter-revolution: *Memoirs to Serve for a History of Jacobinism*. Barruel built upon a startling claim made to him by a Scottish nutcase called John Robison that Crusaders in the medieval order of Knights Templar had gone underground and plotted for five centuries to do nothing less than take over the world.

Allow me to explain. The Templars Barruel seized on had been the richest of the military-monastic orders in medieval Europe. Their banks lent to kings and popes, and their hostels and castles peppered Christendom. In 1307, Philip the Fair of France grabbed their wealth in a proto-totalitarian campaign. His agents rounded up Templar knights and tortured them until they were ready to confess in show trials to the most extraordinary crimes. The knights 'admitted' that Templar initiation ceremonies required new recruits to spit, trample and urinate on the cross, kiss each other obscenely on the lips, navel and base of the spine, deny the sacraments and worship satanic idols. Even the Catholic Church does not defend the persecution of the Templars today, but Barruel believed the accusations of diabolism and homosexuality wholeheartedly, and used them to explain the revolutions of the 1780s.

What had happened was this, apparently. The Templars had gone into hiding and formed a secret society after their persecution. Over the centuries, they had nursed their hatred of monarchy and of the Catholic Church, which had supported Philip the Fair. They lived in a shadowy world behind the scenes, and worked under cover names – the Freemasons, the Bavarian Illuminati – to confuse their enemies. They waited until the eighteenth century, and then struck back by manufacturing consent for their occult doctrines of liberty, equality and fraternity. 'Your whole school,' thundered Barruel at the Freemasons

> and all your Lodges are derived from the Templars after the extinction of their Order, a certain number of guilty knights, having escaped the proscription, united for the preservation of their horrid mysteries. To their impious code, they added the vow of vengeance against the kings and priests who destroyed their Order, and against all religion, which anathematised their dogmas. They made adepts, who should transmit from generation to generation the same hatred of the God of the Christians, and of Kings, and of Priests. These mysteries have descended to you, and you continue to perpetuate their impiety, their vows, and their oaths. Such is your origin. The lapse of time and the change of manners have varied a part of your symbols and your frightful systems; but the essence of them remains, the vows, the oaths, the hatred, and the conspiracies are the same.

Barruel was convinced that this ancient satanic plot could explain the loss of his world. If people asked for proof that the Freemasons had 'sworn hatred to the altar and the throne, had sworn to crush the God of the Christians, and utterly to extirpate the Kings of the Earth', he replied that Voltaire, George Washington and Benjamin Franklin were all Freemasons (or, rather, Knights Templar). His book was a hit, and bemused British Freemasons had to issue angry denials. They did no good, and Barruel's fantasy that human rights and democracy were a front for a cosmic conspiracy against monarchy and religion passed into the bloodstream of the European far right: not respectable conservatism, which naturally had many Masonic sympathizers, but into the underworld of ultra-Catholicism and counter-revolutionary fantasy and thuggery.

Barruel's theory sounds insane when you write it out – actually, it is insane – but it appealed to those whose political certainties went with the loss of the divinely blessed monarchical order, and whose economic certainties were being destroyed by the new capitalist ways of doing business.

We flatter ourselves if we regard their embrace of conspiracy theory as outlandish. Democracy is not an easy system of government. It has been despised as mob rule or the manipulation of the mob by demagogues ever since Plato. If I were to address a leftish meeting in London and say that the Knights Templar had been plotting to take control of the world since 1307, I would be laughed off stage – at any rate I hope I would. If I were to say that democracy was a charade because there were no serious differences between parties that were the playthings of corporate America, I'd be applauded, and not only at leftish meetings. What would happen if I were to say that Jews featured disproportionately among the bankers and chief executives of global capitalism? Thirty years ago, the audience would have booed me as a Nazi. Today, I'm not so sure. Maybe there would just be a shuffling of feet as the audience willed me to substitute 'Zionist' for 'Jew'.

For it doesn't take much to lose your balance and fall into conspiratorial ways of thinking, particularly when you are on the losing side or suspect your apparently powerful traditions are under threat. The success of market economies, the decline of trade unions and the fraying of welfare states make many on the liberal-left feel that they are losing today, but for most of the two centuries after the Enlightenment, the monarchical and religious right were history's losers. Traditionalists terrified by the prospect of democracy, second-rate intellectuals unable to find the work to match their expectations and small business people and peasants squeezed between the trade unions and conglomerates, supplied the bulk of fascism's recruits.

Just before his death in 1820, Barruel became the first counter-revolutionary thinker to concentrate on Jews, not as individuals, but as *the* Jews, a diabolic sect united in a common conspiracy. If you accept his logic that modernity is a plot, then his shift to antisemitism made sense. The promise of the Enlightenment was set out in the American Declaration of Independence. The belief that 'all men are created equal, that they are endowed by their Creator with certain unalienable Rights, that among these are Life, Liberty, and the Pursuit of Happiness' necessitated freeing subject peoples in the long run. The Jews were the first beneficiaries, and the sight of the revolutionary governments putting a religious group that church and state had persecuted since the Romans on an equal legal footing with Christians infuriated the ultra-right.

Traditional Christian hatred casts Jews as the ultimate outsiders – the Christ-killers, the well-poisoners, the child-murderers and the usurers. The new political hatred retained many features of the old, but stood the original accusation on its head. Political antisemitism produced a theory of power in which Jews had obtained their freedom because they were the ultimate insiders – the manipulators of governments and peoples, the secret organizers of revolutionary chaos, the real rulers of the Earth.

Counter-revolutionaries can never go back, which is why Islamism shouldn't be seen as an early medieval ideology that has jumped from the seventh to the twenty-first century, or Christian, Hindu and Jewish fundamentalism as a return to the past. Revolutionary times force reactionaries to become revolutionary themselves and to find new ways of appealing to the publics which the spread of education and democracy bring. Throughout the nineteenth century, religious ultras and racist conmen declared that the Jews were trying to conquer the world. A handful went further and ruled that only 'the complete extermination of the Jewish race' could frustrate their evil ways.

The reactionaries of tsarist Russia were the most splenetic because they had the greatest need to manufacture a racist campaign to distract subject peoples. The autocracy was buckling before the new forces of liberalism, socialism and nationalism, and had to rally support. Tsar Nicholas II's secret police wrote *The Protocols of the Learned Elders of Zion*, and presented it as a true account of a vast Jewish plot. The policemen's efforts read like a bad Monty Python sketch today. The Elders scheme to spread every dangerous political creed and, for good measure, pornography and alcoholism. The Jews gloat that liberal freedom is a charade that hides their power. 'What is the part played by the press today?' the Elders intone. 'It serves to excite and inflame those passions which are needed for our purpose or else it serves the selfish ends of parties. It is often vapid, unjust, mendacious, and the majority of the public have not the slightest idea what ends the press really serves.' The fools!

The attack on press freedom and all other freedoms makes it obvious that political antisemitism is not about Jews, it is about power. It would still exist if the Nazis had killed every Jew on earth, and does exist in countries where there are no Jews. The tsars used it to oppress all the peoples of the Russian

Empire and deny them constitutional government. Then as now, state-sanctioned racism against a minority appeared to be defending the majority while working to keep it subjugated.

Yet as Norman Cohn, a historian of the *Protocols*, says, 'incredibly yet incontestably' a ludicrous and self-serving forgery produced by the 'counter-revolutionary agents and pseudo-mystics that flourished on the decay of the Tsar's empire' was believed by millions and helped inspire the murder of millions in the twentieth century. At one point in the Thirties, sales of the *Protocols* were second only to sales of the Bible. For Adolf Hitler they were a bible. In *Mein Kampf* he said that 'the important thing is that with positively terrifying certainty they reveal the nature and activity of the Jewish people and expose their inner contexts as well as their ultimate final aims'.

As incredible and incontestable is how much of their story of 1905 the tsarist agents took from the original ravings of the European counter-revolution in 1797. Once again, there is an ancient conspiracy that seeks to overthrow the established order of kings and tsars, popes and patriarchs. Political liberty is once more revealed as a fraud. Like the Freemasons, the Elders use democratic ideas to create corrupt parties that act as their front organizations. In the villages my great-grandparents fled, proclamations appeared which read: 'The efforts to replace the autocracy of the divinely appointed Tsar by a constitution and a parliament are inspired by those bloodsuckers, the Jews, the Armenians and the Poles. Beware of the Jews! All the evil, all the misfortune comes from the Jews. Down with the traitors, down with the constitution!'

When the fascist wave broke over Europe, its supporters explicitly acknowledged their debt to Barruel. His satanic Freemasons were still there in the updating of his conspiracy theory; in a minor role certainly – but still there. 'Gentile Masonry blindly serves as a screen for us and our objects,' the Elders of Zion cackle in the *Protocols*. Or as Hitler elaborated in *Mein Kampf*, 'the governing circles and the higher strata of the political and economic bourgeoisie are brought into his [the Jew's] nets by the strings of Freemasonry, and never need to suspect what is happening'.

As he annihilated European Jews by their millions, Hitler honoured the memory of the counter-revolutionaries of the 1790s by murdering European Freemasons in their tens of thousands. Mussolini banned them, and Franco hated them for corrupting Catholic Spain with Enlightenment ideas and murdered maybe as many as 7,000.

And – incredibly yet incontestably again – the ideas that destroyed Europe in the Thirties and Forties survive to this day. The Muslim far right quite deliberately took the ideology of L'Abbé Augustin Barruel, Tsar Nicholas II, Benito Mussolini, General Francisco Franco and Adolf Hitler, and transferred it to the Middle East; not just in part, but in every detail right down to the paranoid fear of men who roll up their trouser legs.

The resurgence of fascistic ideologies in the Middle East was explained away by the liberal-left and just about everyone else with the assertion that its 'root cause' was the Israeli occupation of the West Bank and Gaza. Very few stopped to think how bewildered they sounded. They had to pretend that from the 1790s until the 1940s, fascistic ideas were deranged conspiracy theories employed by the ultra-right, and ultra-left on occasion, to justify tyranny, censorship, the suppression of the rights of women and genocide. As soon as the Second World War ended and the state of Israel was established, however, the madness vanished, and fascistic ideas became rational responses to a colonial venture by refugees from Europe.

As a result of this rationalization of the irrational, a dirty little war in a patch of land smaller than Wales acquired huge explanatory power. Palestine became the justification for everything that was going wrong in the Middle East and, increasingly, everything that was going wrong with Europe's Muslim minority. To say that the 'root cause' of the Israeli–Palestinian conflict explained Islamism was to make a very large assumption about a very small war, and its adherents had to dodge three big questions as they made it.

The first is why did fascist ideas take off in the Middle East? Why not a standard anti-colonial hatred of immigrant settlers? The short answer is that right-wing Arabs who had to cope with the flight of Jewish refugees from the Nazis to Palestine turned to the Nazis for support. (Not all Arabs did; the sensible ones made the unanswerable point that there were no good grounds for making Palestinians pay for the crimes of Europeans.) Hitler's Germany responded by pumping money and propaganda into the Middle East, in part because it wanted to stop the creation of a Jewish state that could act as a voice for persecuted Jews as the Vatican acted as a voice for persecuted Catholics, and in part because it just hated Jews. The Nazis' *Zeesen* radio service mingled antisemitic propaganda with quotations from the Koran. 'The Jew since the time of Mohammed has never been a friend of the Muslim, the Jew is the enemy and it pleases Allah to kill him,' it declared. It presented the Allies in the Second World War as the lackeys of the Jews and drummed into its audience the notion that the international community was the 'United Jewish Nation'. Haj Amin el-Husseini, the Mufti of Jerusalem, and the senior religious figure in Palestine, became an agent of the Nazi empire. Hitler received him and he encouraged European Muslims to join SS battalions.

That was more than half a century ago and you can understand it as a reaction to the push towards an Israeli state if you wish. The persistence of fascist ideology is harder to dismiss.

Writing in the Fifties, Sayyid Qutb, who inspired the Sunni Islamist movement, described Judaism not as a religion but as the force behind all the secular ideas that threatened the sacred power. In *Our Battle with the Jews*, he decided that Karl Marx, Sigmund Freud, Emile Durkheim and Jean-Paul Sartre were Jews and consequently 'behind the doctrine of atheistic materialism was a Jew; behind the doctrine of animalistic sexuality was a Jew; and behind the destruction of the family and the shattering of sacred relationships in society was a Jew'. (Sartre wasn't Jewish, but then, as I found, a feature of modern anti-semitism is that anyone can be Jewish. It is a universal religion.)

Meanwhile Adolf Hitler might have written Article 22 of the Hamas constitution of 1988.

For a long time, the enemies [the Jews] have been planning, skilfully and with precision, for the achievement of what they have attained. They took into consideration the causes affecting the current of events. They strived to amass great and substantive material wealth which they devoted to the realisation of their dream. With their money, they took control of the world media, news agencies, the press, publishing houses, broadcasting stations, and others. With their money they stirred revolutions in various parts of the world with the purpose of achieving their interests and reaping the fruit therein. They were behind the French Revolution, the communist revolution and most of the revolutions we heard and hear about, here and there. With their money they formed secret societies, such as Freemasons, Rotary Clubs, the Lions and others in different parts of the world for the purpose of sabotaging societies and achieving Zionist interests. With their money they were able to control imperialistic countries and instigate them to colonise many countries in order to enable them to exploit their resources and spread corruption there.

I can just about understand how the survival of the ultra-right tradition of the 1790s made the Palestinian branch of the Muslim Brotherhood fantasize about the octopus-like grip of the Freemasons, but why the Rotary clubs? Why the Lions clubs?

You might as well ask why the Freemasons? Why the Jews? To seek a rational root cause, is to miss the point that there always has to be someone. Freedom must be a conspiracy; failure must be someone else's fault. Why the Rotarians? Why not the Rotarians?

You may want to excuse Hamas by saying it is a vile organization created by the vile behaviour of the Israelis, although I would caution against it. But you shouldn't dodge a second question: why are fascist ideas being parroted hundreds of miles away, indeed thousands of miles away, from a disputed territory on the edge of the eastern Mediterranean?

The Syrian Ministry of Information authorized publication of the *Protocols of the Elders of Zion*, and it is on the school syllabus in Saudi Arabia. Elements in the state-controlled Egyptian media treat the forgery as fact, and as we have seen, Saddam Hussein used them to justify his totalitarian persecutions. Meanwhile Egyptian, Iranian and Syrian television have run series based on the *Protocols*. 'Listen!' says a rabbi to a young Jew, in a typical scene. 'We have received an order from above. We need the blood of a Christian child for the unleavened bread for the Passover feast.' Jews seize a terrified child. Then the camera zooms in for a close-up of his throat being cut.

In this reactionary culture, a Jewish conspiracy is responsible for just about every perturbation the pagan world inflicts on the godly. The Saudi Arabian religious police in the Committee for the Propagation of Virtue and Prevention of Vice declared in 2003 that Jews were even corrupting the toys of innocent children when they announced that 'Jewish Barbie dolls, with their revealing clothes and shameful postures, accessories and tools are a symbol of the decadence of the perverted West. Let us beware of her dangers and be careful.'

And 200 years on from Barruel, the rhetoric about the Freemasons 'subverting societies' was still being translated into action. On 9 March 2004, two suicide bombers blew themselves up in an Istanbul restaurant. If their victims had been British, American or Jewish, right-thinking people would have said that the overthrow of the Taliban or the invasion of Iraq or the humiliation of the Palestinians was the 'root cause' of the murders. As it was, the dead were members of a party of diners from a Masonic lodge, and the story died as quickly as they did.

It is straining credulity to say this is all the fault of Israel. If you do, you are in danger of agreeing with a cod line of consolation peddled by the Arab nationalists and Islamists. Their answer to the question of how a culture that was once the very fulcrum of civilization became dependent, defeated, backward, corrupt and poverty-stricken is: 'They did it! The Westernizers, the uppity women, the Freemasons and the Jews.'

Syria, Egypt, Iraq and Iran are all Middle Eastern countries, so even if you wanted to strain credulity by saying their official antisemitism was nothing more than a rational reaction to Israeli oppression, you might not be straining it to breaking point.

But then we have the Malaysian Prime Minister Mahathir Mohamad damning the 'Jews who determine our currency levels, and bring about the collapse of our economy'. The spokesman for the Muslim Brotherhood's Asian equivalent, the Jamaat-i-Islaami party in Pakistan, decided that 'most anything bad that happens, prices going up, whatever, this can usually be attributed to the IMF and the World Bank, which are synonymous with the United States. And who controls the United States? The Jews do.' In a different hemisphere, Robert Mugabe blamed the collapse of the Zimbabwean economy he had wrought on 'Jews in South Africa, working in cahoots with their colleagues here'. Abu Hamza, who incited terrorism from his Finsbury Park mosque in London, sounded like a ghost from Nazi Germany when he told the press: 'I am not saying every American government figure knew about [9/11]. But there are a few people [in the US government] who want to trigger a third world war. They are sponsored by the business lobby. Most of them are Freemasons, and they have loyalty to the Zionists.' A poll for *The Times* in 2006 found that 46 per cent of the British Muslims sampled believed that Jews were 'in league with the Freemasons to control the media and politics'.

All of these echoes of fascism passed without comment from the majority of the liberal-left. I'm not saying their anti-Zionism was the same as classic antisemitism because with a few dishonourable exceptions the Jewish obsession of most people on the Left didn't degenerate into a visceral loathing of all Jews. Rather, they behaved as if they were antisemites. When they designated Israel the world's only pariah state and the 'root cause' of terrorism and war, they once again ascribed to Jews the supernatural power to bring chaos. When they blamed a coterie of 'neo-conservatives' for protecting it, they slipped into the mental habits of Barruel.

As they did, they had to dodge the third and final question: how did they think they were helping the alleged objects of their concern? The twentieth century ought to have taught them that racism is about not only the racist's victims, but also a means for tyrannical governments and movements to oppress others. Saddam Hussein's regime found fascist ideas appealing because Baathism was committed to wars of aggrandizement abroad and tyranny at home. Al-Qaeda and the Muslim Brotherhood could happily use secular fascist ideas as well as an apocalyptic version of Islam because if you want to repress women, kill gays, impose an imperial tyranny and justify terrorism, the fascist tradition is a natural source book to turn to. For all the guards around the world's synagogues, the Jews weren't the main victims of Baathism or Islamism. Nor was their state terrorist and terrorist violence a response by 'the Muslims' to the injustices perpetrated upon them by 'the West' or 'the Jews' however real those had been. The vast majority of the victims of Shia and Sunni Islamism and Baathist violence were Muslims. The people whose rights they denied and lives they dominated were Muslims.

If Islamism and Baathism were the heirs of fascism, Egypt and the milder authoritarian regimes that used antisemitism had the same interest as the tsars in keeping the hatred burning. The Moroccan Foreign Minister, Mohamed Benaissa, was blunter than most of his colleagues when he stated that governments in the region cannot 'carry out reforms' without 'putting an end to the Palestinian tragedy and to the war waged against the Palestinian people'. Why not? Did the plight of the Palestinians so enrage Moroccans that they would reject any moves towards democracy by their government? Didn't they want freedom for the Palestinians and freedom for themselves? The same question might have been addressed to the rich world's liberal-leftists. Why couldn't they support democracy in Iraq, Syria, Iran and North Africa – not to mention China and North Korea – along with the withdrawal of Israeli forces and settlers? Why did they, like Western governments at their worst, ignore dictatorial and genocidal regimes? No liberal would want to live in a state ruled by al-Qaeda or the Muslim Brotherhood. Liberals, socialists, women, gays, freethinkers and Christians could not possibly prosper in an Islamist Palestine or Islamist anywhere. Rather than think about what life would be like under the new far right, they revived the old racist belief of the Left that what was intolerable for white-skinned peoples was fine for lesser breeds.

There was a motive beyond the usual singling out of democracies for special treatment which explained the focus on Israel, although few liked to admit it. Because totalitarian movements of the Right said that Israel was their greatest grievance, there was a temptation to appease them by pretending that Israel was the worst abuser of human rights in the world. Leaving aside the dangers of allowing Islamists to determine a liberal political agenda, the myopia the fixation brought ignored the fact that a solution to the conflict required a confrontation with both the Jewish and the Muslim ultras who could accept no compromise in their contested 'holy' land. From the point of view of the practical politics of dividing territory, the liberal argument on Israel wasn't a great help because it could call for concessions from only one side.

The bigger question was whether it would help calm the Islamist explosion. I've been very hard on today's liberal-left, so I will end with the hope that it is right. A just settlement for the

Palestinians is a good thing in itself and should be pursued regardless of whether fanatics want it or not. Everyone knows what it is – a return to the 1967 borders, the tearing down of walls, a confrontation with maniacs from all religions who regard the holy land as the exclusive preserve of their god. Maybe if the international community were to deploy troops to safeguard Israel's borders, it will happen. If it does, we will see if a settlement vindicates the current liberal view. Perhaps it will. Perhaps it will satisfy all the Islamists who are currently saying that their wars in Chechnya, the Philippines, Indonesia, Kashmir and Somalia, and their terrorist campaigns in Iraq, Afghanistan, India, Britain, France, Spain, the United States, Denmark, Holland, Canada and Australia are a part of a unified war against paganism and for a Caliphate. Maybe they will shake themselves and say 'fair enough, we realize that now you've addressed our root cause, we don't want a theocratic empire after all and will return to civilian life'.

If the liberals and leftists are wrong, and there are good grounds for thinking that they are horribly wrong, history will judge them harshly. For they will have gazed on the face of a global fascist movement and shrugged and turned away, not only from an enemy that would happily have killed them but from an enemy which already was killing those who had every reason to expect their support.

CHAPTER THIRTEEN

Why Bother?

*They talked and wrote as if they could not imagine them-
selves responsible for the lives of their fellow-citizens. That
was someone else's business; the business of the Left was...
what? To oppose the authorities, whatever they did.*

Michael Walzer, 2002

A COMPLAINT about my argument could be that 'you can
always do this'. You can always discredit decent people by
isolating the malevolent hangers-on who join them in upsurges
of radicalism. These eruptions come once or twice in an
average lifetime. Every thirty or forty years, a wave of protest
that you can plausibly describe as 'left wing' in the terms of its
day sweeps through the hearts of men and women. Each
upsurge has its dark side but that does not negate the good it
brings. The Enlightenment of the eighteenth century brought
new ideas about human freedom, market economics and the
separation of church and state, but also the Terror of the
French Revolution. The failed revolutions of 1848 inspired
the subject peoples of the European empires to free themselves,
but also stimulated militaristic nationalism. The socialist
explosion of the 1880s and 1890s created the modern trade
union movement and the beginnings of the welfare state and
anti-colonialism, but it also created Lenin and the Bolsheviks.

The Thirties generation resolved that the hardships of the Great Depression must never recur, but assumed this noble goal required planners to treat the working class as guinea pigs in vast social experiments. The campaigners of the Sixties fought racism, sexism and homophobia, but they also fostered an aggressive individualism that dissolved the bonds of mutual support and balanced it with an aggressive identity politics that threatened basic freedoms.

Right now, it feels as if we are living through another radical upsurge. There is a counter-culture and there are marches through the streets. Usually sedate members of the liberal establishment have gone ape in the pages of the press and made ringing declarations of radical anger on the broadcasters' talk shows. I have covered the malignant side, but need to search for the good in it, and ask whether the next generation will look with gratitude at benign aspects of their lives and be able to say that the ideas that brought them began with the liberal-left of the early twenty-first century, with what is happening now.

First on the list must be the environment. Although the green movement is impossible to categorize in the old political language as it attracted the support of people of all political affiliations and none, most of the deniers of global warming have come from the free-market right. My guess is that generations as yet unborn will look back with gratitude to the efforts of today's environmental campaigners and in a hazy way see them as members of the Left. There have also been admirable efforts to defend civil liberties, but their integrity has been compromised by the refusal of many to stand up for the civil liberties of those who are oppressed by the various anti-Western tyrannies and terrorist movements. The anti-globalization movement has provided intellectual support to governments in South America and elsewhere who want to nationalize their energy industries or impose higher taxes on multi-nationals. The economic record of nationalized industries outside the advanced countries is dire, and the poor world's political elites often use nationalization as an excuse to divert revenues into their bank accounts. But if pervasive jobbery and corruption are avoided, then the change may be for the better. Anti-war protesters and leftish political parties have upheld the authority of the United Nations, but as the United Nations is a club with no membership restrictions and admits the worst regimes on earth, that gain seems insignificant to me. Finally, the disasters of the second Iraq war and the protests against it will doubtless deter the United States and others from charging in and overthrowing tyrannous regimes in future, but clearly that outcome will please tyrants above all others.

After that, I'm struggling, for a reason which I emphasized earlier. The best side of previous outbreaks of leftish passion was found in their concern for the underdog. You can see a hatred of sadistic authority running through my list of radical eruptions from the Enlightenment's detestation of priests with the power to persecute to the Sixties generation's confrontations with racists. Today's upsurge stands in a dishonourable contrast. For where are the underdogs on whose behalf it is speaking? Answer comes there none, because to maintain the illusion that totalitarian movements would stop threatening their comfortable lives if only the 'root cause' of Western provocation was removed, the protesters of the rich world ignored the victims of the far right.

The Iranian feminist, Azar Nafisi, had to confront the postmodern Left's queasiness about women who were fighting for the causes it once cared about after she published *Reading Lolita in Tehran* in 2003. It is an account of educated Iranian women escaping from the repression of the ayatollahs to talk about *Madame Bovary, Pride and Prejudice, The Great Gatsby*, as well as *Lolita*, at a reading circle Nafisi organized at her home each Thursday. Living under theocratic rule was like 'having sex with a man you loathe', she said, and in the work of authors from other continents and other times, she and her friends could briefly get away from the men who abused them. Nafisi had suffered for the principles. The Islamists had expelled her from the University of Tehran for refusing to wear the mandatory veil and banned her from teaching for six years. She fled to America and wondered where to look for support in her new home. To Western liberals who had never spent a second of their time thinking about the Iranian opposition or protesting against the Iranian regime? To the graduates of Western universities who thought that their cultural justification for the oppression of women was a proof of their liberalism? Nafisi found that people who would complain to the authorities about the mildest sexual innuendo couldn't be counted on to fight a patriarchal state. She told an American who interviewed her in Boston, Massachusetts: 'I very much resent it in the West when people – maybe with good intentions or from a progressive point of view – keep telling me, "It's their culture"... It's like saying, the culture of Massachusetts is burning witches.'

Asking how long these double standards can persist, takes me into the tricky business of prediction. My guess is that the time will come soon when the liberal-left's escape routes will close. George W. Bush, their bogeyman, will be gone and they will be all alone in a frightening world without the enemy who has defined them and held them together for so long. After the signing of the Hitler – Stalin pact made a nonsense of so many of the hopes of his radical generation, W. H. Auden went for a drink in New York and wrote:

Faces along the bar
Cling to their average day:
The lights must never go out,
The music must always play,
All the conventions conspire
To make this fort assume
The furniture of home;
Lest we should see where we are,
Lost in a haunted wood,
Children afraid of the night
Who have never been happy or good.

I can hear the same being said about today's radical generation and almost feel sorry for the poor dears. For when their fury passes, what will they have left? They will look to their core principles for guidance, only to find that they, rather than their conservative opponents, have battered them to the point of destruction. If they talk about the urgent task of combating terror by spreading the freedoms they enjoy, the audience they taught to sneer at others will sneer at them. If they provide evidence of a totalitarian menace, the accusation of lying they have thrown so freely at others, will be thrown back in their faces. If they belatedly rediscover the moral imagination to show solidarity with those who share their values, their own charges of consorting with the dupes of American imperialism will be used in evidence against them.

For you don't have to spend too much time looking at modern Islamism to realize that Tony Blair and George W. Bush may have been mistaken about much but are right about one big thing. We will still have to confront a psychopathic totalitarian movement that will murder without limit for decades. At the time of going to press, it has seized power in Somalia, and the prospect of it making further advances and linking up with states manufacturing weapons of mass destruction won't go when Bush and Blair go. As I said, I hope I am wrong, but I do not think a quiet life is an option, and not only because of Islamism. You should not underestimate the possibility of envious imitation from other apocalyptic creeds. We have seen it already in Britain in a mild way. Extreme Christians, Hindus, Sikhs and Jews have copied the successful use of the threat of intimidation by Muslim extremists to prevent satires or critiques of Islam. There's no reason why the competition between religious extremists should stop there.

Ten years ago, I would have said that the liberal-left understood best how to challenge totalitarian movements of the secular and religious right and offer succour to its victims: now I am not sure. In our time, the notion of camaraderie has been at its strongest in the old organizations of the democratic socialist movement. We saw it displayed when British trade unionists and Labour MPs who hated the war against Iraq nevertheless stood by their Iraqi comrades when Islamists and Baathists were murdering them. Their socialism is dying, however, and they will probably be the last generation to feel the need for solidarity with suffering strangers in their bones.

If the new left of the twenty-first century is to be a liberal-left worth having, then it must learn from the best of the old traditions. First, it must understand that we are lucky people who have won life's lottery. An accident of birth has given us freedom and the wealth that comes with it. We don't have an obligation to overturn tyranny by military force. But we have no right to turn our backs on those who want the freedoms we take for granted. We have no good cause to scoff at them and make excuses for the men who would keep the knife pressed to their throats. The best reason for offering them support is that we can. We have the freedom to vote, to lobby, to protest, to write and to speak, and there is no point in having freedom unless you use it to a good purpose.

There also needs to be a clean break with totalitarianism: both totalitarian regimes abroad and the totalitarian left – if it is still a left – at home. It is incredible that this point needs to be reiterated after the twentieth century; astonishing that we need to go through all that again. I hope I have shown that we do and that the worst traditions of the liberal-left are flourishing while the best are rusting from underuse. In part, the confusion is brought by confusion about religion. As religious beliefs are deeply held and religious culture produces much of value, many liberal-minded people are wary about having arguments with the religious. They have forgotten what the men and women of the Enlightenment knew. All faiths in their extreme form carry the possibility of tyranny because they place the revealed word of whatever god or gods they happen to worship above the democratic will of electorates.

These are obvious points to make, or so they seem to me, but maybe they are not so obvious. While I was finishing writing, a group of academics, trade unionists and political writers from the Internet blogs was meeting in a pub in Euston. I don't mean to be rude when I say that they weren't intellectual celebrities, just politically aware citizens. Their number included supporters and opponents of the war and representatives of most varieties of leftish opinion. A disenchantment with the liberal mainstream, which bordered on disgust, united them. They asked me to help draw up a manifesto, but because there is no creature on earth more selfish than an author with a deadline to hit, I barely exerted myself. Nevertheless, they emailed me drafts as they went along, and as I looked at them, I found plenty to admire.

The Euston Manifesto begins by declaring its support for democracy and continues: 'We decline to make excuses for, to indulgently "understand", reactionary regimes and movements for which democracy is a hated enemy.' It announces its support for universal human rights and rejects 'the double standards with which much self-proclaimed progressive opinion now operates, finding lesser (though all too real) violations of human rights which are closer to home, or are the responsibility of certain disfavoured governments, more deplorable than other violations that are flagrantly worse'. It emphasizes a commitment to match the globalization of capital with a globalization of labour rights – the first task of a serious left today in my view – and goes on to list many other fine democratic principles that are worth having and worth the bother of defending.

I approved of nearly every word, but I did worry that my friends were producing a bland document that would sink without trace. Did the politically literate really need reminding that they should support those who wanted to vote rather than those who wanted to blow up polling stations?

Of course they did. As the twenty-first century got into its stride, the obvious had become threatening to a frenzied and fragile liberal-left consensus, whose self-image couldn't survive a glance in the mirror. The Euston Manifesto was launched in the *New Statesman* and the heavens fell in. A tidal wave of praise, criticism and scorn swept round the Internet as the phrase 'Euston Manifesto' scored hundreds of thousands of hits. *The Times*, the *Guardian*, the *Hindu*, the *American Spectator*, and other newspapers around the world praised and condemned it in equal measure. You can read it for yourself on the Net, if you want more good arguments against contemporary thinking and positive ideas for the future. My concluding point is merely that it was a symptom of the dismal state of liberal life that a statement of the obvious produced by obscure men and women in a London pub could cause such a fuss.

It is in the hope that no one will ever need to make such a fuss again that I have written this book. Not the expectation, just the hope.

POSTSCRIPT

*Tony Blair: There is global struggle in which we need a
  policy based on democracy, on freedom and on justice...*
*John Humphrys (a BBC presenter): Our idea of
  democracy...*
*Blair: I didn't know that there was another idea of
  democracy...*
Humphrys: If I may say so, that's naïve...
*Blair: The one basic fact about democracy, surely, is that you
  can get rid of your government if you don't like them.*
*Humphrys: The Iranians elected their own government, and
  we're now telling them...*
*Blair: Hold on John, something like 60 per cent of the
  candidates were excluded.*

BBC Radio 4, February 2007

When I published *What's Left?* I did not expect to be universally loved. I have lived among London's liberal intelligentsia long enough to know that while it is hard on others it is always easy on itself, and would not take kindly to a history of how leftish people had ended up apologizing for the ultra-right. The reviewers who praised this book are all over its cover, what surprised me about the critics was their denial. A few said the book was a defence of the second Iraq war, even though every time I mentioned opposition to the war I said the opponents were right in nearly all their arguments but had astonished me and others by their inability to support those Iraqis who wanted something better after thirty-five years of a vile dictatorship. More common was a transparent shiftiness.

All right, critics conceded, a few leftists had flipped over and gone along with Islamism and Baathism. But these people were not worth bothering with. No connection existed between the ideological contortions of the extremes and a liberal mainstream that remained wedded to the highest principles. All I had done was use odious but fringe figures to smear decent and moderate men and women, such as themselves. As an account of my argument, this was partial in the extreme. *What's Left?* looks at how: the Left picked up and then dropped the opponents of Saddam Hussein; the European Union stood by and allowed Slobodan Milosevic to ethnically cleanse the Balkans; the reasons for the liberal middle class's disillusion with democracy and free speech; the instant willingness of respectable writers to excuse Osama bin Laden and al-Qaeda after the 9/11 attacks; the inability of the British Liberal Democrats and European Social Democrats to oppose George W. Bush while supporting a free Iraq; the growth of polite anti-semitism; and the propensity of liberals everywhere to portray a global clerical fascist movement as a rational response to Western provocation. Say what you will, but these were and are mainstream phenomena. Liberal writers did not examine them and explain why I was mistaken. They just ignored what I had written and hoped that if they insisted on their righteousness with sufficient vehemence, others would believe them – and maybe they would believe themselves.

For denial about what had happened to the liberal-left was not confined to the reaction of a few reviewers to one political book. In Europe and North America intellectuals worked ferociously to maintain the illusion that a principled consensus survived the mayhem after 9/11. I can sympathize with them to an extent because although it is essential to realize where the received wisdom is going wrong it is rarely a simple or painless task. Historians have it easy. They can look back at another time and see the faults in what almost everyone took for granted. In theory, we know future historians will do the same to us and find elements of our beliefs as wrong-headed and narrow-minded as we find those of our ancestors. In practice, however, self-examination is psychologically impossible for many. When you live in a consensus, it does not feel as if you have an ideology that needs examining. If the overwhelming majority of people you meet agree with you, your assumptions do not appear tenuous or debatable. They are just there – as natural as the air you breathe and as unquestionable as the weather.

Often it takes a fresh set of eyes to see a stale world anew. In 2006, after two years of living in South America, Martin Amis returned to Britain to find a liberal-left wallowing in self-delusion. When asked by the *Independent* what had shocked him most since he got home he replied: 'The most depressing thing was the sight of middle-class white demonstrators waddling around under placards saying, "We Are All Hezbollah Now". Well, make the most of being Hezbollah while you can. As its leader famously advised the West: "We don't want anything from you. We just want to eliminate you."'

Members of the liberal mainstream could say that leftists boasting of their conversion to Islamism were a fringe phenomenon; although they only ever said that when they were cornered. At all other times, they never discussed the movement from the far left to the far right and their silence implied complicity.

In any case, Amis made it clear that he was talking about the mainstream, not the fringe when he added that he had gone

on *Question Time*, the most popular political discussion programme of the day, and 'a woman in the audience, her voice
quavering with self-righteousness, presented the following
argument. Since it was America that supported Osama bin
Laden when he was fighting the Russians, the US armed forces,
in response to September 11, "should be dropping bombs on
themselves!" And the audience applauded. It is quite an
achievement. People of liberal sympathies, stupefied by relativism, have become the apologists for a credal wave that is
racist, misogynist, homophobic, imperialist and genocidal. To
put it another way, they are up the arse of those that want them
dead.'

So they were, and so they remain, as any honest examination
of mainstream liberal culture would show. To stay only with the
BBC, in the first *Question Time* after 9/11, a section of the audience screamed down the attempts by Philip Lader, the former
US Ambassador to Britain, to express his condolences for the
dead of New York and Washington and left him close to tears.
Even at that early stage, his abusers were convinced that
America had it coming and radical Islam was nothing more
than a rational reaction to Western policy. A follow-up programme dumbfounded ministers in the 2005 Labour government. When one of their number, Hilary Benn, a palpably
decent man, whatever members of the public thought of his
politics, tried to say how much he admired those Iraqis who
daily risked the lives of themselves and their families in the
unequal struggle to build a new society, the audience booed
him. When a slimy tabloid journalist giggled about the failure
of Iraqi democracy, the audience cheered him on.

Meanwhile so consistent was the pro-Islamist party line in
the BBC's drama, it seemed as if a politburo had taken control
of the arts department. The 2006 series of *Spooks* showed

Islamist suicide bombers taking over the Saudi Arabian embassy. Nothing too far-fetched in that, real MI5 agents were running themselves ragged as they tried to close down terror cells. The BBC's novel twist was that its fictional MI5 agents discovered that the Islamists were Mossad agents in disguise. Was the BBC agreeing with Mohammed Atta's father and saying that Islamist terrorism was a Jewish conspiracy? Up to a point it was. As the *Guardian*'s critic put it, liberal broadcasters were positing 'a kind of moral equivalence – albeit a qualified one – between the legitimate if not always overly legalistic secret security service of a democratically elected government and stateless Jihadists whose aim is the destruction of everything they don't believe in'.

Even children were not spared. The BBC's reworking of *Robin Hood* turned the Sheriff of Nottingham and Guy of Gisborne into pastiches of George W. Bush and Tony Blair. The actor playing Sir Guy explained that in the twenty-first-century version of Sherwood Forest, Robin returns from a war in the Middle East to find Nottinghamshire controlled by an unpopular leader who has imposed heavy taxes and a climate of fear. The story is about 'the perpetuation of terror' in which Robin and his men are the terrorists, he said. 'It's in the Sheriff's interests to keep fear of the outlaws alive so he can control the populace.'

Did the BBC mean that Robin Hood and his Merry Men were Osama bin Laden and his Merry Islamists? Or that the Government was inventing a non-existent Islamist threat to justify placing the British under the iron heel of the national security state? Possibly a bit of both, but I doubt the BBC worried about the contradiction. When a consensus takes hold, believers do not feel the need to think about what they say. The assurance that all their right-thinking friends agree with them produces a bad case of verbal diarrhoea in which sufferers blurt out half-thought-out declarations and accusations without worrying about how they will sound to those outside the consensus, because they do not believe that anyone worth thinking about is outside it.

I have quoted a few of thousands of examples from the BBC because even its opponents do not pretend that its staff are anything other than conventionally minded members of the middle-class mainstream. But if you are still not convinced that there is more to be worried about than a few loons on the fringe, allow me to hand you over to a group I suspect we are going to be hearing a lot more from: British Muslims who converted to Islamism and came out the other side to tell their stories.

In his memoir, *The Islamist*, Ed Husain marvelled at how the Labour government, the liberal media and supposedly anti-fascist leftists had aided movements that represented everything they purported to be against. He described how he broke with the gentle religion of his parents when he was a teenager and joined a mosque in the East End of London dominated by Jamaat-i-Islaami, the south Asian sister organization of the Muslim Brotherhood. They immersed him in the totalitarian thought of Jamaat's founder Abul Ala Mawdudi, and of Sayyid Qutb, the Muslim Brotherhood's theorist of total jihad against a world sunk in paganism. On his bedroom wall, he stuck the motto of Jamaat and the Brotherhood:

> *Allah is Our Lord*
> *Muhammad is Our Leader*
> *The Koran is Our Constitution*
> *Jihad is Our Way*
> *Martyrdom is Our Desire*

He moved on to the Hizb-ut-Tahrir, which wanted a theo-cratic empire, and used the indifference of Hurd and Major to the massacres of Bosnia's Muslims to nurture the ideas of 'jihad, martyrdom, confrontation and anti-Americanism' in the Nineties. On every step of his journey, he found the forces of the liberal mainstream melting before him. When he organized students in London colleges, he found intimidating liberal academics a simple task. They did not know how to respond to the ever more provocative demands of the Islamic societies he set up. Multi-culturalism can only work if public institutions are secular spaces where all are welcome and sectarianism has no place. However, the university administrators' commitment to liberal secularism was undermined by the worry that it was racist – 'Islamophobic' – to oppose extremists; so they backed off from the necessary confrontations and allowed the Islamists free rein. 'Our magnetism and vitality drew people to us,' Husain remembered. 'A visible Muslim presence everywhere, women veiled, ubiquitous posters of Islam and the student population, almost without exception, under our control.'

Just before he released *The Islamist*, Husain went back to his old mosque. In the bookshop,

> I bought an updated copy of Qutb's *Milestones*, published not in Riyadh but in Birmingham…with chapter headings such as 'The virtues of killing a non-believer', and ideas such as 'Attacking the non-believers in their territories is a collective and individual duty'. Just as I had done as a sixteen-year-old, hundreds of young Muslims are buying these books from Islamist mosques in Britain and imbibing the idea that killing non-believers is not only acceptable but the duty of a good Muslim.

Husain was shocked that Jamaat and the Muslim Brotherhood were the allies of the leaders of the nominally left-wing anti-war movement, although readers of this book will not be. More telling, was his description of how the Labour government turned its back on moderates and treated members of Jamaat and the Brotherhood as the legitimate voice of British Islam; invited them into Whitehall to guide government policy and to Buckingham Palace to receive knighthoods, even if they had said that they supported the murder of Salman Rushdie. Labour, like many who voted for it, was anti-racist and anti-sexist, yet when confronted with the Muslim versions of the European far-right parties it strived to accommodate them.

A second British refugee from Islamism remembered the contempt with which his former associates held the leftists who tried to appease them. Hassan Butt, who had been a recruiter for jihad, described

> how we used to laugh in celebration whenever people on TV proclaimed that the sole cause for Islamic acts of terror like 9/11, the Madrid bombings and 7/7 was Western foreign policy. By blaming the government for our actions, those who pushed the 'Blair's bombs' line did our propaganda work for us. More important, they also helped to draw away any critical examination from the real engine of our violence: Islamic theology.

He explained that theology succinctly:

> What drove me and many of my peers to plot acts of extreme terror within Britain, our own homeland and abroad, was a sense that we were fighting for the creation of a revolutionary state that would eventually bring Islamic justice to the world.

The foundation of extremist reasoning rests upon a dualistic model of the world. Many Muslims may or may not agree with secularism but at the moment, formal Islamic theology, unlike Christian theology, does not allow for the separation of state and religion. There is no rendering unto Caesar in Islamic theology because state and religion are considered to be one and the same. The centuries-old reasoning of Islamic jurists also extends to the world stage where the rules of interaction between Dar ul-Islam (the Land of Islam) and Dar ul-Kufr (the Land of Unbelief) have been set down to cover almost every matter of trade, peace and war. What radicals and extremists do is to take these premises two steps further. Their first step has been to reason that since there is no Islamic state in existence, the whole world must be Dar ul-Kufr. Step two: since Islam must declare war on unbelief, they have declared war upon the whole world. Many of my former peers, myself included, were taught by Pakistani and British radical preachers that this reclassification of the globe as a Land of War (Dar ul-Harb) allows any Muslim to destroy the sanctity of the five rights that every human is granted under Islam: life, wealth, land, mind and belief. In Dar ul-Harb, anything goes, including the treachery and cowardice of attacking civilians.

Why could not liberals stand up to the nightmare of sexism, racism, homophobia and tyranny this psychopathic ideology brought? Why did they deny its existence and pretend that its massacres and repression were somehow understandable protests rather than a single-minded effort to implement an apocalyptic creed?

If you have reached this far, I hope you feel that you have read a book rather than a theoretical pamphlet with a formal statement of its premises. However, perhaps the closing pages are the place to draw together the reasons for the liberal-left's predicament that come out in the narrative.

On the rare occasions mainstream commentators discussed it, they breezily said that if leftists seemed to be heading to the far right occasionally, they were simply reacting against the catastrophic Bush administration. This was a part of the answer, but could not be the whole truth. It did not explain why Western liberals and leftists could not oppose Bush while supporting those who shared their values in the poor world and took no account of the treacheries within leftism long before Bush came to power. To understand that long betrayal we have to look for deeper causes.

1. Socialism for Shoppers: The Rise of Consumer Leftism

It is hard to define what it means to be left wing in the twenty-first century. Generally, people who say they are on the Left favour higher rates of taxation and the provision of public services by state monopolies, and are wary of private corporations and financial markets. Yet when their social democratic politicians take power they often turn to the market for solutions to the practical problems of running modern societies. They recognize that socialism in its extreme and moderate forms has gone. Parties of the Left in the democratic world are everywhere cautious and flexible, and can no longer inspire enthusiasm for state control because they no longer believe in it – and nor do most of their supporters when they are honest with themselves. Political writers have discussed the death of socialism and the triumph of market liberalism at length, but few have noticed a morbid consequence.

In the twentieth century, many on the Left were willing to support or minimize the crimes of the communists. To condemn Pinochet's dictatorship in Chile, say, but ignore the victims of the Soviet Union and its satellite states was one characteristic double standard. To demand that the West scrap its nuclear weapons while implying that the Soviet arsenal was purely defensive was a second. In a usually ill-defined manner, they did not believe that communism was wholly rotten and that the progressive rhetoric in communist propaganda was all lies. Bar a few exceptions we discussed, however, they were resolute in their opposition to the fascist tradition.

In the twenty-first century, with socialism gone, the main threat to the status quo comes from Islamists whose attitudes towards women, Jews, homosexuals and free thought do not even pretend to be progressive. Indeed, in Iran, Afghanistan, the Gaza Strip and everywhere else they take power, they persecute leftists. Yet people who call themselves left wing cannot bring themselves to oppose them.

Far leftists go further and are open in their support for jihadis. The apologias from some liberals are so comprehensive that they must also support radical Islam in their hearts. Far leftists have to head to the far right because there is simply nowhere else for them to go now that the revolutionary guerrillas and communist regimes of the twentieth century are history. A love of violence and hatred of their own societies – well merited or otherwise – leads them to conclude that any killer of Americans is better than none.

To explain the catastrophic collapse of their hopes they have revived the false consciousness conspiracy theory, which has been present in socialist thought since the early defeats at the turn of the twentieth century, and given it an astonishing prominence. They hold that the masses rejected the Left because brainwashing media corporations 'manufactured consent' for globalization. Democracy is a sham, the political parties are all the same and human rights are meaningless. What fools call freedom is a smokescreen to hide the machinations of the real rulers of the world. The theory of false consciousness is very close to the antisemitic conspiracy theory of classic Nazism. Indeed its adherents often topple over into the antisemitic conspiracy theory of classic Nazism.

These may seem like fringe developments but the new ideology that emerged in dark, barely noticed corners of the Left fitted the consumer society well. Because there was no coherent left-wing political programme the most unlikely people could affect a leftish posture.

If I were a socialist writing fifty years ago, you might have read me and found yourself agreeing with a proposal I was making. But because I believed in socialism I would have to interject and say that I also wanted the nationalization of the commanding heights of the economy, penal taxation, stronger rights for trade unions and workers' control. If not you, then other readers would have backed away at that moment, muttering that my ideas would lead to disaster. Modern leftists do not have to risk alienating readers with proposals that might be uncomfortable. They rarely have proposals for a new ordering of society. They are merely against the West in general or America in particular, both of which, God knows, provide reasons aplenty for opposition. The collapse in ideology also explains the general inability to support feminists, democrats and leftists in the poor world. If you do not have a positive programme yourself, how can you see strangers as comrades who must be supported? These betrayals may be scandalous but they chime with the psychology of consumerism. Shoppers have little time for Auden's flat ephemeral pamphlets and boring meetings. They are commitment-phobes, with no appetite for the hard slog and the long haul.

Even leftish conspiracy theories do not feel as absurd as they once might have done. In the age of globalization, people who are prosperous and free can still feel that vast powers beyond democratic control run the world.

The result is that almost anyone can strike a leftish pose now. When I go into the homes of the richest people I know, I see Noam Chomsky and Michael Moore on their shelves and think, 'Why am I surprised? Of course, they read them. The Left is no threat to them any longer. Being a leftist carries no costs.'

2 Multi-Culti Going Faulty

Whoever said of the late twentieth century that 'the Right won the economic war but the Left won the cultural war' deserves a prize. Just as market liberalism triumphed in economics, so social liberalism triumphed in wider society. It was routine for each side to accuse each other of hypocrisy. 'How can you support social liberalism but not economic liberalism,' conservatives asked leftists. 'Well *tu quoque* and vice versa,' leftists replied.

Although the extraordinary success of campaigns against sexism and racism vastly improved the lives of millions of individuals, the accusation that leftish liberals were hypocrites because they favoured cultural but not economic liberalism was not always right. Post-modern liberals developed an identity politics based on group definitions that was anti-individualist in its assumptions. They treated women, members of ethnic minorities, gays and others as members of blocs with communal interests. Their simplifications were not always pernicious – a campaign to tighten the law on domestic violence, for example, is a campaign for women, not this or that woman.

But as we saw in Chapter 4, post-modernists took the liberal idea of tolerance and pushed group-based identity politics into an extreme relativism. I am unqualified to discuss their philosophy, although I instinctively feel it is wrong, but a child could understand their politics, which is why they had to hide them in such convoluted prose. They held that it was racist and culturally imperialist to criticize 'the Other' even when 'the Other' was engaging in the repression of women, persecution of homosexuals and denial of democracy. Groups or cultures were treated as hermetically sealed boxes that did not have internal conflicts, and whose discourses could not be criticized with universal concepts and standards. The one exception was their own culture, which they dismissed as repressive even when it upheld the rights of women, homosexuals and lived by democratic norms.

A stance against 'the West' or 'the hegemonic' absolved all sins. When the Islamic revolution in Iran began its persecution of leftists, the nominally left-wing Michel Foucault said Europeans should not condemn because Iranians 'did not have the same regime of truth as ours'. His betrayal has run through post-modern politics ever since. Today's Iranian feminists may hold the same beliefs as Western feminists but they are not admirable fighters for universal values against the prejudices of a misogynist autocracy but embarrassments who are failing to fulfil their allotted cultural roles.

As John Maynard Keynes might have predicted, strange ideas that began in the universities in the Seventies were everywhere a generation later. Cultural relativism explains why a Labour government embraced the Muslim Brotherhood and Jamaat-i-Islaami, and why liberal academics refused to confront Islamists on the campuses. As seriously, the emphasis on difference and the denial of universality in post-modern multi-culturalism made a virtue of segregating immigrant communities in Europe. One British Muslim who came close to becoming a terrorist said:

> the result of 25 years of multiculturalism has not been multi-cultural communities. It has been mono-cultural communities. Islamic communities are segregated. Many Muslims want to live apart from mainstream British society; official government policy has helped them do so. I grew up without any white friends. My school was almost entirely Muslim. I had almost no direct experience of 'British life' or 'British institutions'. So it was easy for the extremists to say to me: 'You see? You're not part of British society. You never will be. You can only be part of an Islamic society.' The first part of what they said was true. I wasn't part of British society: nothing in my life overlapped with it.

Official indifference to the treatment of women inevitably followed. Parents pulled Asian girls out of school before they could take the examinations that might lead to an independent career. 'Honour killings' were all too frequent and forced marriages were commonplace. Politically correct state authorities decided to print official literature in translation rather than teach immigrants English. The thought that a foreign wife who could not speak English could be trapped at home with a brutal husband with no means of calling for help or breaking free and forging a new life did not occur to them.

If white-skinned women had been murdered, raped, battered and denied education and independence because of their sex, liberal England would have screamed blue murder, but because the victims had brown skins it maintained a polite silence and felt very liberal when it did so.

Just before he resigned, Tony Blair told the BBC that upholding universal standards of justice and democracy must be an aim of British foreign policy. A man-of-the people interviewer, who was extremely unlikely to have heard of Foucault let alone read him, interrupted with the sneer, '*Our* idea of democracy'. Blair said there was only one idea of democracy, 'that you can get rid of your government if you don't like them'. The interviewer replied that Iran, then in a confrontation with the West, *was* a democracy, and did not seem abashed when Blair pointed out that the religious authorities vetoed candidates and harassed dissidents. From Foucault's different standards of truth to the BBC's different ideas of democracy, supposedly liberal or leftish relativists betrayed the very people who were entitled to expect their support, abroad and at home.

3. Liberal Disillusion

The Virginia Woolf type of liberal intellectual has always disliked the working class. Today a far wider nervousness about the ability of middle-class liberals to mobilize popular support for the causes that mean most to them pervades Europe and North America. The centralization of decision-making in the European Union, the fondness for asking unelected judges to take political decisions, the speech codes and the unwillingness of liberal politicians and journalists to tackle hard subjects that might be deemed as racist, all speak to a belief that the working class is authoritarian and prejudiced and not to be trusted.

You can see how my class got that way. Successive Conservative and New Labour governments in Britain and successive Democrat and Republican administrations in the United States had shown that 'populist' politics was always popular. Meanwhile the necessary campaigns for equality for women, ethnic minorities and homosexuals carried with them a distasteful and tactically disastrous suggestion that the working class, and working-class men especially, were the most pernicious enemies of the new freedoms.

Beyond a fear that they could not win majorities in open elections, the liberal middle classes across the developed world felt a far deeper unease that history was no longer on its side. Market economies undermined the status and comparative wealth of the public sector managers who dominated modern states at the high tide of social democracy in the mid-twentieth century. Financiers and industrialists accrued fantastic wealth and political status, while the liberal middle classes lingered in jobs their rulers despised for their failure to be market-orientated.

Modern democracy was a system which produced results that no longer pleased them. They were less likely than they once would have been to oppose clerical fascist movements and stand up for the best values of their societies, not dodgy dossiers or privileges for plutocrats but the freedoms the liberal-left once died for, and may have to die for again.

4. Fear

In 1968 at the start of the narrative of this book, no one – not Kanan Makiya and the revolutionary students, nor the politicians, spies and academics who specialized in international affairs – predicted the wars that would follow the Baathist seizure of power or the extraordinary scope and violence of the Islamist explosion that began with the Iranian revolution. From the 9/11 atrocities on, the dimmest citizens of the Western democracies could be in no doubt that forces were swirling around the globe that would murder them without compunction. Yet after 9/11, citizens were not murdered in significant numbers. As I said before, I owe my apologies to the bereaved of the attacks on London and Madrid. But when set against the astonishing scale of the Iraqi massacres or the genocide in Darfur, the rich world could live with these casualties, while all the time knowing that unimaginable violence could be coming not just from foreigners but from neighbours radicalized in unregulated mosques, trained in the badlands of the Pakistan-Afghanistan border and coordinated via the Internet.

A frantic desire to appease would be the natural response in normal circumstances, but it became ubiquitous when citizens saw that America and Britain had launched the second Iraq war on the worst intelligence since the US military dismissed the possibility of a Japanese attack on Pearl Harbor. 'Surely, this was "our" fault,' they said. 'Surely, we were the "root cause", and, surely, if we admitted our responsibility and changed our ways the psychopath would move on and pick on someone else and we would be safe.'

Fear is the most powerful of human motives, and a willingness to rationalize the irrational is a fatal liberal weakness. Add in the despairing and reactionary turn modern leftish thinking took after the collapse of socialism, the tolerance of the intolerable inculcated by post-modernism and the doubts about democracy in the liberal mainstream, and I hope you can see why so many could not oppose totalitarian movements of the far right or even call them by their real names.

However understandable the denial, it remains as pitiful a response to Islamism as climate change denial is to global warming. Both sets of deniers believe that we can carry on as before living our safe, consumerist lives as if nothing has changed. Neither understands that we have no choice other than to face the threats of our time. Reasonable men and women can disagree about how we face them, but we will not be able to see the world clearly until we have swept away the vast mounds of junk that block our view.

NOTES

A full list of sources follows. Before getting to them, I must acknowledge the importance of the Internet blogs, which came of age while I was writing this book. I found many of the references to the conflict between post-modernism and feminism in Chapter 4 via Ophelia Benson's 'Butterflies and Wheels' – www.butterfliesandwheels.com. The task of trying to write an account of what has happened to the liberal-left in Part Two initially appeared next to impossible because of the suffocating conformism displayed by the mainstream liberal media after the second Iraq war. The debates and arguments of the day rarely appeared in the newspapers and journals that are the first port of call for a historian. Fortunately, the bloggers filled the gap, and I found many of the sources cited in Chapters 11 and 12 via Norman Geras's 'Normblog', http://normblog.typepad.com/normblog/ and the team of writers at 'Harry's Place', http://hurry upharry.bloghouse.net/

PART ONE: *Morbid Symptoms*

17 **'Yet it is a great'** Norman Cohn, 'Introduction', in *Warrant for Genocide*, new edn, London: Serif, 1996, p. xiv.

Chapter One

21 **'He didn't look'** Lawrence Weschler, *Calamities of Exile*, Chicago and London: University of Chicago Press, 1998, p. 15.
23 **'This is crazy'** Ibid., p. 16.

26 **'This is for history'** Ibid., p. 27.

27 **'We have criticised'** Robert Fisk, *The Great War for Civilisation*, London: Fourth Estate, 2005, p. 148.

30 'a bureaucratic bourgeoisie' CARDRI (Commission Against Repression and for Democratic Rights in Iraq), *Saddam's Iraq*, London: Zed Books, 1986, pp. 73–84.

31 **'the proclivity of'** Kanan Makiya, 'Note to the Reader', in *Republic of Fear*, 2nd edn, Berkeley and London: University of California Press, 1998. Unless otherwise indicated all remaining quotes in this chapter are from this edition of *Republic of Fear* and its new introduction by the author.

34 **'Why didn't you'** Sarah Smiles, 'Why a Little Girl's Parents Didn't Tell Her the Truth about "Baba" Saddam', *The Age*, 27 April 2003.

43 **'After the arrest'** Con Coughlin, *Saddam: The Secret Life*, London: Macmillan, 2002, pp. 155–8.

Chapter Two

46 **It was tosh** SIPRI (Stockholm International Peace Research Institute) Arms Transfers Database, 'Imported Weapons to Iraq (IRQ) in 1973–2002', 5 March 2003.

Country	$US millions, 1990	Percentage of total
USSR	25,145	57.26
France	5,595	12.74
China	5,192	11.82
Czechoslovakia	2,880	6.56
Poland	1,681	3.83
Brazil	724	1.65
Egypt	568	1.29
Romania	524	1.19
Denmark	226	0.51
Libya	200	0.46
USA	200	0.46

49 **'Comrade al-Majid's decisions'** Samantha Power, *A Problem from Hell*, London: Flamingo, 2002, p. 171.

49 **'Who's going to remember...massacre of the Armenians?'** Simon Sebag Montefiore, *Stalin: The Court of the Red Tsar*, New York: Knopf, 2004, p. 236.

49 **'A few children'** Jung Chang and Jon Halliday: *Mao: The Unknown Story*, London: Jonathan Cape, 2005, p. 462.

51 **'I wanted to'** Power, *A Problem from Hell*, p. 187.

54 **There are plenty** 'One of the reasons I love you,' Woodrow Wyatt told Margaret Thatcher, 'is that you don't have enough cunning and you're not a devious person.'

    'Neither of us can be ill,' Margaret Thatcher told Woodrow Wyatt. 'We have to keep on fighting.'

    He rewarded her with obsequious columns in the *News of the World*. She rewarded him with the sinecure of the Chairmanship of the Tote, which allowed Wyatt to draw a maximum salary for a minimal amount of work and entertain his cronies at the best racecourses. Woodrow Wyatt, *The Journals of Woodrow Wyatt*, vol. I, ed. Sarah Curtis, London: Macmillan, 1998.

56 **'I've been expecting...ultra-high unemployment'** Richard Weight, *Patriots*, London: Pan, 2003, pp. 517–37.

56 **'wholesale domestic liquidation'** Records of the Prime Minister's Office, 1974, reported in *Daily Telegraph*, 29 December 2005.

58 **'realized early in'** John Sullivan, *As Soon as this Pub Closes*, 1988, available at http://www.whatnextjournal.co.uk/Pages/Sectariana/Pub.html

58 **'to frustrate the'** Peter Paterson, 'More Sinister than a Mere Sex Scandal', *Daily Mail*, 5 November 1985.

59 **'Then they started'** Colin Smith and Robert Chesshyre, 'Vanessa and the Red House Mystery', *Observer*, 28 September 1975.

61 **'I was suddenly'** Paul Callan, 'How the Reds Bedded Their Recruits', *Daily Mirror*, 31 October 1985.

62 '**Natasha appealed to**' Vanessa Redgrave, *Vanessa Redgrave: An Autobiography*, New York: Random House, 1994, p. 203.

63 '**[He] opened the**' Dennis Tourish and Tim Wohlforth, *On the Edge*, Armonck, NY, and London: M. E. Sharpe, 2000, pp. 163–5.

64 '**It's Christmas**' Ibid., pp. 165–7.

65 '**A powerful Zionist**' 'The Zionist Connection', *News Line* editorial, 9 April 2003.

65 '**To my shame**' Charlie Pottins, letter to the *Weekly Worker*, 18 December 2003.

67 **about £20,000 from Iraq** Tom Burns, 'The Revolution Betrayed', *Solidarity*, Spring 1988. Available via http://libsoc.blogspot.com/

68 '**I haven't the slightest**' Ken Livingstone, 'The Tribute and Concert in Memory of Comrade Gerry Healy at the Adelphi Theatre, London, on March 4th, 1990', *Marxist Monthly*, April 1990.

Chapter Three

73 '**Everyone I respected**' Lawrence Weschler, *Calamities of Exile*, Chicago and London: University of Chicago Press, p. 48.

73 '**out of despair…astonishing**' Ibid., p. 52.

74 '**Tony Blair's legacy**' Report of Emergency Committee on Iraq Meeting, 13 February 1998.

74 '**used by the regime**' 'Iraq: Call to End Non-military Sanctions', BBC News Online, 18 September 2000.

75 '**Arabs feel contented**' Kanan Makiya, *Cruelty and Silence*, New York: W. W. Norton, 1993, pp. 317–19.

75 '**guinea pig witness**' Makiya, *Cruelty and Silence*, p. 21.

76 '**a man of vanity**' Quoted in Charles Paul Freund, 'Dropping Insults over Iraq', *Reason*, 4 December 2000.

76 '**was the one Arab**' Edward Said, 'The Academy of Lagado', *London Review of Books*, 17 April 2003.

77 '**one needs some kind**' Makiya, *Republic of Fear*, p. xxix.

78 'allowing ourselves to' Ibid.

79 'Iraq was a state' Ibid., p. xxxii.

81 'the obvious question' George Packer, *The Assassin's Gate*, New York: Farrar, Straus and Giroux, 2005, p. 28.

84 'US foreign policy' Ian Johnson, 'Putting Cruelty First: An Interview with Kanan Makiya, Part 2', *Democratiya*, March–May 2006.

85 'no curiosity about' Packer, *The Assassin's Gate*, p. 65.

Chapter Four

92 'Enlightenment: Sinister, destructive' Ophelia Benson and Jeremy Stangroom, *The Dictionary of Fashionable Nonsense*, London: Souvenir, 2004, p. 36.

94 'resoundingly re-asserted its' Perry Anderson, 'Renewals', *New Left Review*, January–February 2000.

95 'There's so much hatred' James Buchan, *High Latitudes*, London: Harvill Press, 1996, pp. 146–7.

95 'a fluent popular style' Anderson, 'Renewals'.

97 'an outstanding psychiatrist' Donald H. Naftulin, John E. Ware, Jr and Frank A. Donnelly, 'The Doctor Fox Lecture: A Paradigm of Educational Seduction', *Journal of Medical Education*, vol. 48, July 1973, pp. 630–5.

98 'overall, the evidence' J. Scott Armstrong, 'Unintelligible Management Research and Academic Prestige', *Interfaces*, vol. 10, no. 2, April 1980, pp. 80–6.

99 'No one denies the need' Denis Dutton, 'Language Crimes: A Lesson in How Not to Write, Courtesy of the Professoriate', *Wall Street Journal*, 5 February 1999.

100 'artificially difficult style' Frank Lentricchia and Thomas McLaughlin (eds), *Critical Terms for Literary Study*, 2nd edn, Chicago and London: University of Chicago Press, 1995.

101 'Ah – so that's it' Ophelia Benson, 'Bad Writing', butterfliesandwheels.com

102 **'Narayan's preoccupations with'** Azfar Hussain, Review of Uma Narayan, *Dis/locating Cultures/Identities, Traditions, and Third World Feminism*, 1997, *Rocky Mountain E-Review*, vol. 54, no. 2, Fall 2000.

103 **'would be exceedingly...Yes'** Robert Conquest: *Reflections on a Ravaged Century*, London: John Murray, 1999, pp. 9–11.

106 **'There is no such'** Quoted in Richard Wolin, *The Seduction of Unreason*, Princeton, NJ: Princeton University Press, 2004, p. 287.

107 **'an Islamic movement'** Wesley Yang, 'The Philosopher and the Ayatollah', *Boston Globe*, 12 June 2005.

109 **'In ways both'** Naomi Klein, 'Introduction', in *No Logo*, London: Flamingo, 2000.

110 **'Disneyland is presented'** Quoted in Wolin, *The Seduction of Unreason*, p. 305.

111 **'In Butler, resistance'** Martha Nussbaum, 'The Professor of Parody', *New Republic*, 22 February 1999.

114 **'The ideas of'** J. M. Keynes, 'Concluding Notes', in *The General Theory of Employment, Interest and Money*, London: Macmillan & Co., 1936.

115 **'wrong to force'** Simon Blackburn, 'The Lie of the Land', *Financial Times*, 28 July 2006.

117 **who 'demonised' Mugabe** John Vidal, 'Monster of the Moment', *Guardian*, 1 July 2005.

119 **'They operate on'** John Lloyd, *The Protest Ethic*, London: Demos, 2001, p. 11.

125 **'Its cloying self-regard'** Ian McEwan, *Saturday*, London: Jonathan Cape, 2005, p. 72.

Chapter Five

127 **'Douglas, Douglas, you'** John Campbell, *Margaret Thatcher: The Iron Lady*, London: Jonathan Cape, 2003, p. 770.

128 **'This was a deliberate'** Samantha Power, *A Problem from Hell*, London: Flamingo, 2002, p. 251.

130 'The camp guards' International Criminal Tribunal for the
     Former Yugoslavia, Mejakic et al., Case no. IT-02-65,
     'Omarska and Keraterm Camps', Consolidated Indictment,
     21 November 2002.

131 'I don't want' Ed Vulliamy, 'Shame of Camp Omarska',
     Guardian, 7 August 1992.

132 'Remember, you will' US State Department, *Sixth Report on
     War Crimes in the Former Yugoslavia*.

134 'We had all the demonstration' Power, *A Problem from Hell*,
     p. 274.

135 'in terms of' Ibid., p. 288.

136 'the postmodern world' Robert Cooper, *The Breaking of
     Nations*, London: Atlantic Books, 2003, p. 39.

141 'there were clearly' Douglas Hurd, *Hansard*, 24 May 1993.

143 'Divide and quit' Christopher Hitchens, 'Divide and
     Misrule', *The Nation*, 17 January 2002.

144 'already a killing' Brendan Simms, *Unfinest Hour*, London:
     Allen Lane, 2001, p. 50.

147 'I never saw' Ibid., p. 64.

147 'You Americans know' Ibid., p. 96.

Chapter Six

154 'much of the bad news' Brendan Simms, *Unfinest Hour*,
     London: Allen Lane, 2001, p. 196.

155 'Growing up in' Tim Adams, 'Question Time', *Observer*,
     30 November 2003.

157 'to me it seems' Noam Chomsky, *American Power and the
     New Mandarins*, New York: Pantheon Books, 1969, p. 17.
     There is an exchange of letters between Chomsky and the
     British writer Oliver Kamm on the passage at
     http://oliverkamm.typepad.com/blog/2006/01/chomskys_sel
     fre.html

157 'Two atom bombs' Chomsky, *American Power and the New
     Mandarins,* pp. 136–7.

158 'when you send' Maya Jaggi, 'Conscience of a Nation',
    Guardian, 20 January 2001.

159 'by capitalist newspaper... any such obligation' Quoted in
    Geoffrey Wheatcroft, *The Strange Death of Tory England*,
    London: Penguin, 2005, p. 217.

163 'The alleged Hitlerite' Robert Faurisson, 'Revisionism on
    Trial', *Journal of Historical Review*, vol. 6, no. 2, 1985.

165 'if a person ignorant' Noam Chomsky, 'The Faurisson
    Affair', Letter to Lawrence K. Kolodney, 1989, available at
    www.chomsky.info/letters/1989—.htm

166 'The simple truth' Pierre Vidal-Naquet, 'De Faurisson et de
    Chomsky', *Esprit*, 1981.

170 'More striking even' Marko Attila Hoare, 'Genocide in the
    Former Yugoslavia: A Critique of Left Revisionism's Denial',
    Journal of Genocide Research, vol. 5, no. 4, December 2003.
    Available at http://www.glypx.com/balkanwitness/hoare.htm

170 'massive atrocities' Noam Chomsky, *A New Generation
    Draws the Line*, London: Verso, 2000, pp. 11, 21, 23, 110.

172 'In the deep' Nerma Jelacic: 'At Last, the Man I Hunted for
    Years Has Been Caught', *Bosnia Report*, No. 47–8,
    September–November 2005.

173 'There was no camp... they never come' Ed Vulliamy, 'We
    Can't Forget', *Guardian*, 1 September 2004.

174 'Why was this wire' Thomas Deichmann, 'The Picture that
    Fooled the World', *LM*, February 1997.

175 'collection centre' Ibid.

176 *LM* didn't fight David Campbell, 'Atrocity, Memory,
    Photography: Imaging the Concentration Camps of Bosnia
    – the Case of ITN versus Living Marxism, Part 2', *Journal of
    Human Rights*, vol. 1, no. 2, June 2002, pp. 1–33.

177 'provided the background' Diana Johnstone, *Fools' Crusade*,
    London: Pluto, 2002, p. 72.

177 'were presumed to' Ibid., p. 115.

177 'Muslim authorities never' Diana Johnstone, 'Using War as
    an Excuse for More War', *Counterpunch*, 12 October 2005.

178 **'I'm guilty for'** Vesna Peric Zimonjic, 'Bosnian Serbs Finally Admit Truth of Srebrenica Deaths', *Independent*, 5 November 2003.

178 **'an outstanding work'** Noam Chomsky, Harold Pinter et al. Available at http://www.hagglundsforlag.se/forfattaredok/Johnstone/ChomskyDararnas.htm

178 **'there was one famous incident'** Noam Chomsky, 'On the NATO Bombing of Yugoslavia', interview with Danilo Mandic, RTS Online, 25 April 2006.

179 **'related entirely to'** One of the protests to the *Guardian* can be found at http://srebrenica-genocide.blogspot.com/2006/01/srebrenica-defending-truth.html/ and a second with a link to the Readers' Editor's judgement can be found at http://oliverkamm.typepad.com/blog/2006/03/chomsky_the_gua.html

Chapter Seven

181 **'Every time I've'** Michael Moore, *Stupid White Men*, New York: Regan Books, 2001, p. 250.

181 **'Obviously'** Martin Amis, *The Information*, London: Flamingo, 1995, pp. 21–2.

182 **'The radical middle-classes'** Michael Frayn, 'Festival', in Michael Sissons and Philip French (eds), *Age of Austerity*, London: Hodder and Stoughton, 1963, pp. 319–20.

183 **'Justices . . . are people'** Naomi Wolf, 'We Americans Are Like Recovering Addicts after a Four-Year Bender', *Guardian*, 7 November 2005.

190 **'a life of labour'** Walter Bagehot, *The English Constitution*, World's Classics edn, London: Oxford University Press, 1928, p. 240.

190 **'Extermination must . . . fecundity'** Quoted in Donald J. Childs, *Modernism and Eugenics*, Cambridge: Cambridge University Press, 2001, p. 9.

190 **'Everyone seemed half drunk'** Virginia Woolf, *Selected Letters*, quoted in Ferdinand Mount, *Mind the Gap*, London: Short Books, 2004, p. 144.

191 **'What rather appals'** Ibid., p. 149.

192 **'This seems to'** Ibid., p. 147.

195 **'Faced with the choice'** George Orwell, *Observer*, 9 April 1944.

195 **'the Kennedy administration'** John Micklethwait and Adrian Wooldridge, *The Right Nation*, London: Penguin, 2004, p. 9.

198 **'responsible for a substantial'** James Bartholomew, *The Welfare State We're In*, London: Politico's, 2004, p. 281.

200 **'An army of social'** Geoff Dench, Kate Gavron and Michael Young, *The New East End*, London: Profile Books, 2006.

202 **'Perhaps surprisingly Conservative'** Anthony King, '95 Per Cent Believe an Attack on This Country is Likely', *Daily Telegraph*, 26 March 2004.

203 **An international survey** Anne Applebaum, 'In Search of Pro-Americanism', July–August 2005, www.anneapplebaum. com/politics/2005/07_fp_pro-aht

204 **'Socially and culturally'** 'On Europe, vote, vote and vote again', *New Statesman*, 26 April 2004.

205 **Researchers from the London** Nick Cohen, 'Britain's Rich Kids Do Better Than Ever', *New Statesman*, 21 March 2005. Jo Blanden of the London School of Economics, Stephen Machin of University College London and Paul Gregg of Bristol University examined the two big generational surveys from the past half-century – the National Child Development Study of 1958 and the British Cohort Study of 1970 – which followed newborn babies through schooling and into adulthood. They looked at how children had done compared to their parents: whether they had risen or fallen in the pecking order, or stayed pretty much where their mothers and fathers once were. They found that, on

average, a boy born to a well-to-do family in 1958 earned 17.5 per cent more than a boy born to a family on half the income of the rich boy's parents. If the equivalent Mr and Mrs Moneybags produced a son in 1970, he would grow up to earn 25 per cent more than his contemporary from the wrong side of the tracks. In other words, far from decreasing, class advantage grew as the twentieth century progressed.

206–7 **'Old Jamaicans wear... previous Utopian fantasies'** Michael Collins, *The Likes of Us*, London: Granta, 2004, pp. 222–9.

207 **'as brief a shelf-life... traditional manual workers'** Jonathan Rose, *The Intellectual Life of the British Working Classes*, New Haven, CT, and London: Yale University Press, 2001, pp. 452–4.

210 **'For decades Americans'** Thomas Frank, *What's the Matter with America?*, London: Vintage, 2006, p. 109.

212 **'demonstrated in no'** Ibid., pp. 199–200.

INTERMISSION

215 **'*In old Moscow*'** Walter Gourlay, *Songs for Political Action*, Bear Family Records BCD 15 720 JL 1996.

Chapter Eight

217 **'One of the easiest pastimes'** George Orwell, 'Fascism and Democracy', in Victor Gollancz (ed.), *The Betrayal of the Left*, London: Victor Gollancz, 1941.

219 **'a mixture of gangsters'** Richard Davenport-Hines, *W. H. Auden*, London: Vintage, 2002, p. 159.

220 **'safe, mediocre, hollow'** Piers Brendon, *The Dark Valley*, London: Jonathan Cape, 2000, p. 397.

220 **'often I am speaking'** Ronald Blythe, *The Age of Illusion*, London: Penguin, 1964, p. 249.

221 'that almost everything' Claud Cockburn, *The Devil's Decade*, London: Sidgwick and Jackson, 1973, p. 84.

224 'I turned to Auden' Christopher Isherwood, *Diaries*, vol. 1, *1939–1960*, ed. Katherine Bucknell, London: Methuen, 1996.

225 'Our great error' Davenport-Hines, *W. H. Auden*, p. 157.

226 'doomed before they' Cato, *Guilty Men*, London: Victor Gollancz, 1940.

228 'brigand powers who' J. M. Keynes, letter to the *New Statesman*, July 1936.

229 'Are they both' Quoted in Theodore Dalrymple, *Our Culture, What's Left Of It*, Chicago: Ivan R. Dee, 2005, pp. 71–5.

230 'He was gregarious' Ronald Blythe, *The Age of Illusion*, London: Hamish Hamilton,1963, p.238.

232 'Lansbury's been dressed' Quoted in Ben Pimlott, *Labour and the Left in the 1930s*, new edn, London: George Allen & Unwin, 1986, p. 73.

234 man pale from Paul Schmidt, *Hitler's Interpreter*, 1951, quoted in John Shepherd, *George Lansbury: At the Heart of Old Labour*, Oxford: Oxford University Press, 2002.

235 'uniting the continent' Martin Ceadel, *Semi-detached Idealists*, Oxford: Oxford University Press, 2000, p. 264.

236 'hardly have been' Richard Griffiths, *Patriotism Perverted*, London: Constable, 1998, p. 58,.

238 'I do not envy' Francis Beckett, *Enemy Within*, new edn, London: Merlin Press, 1999.

240 'Can anyone carry' Victor Gollancz (ed.), *The Betrayal of the Left*, London: Victor Gollancz, 1941.

241 'We were given' Raymond Williams, *Politics and Letters*, London: Verso, 1981, p. 43. For a discussion of Hobsbawm and Williams' anti-imperialist case for invading Finland see http://oliverkamm.typepad.com/blog/2004/07/hobsbawm_again.html

242 'case was genuine' D. N. Pritt, 'Introduction', in D. Collard,

Soviet Justice and the Trial of Radek and Others, London: Victor Gollancz, 1937, pp. 7–8.

243 **'in a sort of'** Alan Strachan, *Secret Dreams*, London: Weidenfeld & Nicolson, 2004, p. 197.

243–4 **'gathering of those ... fried at all'** Paul Anderson, 'Orwell's List 2', 22 June 2003, http://libsoc.blogspot.com

244 **'the so-called People's'** George Orwell, in Gollancz (ed.), *The Betrayal of the Left*.

247 **'a body blow'** Paul Lashmar and James Oliver, *Britain's Secret Propaganda War*, Stroud: Sutton Publishing, 1998, p. 96.

247 **'to be blacklisted'** Christopher Hitchens, *Orwell's Victory*, London: Penguin, 2003, p.112.

247 **'overtly a pacifist'** Corin Redgrave, 'Idealists and Informers', *Guardian*, 28 June 2003.

248 **'a Hitlerian Europe'** Ceadel, *Semi-detached Idealists*, pp. 413–23.

250–2 **'The anti-war socialists... Not so long ago'** Paul Berman, *Terror and Liberalism*, New York: W. W. Norton, 2003, pp. 126–8.

PART TWO: *Raging Fevers*

253 **'Only one faction'** Christopher Hitchens, 'Bush's Secularist Triumph', *Slate*, 9 November 2004.

Chapter Nine

255 **'Nobody move'** 'Stay Quiet and You'll Be OK, Atta Told Passengers', CNN, 18 June 2004.

257 **'If they could'** Tony Blair was speaking at the end of September 2001 before the final death toll of 3,000 was established.

259 **'Alana was clinging'** Kim Murphy, 'Militants Offer a Woman and Her Baby Freedom – but Only if She Leaves

Her Other Child Behind', *Los Angeles Times*, 3 September 2004. (Alana Dzandarova survived, fortunately.)

260 'a terrifying new' Kanan Makiya and Hassan Mneimneh, 'Manual for a Raid', *New York Review of Books*, 17 January 2002.

261 'The values of' Transcript of Al-Jazeera October 2001 interview, available in translation at cnn.com/2002/World/

261 'the gays and' 'Falwell apologizes to gays, feminists, lesbians',14 September 2001, cnn.com/2001/US/

262–3 'for the most . . . served humanity' Quoted in Richard Wolin, *The Seduction of Unreason*, Princeton, NJ: Princeton University Press, 2004, pp. 279–81.

263 'My anti-Americanism has' Margaret Drabble, 'I Loathe America and What It Has Done to the Rest of the World', *Daily Telegraph*, 8 May 2003.

264 'The faith of' Wolin, *The Seduction of Unreason*, pp. 295, 298.

264 'Among Europeans America' Ibid., pp. 278, 283.

265 'The hall swarmed' Malise Ruthven, *A Fury for God*, London: Granta, 2002, pp. 80–90.

266 'A state of' Quoted in Michael Gove, *Celsius 7/7*, London: Weidenfeld & Nicolson, 2006, p. 25.

267 'by every Batuso' Ian Buruma and Avishai Margalit, *Occidentalism*, New York: Penguin, 2004, p. 34.

267 'true Islamic values' Quoted in Ruthven, *A Fury for God*, p. 87.

270 'perpetual war between' Amir Taheri, 'Al Qaeda's Agenda for Iraq', *New York Post*, 4 September 2003.

272 'They started by' Robert Fisk, 'My Beating by Refugees Is a Symbol of the Hatred and Fury of This Filthy War', *Independent*, 8 December 2001.

272 'classic piece of' 9 December 2001, andrewsullivan.com

273 'American bond traders' Leading article, 'In Buildings Thought Indestructible', *New Statesman*, 17 September 2001.

273 **'If someone did'** Michael Moore posting on his website 12 September 2001, since removed.

275 **'square it with my'** Ian Jack, 'Censors and Sensibilities – an Everyday Tale of Literary Folk', *Guardian*, 12 March 2002.

278 **'Like generals who'** Francis Wheen, *How Mumbo-Jumbo Conquered the World*, London: Fourth Estate, 2004, p. 299.

278 **'There was, and is'** Geoffrey Wheatcroft, 'Two Years of Gibberish', *Prospect*, September 2003.

Chapter Ten

280 **'Though in neither'** Tony Blair, statement on the Butler Report, *Hansard*, 14 July 2004, col.1433.

282 **'There were, of course'** Euan Ferguson, 'One Million. And Still They Came', *Observer*, 16 February 2003.

283 **'What right does'** Ariel Dorfman, 'Letter to an Unknown Iraq', *Washington Post*, 23 February 2003.

284 **'All this happiness'** Ian McEwan, *Saturday*, London: Jonathan Cape, 2005, pp. 69–70.

286 **'sweets and flowers'** Alan Johnson, 'Putting Cruelty First: Interview with Kanan Makiya (Part 2)', *Democratiya*, March–May 2006.

287 **'an evil principle'** Fawaz A. Gerges, 'Zarqawi and the D-Word: Is Democracy Un-Islamic?', *Washington Post*, 30 January 2005.

287 **'the insurmountable obstacle'** An English translation of Zarqawi's letter to bin Laden can be found at www.state.gov

289 **'Would you like'** Transcript in Audrey Gillan, 'From Firebrand to Pussycat: Galloway's TV Transformation', *Guardian*, 14 January 2006.

291 **'psychic imperialists'** David Aaronovitch, 'So This Is George's Idea of Connecting People and Politics?', *The Times*, 14 January 2006.

291 **'I thought the President'** *The Times*, 20 January 1994.

292 'like sitting beside' Ian Kershaw, *Hitler: 1936–45*, London: Allen Lane, 2000, p. 13.

292 'the crowded dance' *The New Republic*, 22 April 2004.

292 'Your Excellency, very' *Sun*, 22 April 2006

292 'a civil war' George Galloway, *I'm Not the Only One*, London: Penguin, 2005.

293 'just as Stalin' Ibid.

293 'the disappearance of' *Guardian*, 16 September 2002.

293 'the last castle' 25 July 2005, arabicnews.com

293 'I don't believe' *Independent on Sunday*, 16 November 2003.

294 'Hezbollah has never' Speech to anti-war rally in London, 22 July 2006, video available at http://www.youtube.com/watch?v=jg6qWVGqEJ4

294 'In poor third' *Mail on Sunday*, 17 October 1999.

295 'consider themselves *the*' Mike Marqusee, speech given at 'Days of Hope' Seminar organized by Signs of the Times, 21 June 2003.

296 'Zionist plan, which' Second Cairo Declaration. See discussion 14 October 2005 at http://hurryupharry.blog house.net

299 'by this time' Simon Hoggart, 'Heads Down, Comrades: Real Person on Stage', *Guardian*, 1 October 2004.

300 'the best response' 'A Short War Will Boost US Power', *Socialist Worker*, 22 March 2003.

301 'These poor Iraqis' Galloway defends 'martyrs' remark, BBC News Online, 5 August 2005.

301 'All speakers were anti-Islamic racism' John O'Farrell, 'The European Social Forum', *The Blanket*, 24 October 2004.

302 'Iraqi Quisling' George Galloway, *Morning Star*, 2 October 2004.

305 'whoever finds it' Quotes from Qaradawi's Islamonline are collected in 'Mayor's Dossier on al-Qaradawi Distorts the Truth' at www.outrage.org.uk

309 'secretly try to' Chris Harman, 'The Prophet and the Proletariat', *International Socialism Journal*, 1994.

310 **'The victory of'** Lee Barnes, 'The Tide of History is Turning', BNP Online, 6 May 2005.

Chapter Eleven

312 **'The bitter old'** Paul Berman, *A Tale of Two Utopias*, New York and London: W. W. Norton, 1996, p. 73.

315 **'the United States'** John Lloyd, in Thomas Cushman (ed.), *A Matter of Principle*, Berkeley and London: University of California Press, 2005, pp. 224–5.

317 **'Because Americans do'** Robert Kagan, *Paradise and Power*, London: Atlantic Books, 2003, p. 152.

318 **'Now Bush is'** *Guardian* letters, 5 September 2003.

318 **'Suddenly Saddam's haggard'** Stephen Sackur, *From Our Own Correspondent*, Radio 4, 27 December 2003.

319 **'this man destroyed'** 'Vatican Slams Handling of Saddam', BBC News Online, 16 December 2003.

319 **eminent liberal QC** Clare Dyer, 'Saddam May Sue over Sun Pictures', *Guardian*, 29 June 2005.

320 **'The senseless death'** *Independent*, 19 April 2005.

323 **'read about the'** Tony Blair, 'Iraq and Weapons of Mass Destruction', Prime Minister's statement, 24 September 2002.

324 **'has become the Gulag'** *Amnesty International Report 2005*, speech by Irene Khan at the Foreign Press Association.

325 **'no such slaughter'** Ken Roth, 'War in Iraq: Not a Humanitarian Intervention', *Human Rights Watch World Report, 2004.*

325 **'The criteria for'** Norman Geras, 'Pages from a Daily Journal of Argument', in Cushman (ed.), *A Matter of Principle*, p. 206.

326 **'As for us'** Bernard Kouchner, 'The Tomb of My Murdered Friends', *Le Monde*, 22 August 2003.

328 **'Good Social Democrats'** Barham Salih, speech to the Council of the Socialist International, Madrid, 7 February 2004.

329 **Blair was a 'dickhead'** Isambard Wilkinson, 'Spanish
    Politician Labels Blair an "Imbecile" on Live Television',
    Daily Telegraph, 16 January 2004.

329 **'the countless real'** Richard Herzinger, 'Guilt's End', in
    Cushman (ed.), *A Matter of Principle*, p. 240.

Chapter Twelve

333 **'To take only'** George Eliot, *Impressions of Theophrastus
    Such*, Edinburgh: William Blackwood and Sons, 1879.

335 **'free-speech fundamentalist'** Rohan Jayasekera, 'Plan to
    Outlaw Incitement to Religious Hatred Will Turn into a
    Legal Circus', *Index on Censorship*, Autumn 2004.

336 **'For anyone who inhabits'** Christopher Caldwell, 'Liberté,
    Egalité, Judéophobie', *Weekly Standard*, 5 June 2002.

341 **'Your whole school'** Quoted in Robert L. D. Cooper, 'The
    Knights Templar in Scotland: The Creation of a Myth', *Ars
    Quatuor Coronatorum*, vol. 115, 2002.

344 **'the complete extermination'** Norman Cohn, *Warrant for
    Genocide*, new edn, London: Serif, 1996, p. 65.

345 **'counter-revolutionary agents and'** Ibid., p. 117.

345 **'The efforts to'** Ibid., pp. 120–1.

347 **'United Jewish Nation'** Matthias Küntzel, 'National
    Socialism and Antisemitism in the Arab World', *Jewish
    Political Studies Review*, vol. 17, no.1–2, Spring 2005.

350 **'Jewish Barbie dolls'** 'Saudi Police Outlaw Barbie', *Sydney
    Morning Herald*,10 September 2003.

351 **'Jews who determine'** Mark Strauss, 'Anti-globalism's Jewish
    Problem', *Foreign Policy*, 12 November 2003.

351 **'I am not saying every'** Nick Cohen, 'Is Fascism Behind the
    Terror?', *New Statesman*, 12 April 2004.

351 **A poll for** *The Times*, 7 February 2006.

352 **'carry out reforms'** Colum Lynch, 'G-8, Arab Governments
    Sign Democracy Pact', *Washington Post*, 25 September 2004.

Chapter Thirteen

355 **'They talked and'** Michael Walzer, 'Can There Be a Decent Left?', *Dissent*, Spring 2002.

358 **'I very much resent'** Azar Nafisi, 5 February 2004, identitytheory.com

362 **'We decline to'** The Euston Manifesto, available at http://eustonmanifesto.org/joomla/

Postscript

364 **'There is global struggle'** BBC interview with Tony Blair quoted in David Aaronovitch, 'Slavery – What a Lot of Fuss about Nothing', *The Times*, 1 March 2007.

366 **'The most depressing thing'** Martin Amis, 'You Ask the Question', *Independent*, 15 January 2007. The quote is from Hassan Massawi, former leader of Hezbollah, and is usually translated as, 'We are not fighting so that you will offer us something. We are fighting to eliminate you.'

368 **'the perpetuation of terror'** Michael Osborn, 'Robin Hood Given Modern Makeover', BBC News, 8 September 2006.

370 **'Our magnetism and vitality drew people to us'** Ed Husain, *The Islamist*, London: Penguin Books, 2007, p. 65.

371 **'how we used to laugh'** Hassan Butt, 'My Plea to Fellow Muslims: You Must Renounce Terror', *Observer*, 1 July 2007.

378 **'the result of 25 years of multiculturalism'** Quoted in Alasdair Palmer, 'Not in Their Name?' *Sunday Telegraph*, 7 July 2007.

ACKNOWLEDGEMENTS

I could not have written this book without the help of many people who gave me their time without complaint. I owe large debts of gratitude to: Kanan Makiya for allowing me to enter his life; Paul Anderson and Ken Weller, for advising me on the history of the Workers' Revolutionary Party; Marko Attila Hoare, Nerma Jelacic, Oliver Kamm, Brendan Simms and Ed Vulliamy for their advice on the Bosnian and Kosovo conflicts; Jean Seaton for her help on the histories of the Fabians and the Bloomsbury Group; Thomas Frank and Richard D. North for their comments on the relationship between the middle- and working-class lefts; Paul Anderson, Oliver Kamm and Jean Seaton once again, along with Michael Foot, for their help on the story of the Left in the Thirties; Leni von Eckardt, Greg Palast and David Tate for their help on the Left after 9/11; Gary Kent and Abdullah Muhsin for their comments on the history of the Iraqi trade union movement; John Kampfner, the Editor of the *New Statesman*, for allowing me to reprint at the beginning of Chapter 12 work which originally appeared in the *New Statesman* of 10 October 2005; Tom Cordiner for his help on modern antisemitism; Robert Cooper for his advice on the history of the Freemason conspiracy myth; and Roger Alton, the Editor of the *Observer*, for allowing me time off from work. The excerpt from "Newsreel" came from *The Complete Poems* by C Day Lewis published by Sinclair-Stevenson (1992) Copyright © 1992 in this edition The Estate of C Day Lewis. Reprinted by permission of The Random House Group Ltd.

I am also grateful to Faber and Faber for its kind permission to quote from W. H. Auden's *Spain, O What is that Sound, Letters from Iceland*, and *September 1, 1939* – collected in *The English Auden*.

Francis Wheen was this book's midwife and an irrepressible source of encouragement. Natasha Fairweather of the A. P. Watt literary agency had the recklessness to back it when it was nothing more than a vague notion. Oliver Kamm and Norman Geras helped clear away many misconceptions. Ophelia Benson read the proofs and her wise advice saved me from many blunders, while Mitzi Angel of Fourth Estate was a princess among editors. I am indebted to them all, but my greatest debt of gratitude is to Anne-Marie for her heroic efforts to find me the time to write.

All errors of taste and judgement remain, as ever, the author's own.

INDEX